A Reading Skills Book

interactions two

A Reading Skills Book

Third Edition

interactions two

Elaine Kirn
West Los Angeles College

Pamela Hartmann
Los Angeles Unified School District

Boston, Massachusetts   Burr Ridge, Illinois   Dubuque, Iowa
Madison, Wisconsin   New York, New York   San Francisco, California   St. Louis, Missouri

This is an ⌐EBI⌐ book.

McGraw-Hill

A Division of The McGraw·Hill Companies

Interactions Two
A Reading Skills Book
Third Edition

7 8 9 10 DOC/DOC 0 9 8 7 6 5 4 3 2 1 0

ISBN 0-07-035993-8
ISBN 0-07-114373-4

This book was set in Times Roman by Clarinda.

The editors were Tim Stookesberry, Bill Preston, and Karen Davy; the designers were Lorna
Lo, Suzanne Montazer, Francis Owens, and Elizabeth Williamson; the production supervisor
was Phyllis Snyder; the project editor was Stacey Sawyer; the cover was designed by Francis
Owens; the cover illustrator was Susan Pizzo; the photo researcher was Cindy Robinson,
Seaside Publishing; illustrations were done by David Bohn, Axelle Fortier, Rick Hackney, Lori
Heckelman, and Sally Richardson.

R. R. Donnelley & Sons Company, Crawfordsville, IN, was printer and binder.
Phoenix Color Corporation was cover separator and printer.

Library of Congress Catalog Card Number: 95-82435.

INTERNATIONAL EDITION

When ordering this title, use ISBN 0-007-114373-4

Photo credits: *Page 1* © David Weintraub/Photo Researchers, Inc.; *9* © Seth Resnick/Stock,
Boston; © Michael Dwyer/Stock, Boston; *22* © Gilda Schiff-Zirinsky/Photo Researchers, Inc.;
23 © Owen Franken/Stock, Boston; *29* © John Fung; *45* © Richard T. Hewitz/Photo
Researchers, Inc.; *46* (left, top right) © Peter Menzel/Stock, Boston; *46* (bottom right) © John
Fung; *65* © Richard Pasley/Stock, Boston; *72* © Dennis Budd Gray/Stock, Boston; *85* © Bill
Bachman/Photo Edit; *107* © Vanessa Vick/Photo Researchers, Inc.; *108* (top, bottom) ©
Reuter/Bettmann; *109* © Peter Charlesworth/SABA; *117* © Jim Kingshott/Tony Stone
Worldwide; *118* © Bob Daemmrich/The Image Works; *119* © Ilene Perlman/Stock, Boston;

continued on page 286

Contents

Preface   ix
Summary of Reading Skills   xvi

CHAPTER one

Education and Student Life   1

PART ONE   Reading Selection: *Methods of Education: East Versus West*   2

PART TWO   Reading Selection: *College Students in the United States Today*   8

PART THREE   Building Vocabulary and Study Skills   13

PART FOUR   Reading in the Real World: School Documents   16

CHAPTER two

City Life   21

PART ONE   Reading Selection: *The Urban Crisis*   22

PART TWO   Reading Selection: *Sick Building Syndrome*   30

PART THREE   Building Vocabulary and Study Skills   34

PART FOUR   Reading in the Real World: City Maps   39

CHAPTER three

Business and Money   45

PART ONE   Reading Selection: *Banking on the Poor*   46

PART TWO   Reading Selection: *The Psychology of Money*   52

PART THREE   Building Vocabulary and Study Skills   56

PART FOUR   Reading in the Real World: Banking Forms   60

CHAPTER four

Jobs and Professions 65

PART ONE	Reading Selection: *Workaholism*	66
PART TWO	Reading Selection: *Workaholism—A National Syndrome?*	71
PART THREE	Building Vocabulary and Study Skills	76
PART FOUR	Reading in the Real World: Classified Ads	80

CHAPTER five

Lifestyles 85

PART ONE	Reading Selection: *Our Changing Lifestyles—Trends and Fads*	86
PART TWO	Reading Selection: *Breaking Stereotypes—An Inside Look*	92
PART THREE	Building Vocabulary and Study Skills	98
PART FOUR	Reading in the Real World: Advertisements	104

CHAPTER six

The Global Village 107

PART ONE	Reading Selection: *Refugees*	108
PART TWO	Reading Selection: *The New World of Travel*	116
PART THREE	Building Vocabulary and Study Skills	124
PART FOUR	Reading in the Real World: The Global Crime Wave	126

CHAPTER seven

North America: The Land and the People 131

PART ONE	Reading Selection: *North American Indians: Then and Now*	132
PART TWO	Reading Selection: *Regional Customs*	143
PART THREE	Building Vocabulary and Study Skills	151
PART FOUR	Reading in the Real World: From *Lame Deer Seeker of Visions*	156

CHAPTER **eight**

Tastes and Preferences **163**

PART ONE   Reading Selection: *What Can We Learn from Art?*   164

PART TWO   Reading Selection: *Fashion: The Art of the Body*   175

PART THREE   Building Vocabulary and Study Skills   183

PART FOUR   Reading in the Real World: "Scientists Say Aromas Have Major
Effect on Emotions" (from the *Los Angeles Times*)   189

CHAPTER **nine**

Discoveries **193**

PART ONE   Reading Selection: *The Human Brain—New Discoveries*   194

PART TWO   Reading Selection: *The Ethics of Change*   202

PART THREE   Building Vocabulary and Study Skills   207

PART FOUR   Reading in the Real World: From *The Development of Language*   210

CHAPTER **ten**

Medicine, Myths, and Magic **217**

PART ONE   Reading Selection: *The Work of the Traditional Healer*   218

PART TWO   Reading Selection: *The Mind-Body Relationship*   228

PART THREE   Building Vocabulary and Study Skills   233

PART FOUR   Reading in the Real World: *Home Remedies Even Doctors Use*   239

CHAPTER eleven

The Media 243

PART ONE   Reading Selection: *Movie Magic: Then and Now*   244

PART TWO   Reading Selection: *Movie Reviews: The Critics' Choice*   254

PART THREE   Building Vocabulary and Study Skills   257

PART FOUR   Reading in the Real World: Movie Listings   261

CHAPTER twelve

Prejudice, Tolerance, and Justice 267

PART ONE   Reading Selection: *The Concept of Law*   268

PART TWO   Reading Selection: *My Lawsuit That Wasn't*   276

PART THREE   Building Vocabulary and Study Skills   279

PART FOUR   Reading in the Real World: Magazine Articles   282

Contents

Preface
to the Third Edition
The Interactions Two Program

The Interactions Two program consists of five texts and a variety of supplemental materials for low-intermediate to intermediate students seeking to improve their English language skills. Each of the five texts in this program is carefully organized by chapter theme, vocabulary, grammar structures, and, where possible, language functions. As a result, information introduced in a chapter of any one of the Interactions Two texts corresponds to and reinforces material taught in the same chapter of the other four books, creating a truly integrated, four-skills approach.

The Interactions Two program is highly flexible. The texts in this series may be used together or separately, depending on students' needs and course goals. The books in this program include:

- **A Communicative Grammar Book.** Organized around grammatical topics, this book includes notional/functional material where appropriate. It presents all grammar in context and contains many types of communicative activities.
- **A Listening/Speaking Skills Book.** This book uses lively, natural language from various contexts, including dialogues, interviews, lectures, and announcements. Listening strategies emphasized include summarizing main ideas, making inferences, listening for stressed words, reductions and intonation.
- **A Reading Skills Book.** The reading selections contain sophisticated college-level material; however, vocabulary and grammar have been carefully controlled to be at students' level of comprehension.

The text includes many vocabulary-building exercises and emphasizes reading strategies such as skimming, scanning, guessing meaning from context, understanding the structure and organization of a selection, increasing reading speed, and interpreting the author's point of view.
- **A Writing Process Book.** This book uses a process approach to writing, including many exercises on prewriting and revision. Exercises build skills in exploring and organizing ideas; developing vocabulary; using correct form and mechanics; using coherent structure, and editing, revising, and using feedback to create a final draft.
- **A Multi-Skills Activity Book.** New to this edition, this text gives students integrated practice in all four language skills. Among the communicative activities included in this text are exercises for the new video program that accompanies the Interactions Two series.

Supplemental Materials

In addition to the five core texts outlined above, various supplemental materials are available to assist users of the Third Edition, including:

Instructor's Manual

Extensively revised for the new edition, this manual provides instructions and guidelines for using the five core texts separately or in various combinations to suit particular program needs.

For each of the core texts, there is a separate section with answer keys, teaching tips, additional activities, and other suggestions. The testing materials have been greatly expanded in this edition.

Audio Program for *Interactions Two: A Listening/Speaking Skills Book*

Completely re-recorded for the new edition, the audio program is designed to be used in conjunction with those exercises that are indicated with a cassette icon in the student text. Complete tapescripts are now included in the back of the student text.

Audio Program to Accompany *Interactions Two: A Reading Skills Book*

This new optional audio program contains selected readings from the student text. These taped selections enable students to listen at their leisure to the natural oral discourse of native readers for intonation and modeling. Readings that are included in this program are indicated with a cassette icon in the student text.

Video

New to this edition, the video program for Interactions Two contains authentic television segments that are coordinated with the twelve chapter themes in the five texts. Exercises and activities for this video are in the Multi-Skills Activity Book.

Interactions Two: A Reading Skills Books, Third Edition

Rationale

Interactions Two: A Reading Skills Book, Third Edition, is based on the idea that people learn to read by reading. If the material is interesting and not too difficult, students will enjoy reading and will be encouraged to read more; the more they read, the better they will be at it. The problem for academic ESL students is that they want to read more sophisticated material but lack the skills with which to do so.

The solution is twofold: (1) to give students readings that are intellectually stimulating but not beyond their lexical, grammatical, or syntactic understanding; and (2) to teach strategies that make reading easier. The reading selections in this book contain sophisticated material. However, vocabulary and grammar have been carefully controlled to be at the students' level of comprehension. In addition, the exercises guide students toward acquiring the skills of good readers, skills that make reading both easy and fun.

Vocabulary items presented in one chapter are recycled in subsequent chapters to prevent students from forgetting them. This constant recycling enable students to make rapid progress; their vocabulary will increase dramatically as they use the book, and yet this process won't be perceived as difficult.

One of the biggest obstacles to comprehension in many academic ESL readers is that the grammar is too difficult for low-intermediate to intermediate students. In the reading selections of this book, however, the grammar points have been carefully sequenced and contextualized. This text is not only coordinated with the grammar text of the Interactions Two program but is also compatible with the grammar sequencing found in most other low-intermediate to intermediate ESL texts.

The exception to this is the inclusion—new to the third edition—of authentic readings in Part Four of Chapters Six to Twelve. These authentic selections will be more challenging than the controlled reading selections in Parts One and Two, and many students may find them to be above their level. The purpose of these more difficult, authentic pieces is to ease students from the "safe" world of "ESL English" to the more daunting arena of "real world" English in a way that highlights how much they actually can understand, even in material that seems above level.

It should be noted that since this is a reading text, grammar is not taught for the sake of grammar. Instead, it is seen as an aid to comprehension. Other such aids, or strategies, taught in this text include guessing meaning from context, increasing reading speed, understanding stems and affixes, making predictions, learning to accept some uncertainty, making inferences, and distinguishing fact from opinion.

Although the material in this book may look difficult to students, they will find that the tasks they are required to perform with the material are not difficult. As a result students will move through the book with a growing sense of confidence and accomplishment as they discover they can find the main ideas and important details, understand much of the new vocabulary without a dictionary, and successfully apply critical thinking skills to their reading. Moreover, academic students will feel intellectually challenged by material that engages their intelligence.

Chapter Organization

Because its primary purpose is to provide instruction in the reading process, this book offers a large variety of exercises and activities directed toward that end. It is left to individual teachers to choose those sections suited to the specific needs of their students. Each of the twelve chapters is divided into four parts as follows:

- **Part One** consists of a brief prereading exercise and question, a controlled nonfiction reading selection on the chapter theme, and postreading exercises that focus on these important reading skills: getting the main ideas, guessing meaning from context, understanding reading structure, and understanding details, making inferences (Chapters Six, Seven, and Eight), and distinguishing facts from theories. Finally, there are discussion questions that relate the reading selection to the students' own lives and allow for conversation.

- **Part Two** begins with an exercise on skimming for main ideas that guides students in recognizing the main idea of single paragraphs, finding topic sentences, and summarizing. The second controlled reading selection, similar in theme to the first reading, is usually nonfiction but occasionally fiction. It is followed by a variety of postreading exercises on understanding pronoun references (Chapters One to Four), summarizing, understanding idioms (Chapters Six and Seven), making inferences (Chapters Six to Ten, and Twelve), distinguishing facts from theories or opinions (Chapters Nine to Eleven), applying information (Chapter Ten), and personalized discussion questions.

- **Part Three** contains a variety of exercises to help students expand their passive and active knowledge of vocabulary, followed by activities to aid students in acquiring essential skills for academic reading— using a dictionary, marking a book, increasing reading speed, and accepting some amount of uncertainty.

- **Part Four** contains a section of "realia" such as a city map, banking forms, and classified ads (Chapters One to Five) or an authentic reading passage from a newspaper, magazine, or book (Chapters Six to Twelve), accompanied by questions for scanning. Additional exercises include synthesizing information (Chapter Seven), marking a book, and summarizing (Chapter Nine).

Teaching Suggestions

The following suggestions are designed to help teach the reading skills used by good readers, skills essential to students' academic success.

Part One

Before You Read

The skills of anticipation—forming predictions about what is to be read—is an important part of active reading. This skill may be encouraged by having students discuss the pictures and answer the questions in the *Getting Started* section. Add any other questions that are appropriate for your class. The more information about a subject that students can bring to a reading selection, the more they will be able to get out of it; in other words, students will understand a reading better if they realize how much they already know about the topic.

Then read through the *Preparing to Read* question. Tell students that they aren't expected to be able to answer this question *before* reading; instead, they should keep it in mind *as* they read. If students can answer this question after one reading of the selection, they have understood the main idea.

Reading Selection

Each student should read the selection silently, as this is not only the most common form of academic reading but also the fastest. The enormous amount of required reading in college classes makes it crucial for students to read as quickly as possible. Point out to students that moving their lips as they read will slow them down. Tell students not to use a dictionary as they

read the selection the first time but instead to guess the meanings of new words. Emphasize the importance of simply getting the main idea.

If you prefer to have students listen to the reading selection as they read silently in order to reinforce listening comprehension, you might either read it aloud yourself or use the cassette tape which accompanies the book. (Don't have students read aloud, as this would interfere with both comprehension and speed.) The selection should be read straight through without stopping and without explanation.

After You Read

A variety of exercises follow the reading selection. These are intended to help students acquire in English the same skills that good readers already have naturally in their native language. Emphasis is placed on (1) under-standing the main idea and (2) guessing meaning from context. It is with the latter that most students have difficulty. Many students lack the confidence to trust their own guess, and they tend to cling to a dictionary. They need to be told—probably repeatedly throughout the term—that it's not usually necessary to know *exactly* what a new word means, or to know *everything* about it the first time they encounter it.

Although students are instructed to reread the selection after doing the Guessing Meaning from Context exercises, in the last few chapters you might choose instead to have them carefully mark the passage as they read it just *once;* this more closely approximates what happens in many college courses, where the large amount of assigned reading doesn't usually allow students time to read a chapter more than once. If you do have students reread the selection, make sure that they use the dictionary sparingly, if at all, for just those words which are (1) impossible to guess from the context and (2) essential to under-standing a paragraph.

Students can actively practice their newly learned vocabulary words as they express their opinions and share ideas in the Discussing the Reading section. There are a number of ways to handle these discussion questions. Among them:

1. **Ask the questions of the entire class.** The advantage to this technique is that the teacher can control the discussion and encourage students to expand their ideas. The disadvantage, however, is that few students may volunteer to speak in a large group.

2. **Have students discuss the answers in small groups.** A representative from each group can then report that group's ideas to the whole class.

3. **Have students discuss the questions in pairs.** This technique encourages the participation of students who are usually too shy to speak in a larger group.

4. **Choose one question and organize a debate on it.** Divide the class into two sections, each of which will prepare arguments for its team.

(Note: These suggestions may also be applied to the new What Do You Think? sections.)

Part Two

Some of the exercises in Part Two (such as Discussing the Reading) are similar to those in Part One, and the same teaching suggestions apply. However, the main focus of this part is on finding the main idea of individual paragraphs. Students practice finding the topic sentence of a paragraph or, for those paragraphs that have no topic sentence, practice "adding up" details to figure out the implied main idea.

Part Two does not have a specific section on guessing meaning from context, but it is almost impossible to spend too much time on this skill; therefore, after students find the topic sentence or main idea of each paragraph, you might have them work in small groups to identify new words and guess the meanings.

Part Three

The Building Vocabulary exercises can be assigned as homework, but the Study Skills activities should be completed in class, particularly those dealing with increasing reading speed.

Part Four

The ability to find information quickly is an important skill for academic students and is the focus of Part Four. The first five chapters contain a piece of realia. In doing these sections, briefly go over the short glossary with the students. Then have them answer the questions, individually or in groups, from the information found in the realia. Discourage students from reading every word as they hunt for the answers. Instead, they should run a finger over the page (either down or across, depending on the type of realia) until the answer "pops out" at them.

Chapters Six to Twelve contain an authentic article from a newspaper (Chapters Eight, Eleven, and Twelve) or magazine (Chapters Six and Ten), a selection from a textbook (Chapter Nine), or a complete chapter from an autobiography (Chapter Seven). Three of these pieces have been slightly adapted; the other four have not been altered. These pieces should be of high interest to most students, but some students will feel overwhelmed by the perceived level of difficulty. It is extremely important to encourage students to focus on what they *do* understand instead of what they *don't*. The tasks required of students *are* possible to do. If students express frustration at the level of difficulty, remind them that they are able to answer the questions, and, therefore, *do* understand the main ideas and important details. At this point, students don't need to understand anything more than is required of them at these specific tasks. Tell students that for the next several years they may be reading some material that seems too hard; they need to learn how to cope with this difficulty in order to succeed in an academic program. Being able to make the transition from controlled readings to "real" English should give students confidence to tackle more difficult reading material in their academic courses.

New to the Third Edition

1. **Streamlined Design.** The new edition features an attractive two-color design and an extensively revised art program. These

changes were initiated to make the books more appealing, up-to-date, and user friendly. In addition, we made the books easier to use by simplyfying complicated direction lines, numbering exercises and activities, and highlighting key information in shaded boxes and charts.

2. **New Chapter Theme on The Global Village.** The new edition features an entirely new theme for Chapter Six: The Global Village. In addition, the theme for Chapter Nine has been broadened to Discoveries to include new content.

3. **Authentic Reading Material.** Newspaper and magazine articles, a selection from a textbook, and a chapter from an autiobiography have been added to Part Four (renamed Reading in the Real World) of the last seven chapters to help students make the transition from controlled readings to "real" English materials.

4. **Audio Cassette.** New to this edition is a supplemental audio cassette, containing selected readings from the text. Readings included on the cassette are indicated with a cassette icon in the student text.

5. **What Do You Think?** These new boxed features in every chapter present interesting or surprising information designed to stimulate class discussion on topics related to the chapter themes.

6. **Focus on Testing.** Also appearing in each chapter, these new boxed features focus on specific reading and vocabulary skills designed to help students prepare for the vocabulary and reading sections of standardized tests such as the TOEFL.

Acknowledgments

Our thanks to the following reviewers whose comments, both favorable and critical, were of great value in the development of the third edition of the Interactions/Mosaic series:

Jean Al-Sibai, University of North Carolina; Janet Alexander, Waterbury College; Roberta Alexander, San Diego City College; Julie Alpert, Santa Barbara City College; Anita Cook, Tidewater Community College; Anne Deal Beavers, Heald Business College; Larry Berking, Monroe Community College; Deborah Busch, Delaware County Community College; Patricia A. Card, Cheminade University of Honolulu; José A. Carmona, Hudson County Community College; Kathleen Carroll, Fontbonne College; Consuela Chase, Loyola University; Lee Chen, California State University; Karen Cheng, University of Malaya; Gaye Childress, University of North Texas; Maria Conforti, University of Colorado; Earsie A. de Feliz, Arkansas State University; Elizabeth Devlin-Foltz, Montgomery County Adult Education; Colleen Dick, San Francisco Institute of English; Marta Dmytrenko-Ahrabian, Wayne State University; Margo Duffy, Northeast Wisconsin Technical; Magali Duignan, Augusta College; Janet Dyar, Meridian Community College; Anne Ediger, San Diego City College; D. Frangie, Wayne State University; Robert Geryk, Wayne State University; Jeanne Gibson, American Language Academy; Kathleen Walsh Greene, Rhode Island College; Myra Harada, San Diego Mesa College; Kristin Hathhorn, Eastern Washington University; Mary Herbert, University of California–Davis; Joyce Homick, Houston Community College; Catherine Hutcheson, Texas Christian University; Suzie Johnston, Tyler Junior College; Donna Kauffman, Radford University; Emmie Lim, Cypress College;

Patricia Mascarenas, Monte Vista Comunity School; Mark Mattison, Donnelly College; Diane Peak, Choate Rosemary Hall; James Pedersen, Irvine Valley College; Linda Quillan, Arkansas State University; Marnie Ramker, University of Illinois; Joan Roberts, The Doane Stuart School; Doralee Robertson, Jacksonville University; Ellen Rosen, Fullerton College; Jean Sawyer, American Language Academy; Frances Schulze, College of San Mateo; Sherrie R. Sellers, Brigham Young University; Tess M. Shafer, Edmonds Community College; Heinz F. Tengler, Lado International College; Sara Tipton, Wayne State University; Karen R. Vallejo, Brigham Young University; Susan Williams, University of Central Florida; Mary Shepard Wong, El Camino College; Cindy Yoder, Eastern Mcnnnonite College; Cheryl L. Youtsey, Loyola University; Miriam Zahler, Wayne State University; Maria Zien, English Center, Miami; Yongmin Zhu, Los Medanos College; Norma Zorilla, Fresno Pacific College.

Summary of Reading Skills

Note: all chapters contain practice in the reading skills of *prediction* and *main idea* and in the critical thinking skill of *formulating an opinon and supporting it.*

Chapter	Reading Skills	Study Skills & Vocabulary	Focus on Testing
one	• guessing meaning from context: punctuation, synonyms, clues in another sentence • finding topic sentences • pronoun reference	• words in context • scanning for information	• following directions
two	• guessing meaning from context: examples, opposites, details • distinguishing general and specific ideas	• parts of speech • related words • dictionary use • scanning for information	• guessing meaning from context
three	• guessing meaning from context: abbreviations (e.g., i.e.,) part of speech • topics and topic sentences • pronoun reference	• words in categories • parts of speech: suffixes for nouns and adjectives • scanning	• increasing reading speed: reading in phrases
four	• guessing meaning from context: review • topics and topic sentences • analyzing sentence structure: parallelism	• adjective and noun phrases • compound words • scanning	• increasing reading speed: reading in phrases/left-to-right eye movement
five	• guessing meaning from context: review • figuring out the main idea when there is no topic sentence • summarizing	• suffixes (nouns, verbs, adverbs) • prefixes • dictionary use: words with more meaning	• analogies
six	• guessing meaning from context: literal and figurative meanings	• outlining • idioms • scanning • increasing reading speed	• making inferences

Chapter	Reading Skills	Study Skills & Vocabulary	Focus on Testing
seven	• guessing meaning from context: review • making inferences • synthesizing information	• outlining • idioms • categories of words • prefixes and suffixes • word roots • vocabulary learning methods	• comprehension questions
eight	• guessing meaning from context: writing definitions • finding words that fit definitions • making inferences	• outlining • words with similar meanings • dictionary use • connotation • increasing reading speed	• multiple-choice tests
nine	• distinguishing facts from theories • making inferences	• words with similar meanings • categories (content areas) • word roots and affixes • marking a book • summarizing	• guessing meaning from context
ten	• guessing vocabulary from context: review • making inferences • distinguishing facts from theories • applying information	• word categories • word roots and affixes • outlining • summarizing	• analogies
eleven	• guessing vocabulary from context: finding words that fit definitions • recognizing time relationships • distinguishing facts from opinions	• tolerating ambiguity of meaning • hyphenated words	• figurative language
twelve	• guessing vocabulary from context: writing definitions • making inferences	• categories of words • outlining	• comprehension questions

Education and Student Life

The first reading selection discusses some differences between the educational system in much of Asia and the system in the United States and Canada. The second selection discusses how college students in the United States today are different from those of the past. The last part of the chapter teaches you how to find information quickly in an application form and a letter from an American school in Los Angeles.

PART one
Methods of Education: East Versus West

Before You Read
Getting Started

Look at the pictures and discuss them.

1. Where is each scene taking place? What is happening?
2. Compare the methods of education in the two pictures at the top of page 3 with the methods in the two pictures on this page.
3. Which type of class do you prefer? Why?

Preparing to Read

As you read the following selection, think about the answer to this question. How is the educational system in most Asian countries different from the system in Western countries such as the United States and Canada?

Read the following selection quickly. Do not use a dictionary. Then do the exercises that follow the reading.

Methods of Education: East Versus West

A *A* teacher from a Western country recently visited an elementary school in an Asian country. In one class, she watched sixty young children as they learned to draw a cat. The class teacher drew a big circle on the blackboard, and sixty children copied it on their papers. The teacher drew a smaller circle on top of the first and then put two triangles on top of it. The children drew in the same way. The lesson continued until there were sixty-one identical cats in the classroom. Each student's cat looked exactly like the one on the board.

B The visiting teacher was startled by the lesson. She was surprised because the teaching methods were very different from the ways of teaching in her own country. A children's art lesson in her own country produced a room full of unique pictures, each one completely different from the others. Why? What causes this difference in educational methods? In a classroom in any country, the instructor teaches more than art or history or language. He or she also teaches culture (the ideas and beliefs of that society). Each educational system is a mirror that reflects the culture of the society.

C   In a Western society such as the United States or Canada, which has many national, religious, and cultural differences, people highly value individualism—the differences among people—and independent thinking. Teachers place a lot of importance on the qualities that make each student special. The educational systems in these countries show these values. Students do not often memorize information. Instead, they work individually and find answers themselves, and they express their ideas in class discussion. At an early age, students learn to form their own ideas and opinions.

D   In most Asian societies, by contrast, the people have the same language, history, and culture. Perhaps for this reason, the educational system in much of Asia reflects society's belief in group goals and traditions rather than individualism. Children in China, Japan, and Korea often work together and help one another on assignments. In the classroom, the teaching methods are often very formal. The teacher lectures, and the students listen. There is not much discussion. Instead, the students recite rules or information that they have memorized.

E   There are advantages and disadvantages to both these systems of education. For example, one advantage to the system in Japan is that students there learn the social skill of cooperation—of working together. Another advantage is that they learn much more math and science than American students learn by the end of high school. They also study more hours each day and more days each year than North Americans do. The system is difficult, but it prepares students for a society that values discipline and self-control. There is, however, a disadvantage. Memorization is an important learning method in Japanese schools, yet many students say that after an exam, they forget much of the information that they have memorized.

F   The advantage of the educational system in North America, on the other hand, is that students learn to think for themselves. They learn to take the initiative—to make a decision and take action without someone telling them what to do. The system prepares them for a society that values creative ideas. There is, however, a drawback, a disadvantage. When students graduate from high school, they haven't studied as many basic rules and facts as students in other countries have.

After You Read

Getting the Main Ideas

Answer the questions according to the reading selection. Which statements apply
to which systems of education? Write W (Western) or A (Asian) on the lines.
Don't look back at the reading.

1. $\underline{A}$ The teacher draws pictures that the children copy exactly.

2. $\underline{W}$ Each child draws a different picture.

3. _____ The society values individualism, independent thinking, and
initiative.

4. _____ Students have to find information themselves, and there is discussion
in class.

5. _____ Most of the people in the country have the same language, history,
and culture.

6. _____ Students listen to the teacher and memorize information and rules.

7. _____ The system prepares students for a society that values discipline and
cooperation.

Guessing Meaning from Context

When you read, you do not need to look up the meanings of all new
words in a dictionary. You can often guess the meanings of many new
words from the context—the other words in the sentence and the other
sentences in the paragraph.

Sometimes a sentence gives a definition of a new vocabulary item or
information about it. This information may be in parentheses ( ), after a
dash (—), or after a comma (,).

example: There were sixty-one <u>identical</u> cats in the classroom, each one
exactly like the one on the board.
(What does <u>identical</u> mean? It means "exactly like.")

exercise **2** Find the meanings of the underlined words in the sentences below and on page 6.
Write them on the lines.

1. A children's art lesson produced a room full of <u>unique</u> pictures, each one

completely different from the others. _____

2. People highly value <u>individualism</u>—the differences among people.

_____ _____

3. Most Asian societies value <u>discipline</u>, or self-control.

_____

4. Students learn the social skill of <u>cooperation</u>—of working together.

_____

5. They learn to <u>take the initiative</u>—to make a decision and take action

without someone telling them what to do. _____

6. There is a <u>drawback</u>, a disadvantage. _____

Sometimes the meaning or a clue to the meaning of a new vocabulary
item is in another sentence or sentence part.

example: The <u>teaching methods</u> were very different from the ways of
teaching in her country.
(What are <u>teaching methods</u>? They're ways of teaching.)

 Write the meanings of the underlined words on the lines.

1. The visiting teacher was <u>startled</u> by the lesson. She was surprised because
the teaching methods were very different from the ways of teaching in her
country. _____

_____

2. Students <u>memorize</u> information; they learn and remember basic rules and
facts. _____

_____

3. They work <u>individually</u> and find answers by themselves. _____

_____

4. Each educational system is a mirror that <u>reflects</u> the values of the society. In
the Far East, it shows society's beliefs in group goals rather than individualism. _____

_____

5. People in Western cultures <u>value</u> individualism highly. Teachers place a lot
of importance on the qualities that make each person special. _____

_____

exercise 4   Read the selection "Methods of Education: East Versus West" again carefully. Try to guess the meanings of new words from the context. Use your dictionary only when absolutely necessary. As you read the selection again, check your answers to the Getting the Main Ideas exercise. Correct your errors if necessary.

Understanding Reading Structure

exercise 5   Paragraphs divide reading material into topics, or subjects. In the selection "Methods of Education: East Versus West," there are letters next to the six paragraphs. One paragraph is usually about one topic. Match the paragraphs with their topics and write the letters of the paragraphs on the lines as in the example.

1. _C___ How Western school systems reflect the value of individualism

2. _____ The advantages and disadvantages of the North American system

3. _____ Reasons for differences in educational systems

4. _____ How Asian school systems reflect group goals

5. _____ Introduction: A classroom in an Asian country

6. _____ The advantages and disadvantages of Asian methods of education

exercise 6   A reading selection expresses one main idea. The main idea is the most important idea of the reading: It sums up the topics and ideas of all the paragraphs. Circle the number of the main idea of the reading selection "Methods of Education: East Versus West."

1. In elementary schools in Asia, children copy pictures of cats from the blackboard.
2. There are advantages and disadvantages to different educational systems, which reflect culture.
3. In a society such as that in the United States or Canada, teachers value individualism highly.
4. Students from Japan can memorize information better than students from the United States can.

exercise 7   Turn back to the Preparing to Read section on page 3 and answer the question.

Discussing the Reading

activity   In small groups, talk about your answers to these questions.

1. What is the system of education like in your country? How is it different from the North American system?
2. Which system do you prefer? Why?
3. What other educational methods are there? Describe them and tell some of their advantages and disadvantages.

PART two

College Students in the United States Today

Before You Read

Skimming for Main Ideas

A paragraph usually tells about one topic (subject). Often one sentence is the topic sentence. It tells the topic and the main idea of the paragraph. The other sentences give details about the main idea. For example:

Life on U.S. college campuses is always changing. One change these days is that there are more foreign students than ever before, especially in certain majors and in graduate schools. There are almost half a million foreign students in colleges and universities in the United States. Over 100,000 international students attend graduate school—more than 25 percent (%) of the total graduate enrollment. Most of these students are studying business and management. Almost as many are majoring in engineering. Other practical courses—mathematics, computer science, and some life sciences (such as biology)—are also popular majors. Not many foreign students are majoring in the humanities (literature, art, drama, philosophy, etc.) or the social sciences (anthropology, psychology, and so on), probably because they don't believe these fields offer the best job opportunities.

Topic: foreign students in the United States
Topic sentence: One change these days is that there are more foreign students than ever before, especially in certain majors and in graduate schools.

exercise Read the following paragraphs quickly. Do not use a dictionary, and don't worry about the details. When you finish, write the topic and topic sentence of each paragraph. (*Hints:* The topic is just a word or noun phrase—a few words. It is not a sentence. The topic sentence can be found in different places in the paragraph: beginning, middle, or end.)

College Students in the United States Today

A   **F**or many years in the United States, most undergraduate students (in their first four years of college) were 18 to 22 years old. They attended college full time, lived in a dormitory on campus, and expected many "extras" from their colleges, not just classes. But things began to change in the 1970s and are very different now. Today, these "traditional" students are less than one-quarter (1/4) of all college students. These days the nontraditional students are the majority; they are different from traditional undergraduates in several ways. They are older. Many attend college parttime because they have families and jobs. Most live off campus, not in dorms. These nontraditional students don't want the extras that colleges usually offer. They aren't interested in the sports, entertainment, religious groups, and museums that are part of most U.S. colleges. They want mainly good-quality classes, day or night, at a low cost. They also hope for easy parking, short registration lines, and polite service. Both time and money are important to them.

Topic: _____

Topic sentence: _____

_____

B   Psychological tests reflect different learning styles in this new student population, too. Each person has a certain learning style, and about 60 percent (%) of the new students these days prefer the *sensing* style. This means that they are very practical. They prefer a practice-to-theory method of learning—experience first and ideas after that. They often have difficulty with reading and writing and are unsure of themselves. Most of these students are attending college because they want to have a good job and make a lot of money.

Topic: _____

Topic sentence: _____

_____

C   In contrast, other students (but not as many) prefer the *intuitive* learning style. These students love ideas. They prefer a theory-to-practice method of learning and enjoy independent, creative thinking. These "intuitives" are not very practical. They are attending college because they want to create unique works of art or study philosophy or someday help in the field of science.

Topic: _____

Topic sentence: _____

_____

D   There is a drawback for the students who prefer the sensing style of learning. A majority of college professors prefer the intuitive learning style. These teachers value independent thinking and creative ideas. Students in the sensing group are at a disadvantage because their way of thinking doesn't match their teachers'.

Topic: _____

Topic sentence: _____

_____

E   In another way, also, students these days are different from students in the past. In the 1960s and 1970s, many students demonstrated against the government and hoped to make big changes in society. In the 1980s, most students were interested only in their studies and future jobs. Today, students seem to be a combination of the two: They want to make good money when they graduate, but they're also interested in helping society. Many students today are volunteering in the community. They are working to help people, without payment. For example, they tutor (teach privately) children in trouble, or they work with organizations for homeless people. In these ways, they hope to make changes in society.

Topic: _____

Topic sentence: _____

_____

Interactions II • Reading

After You Read

Understanding Pronoun Reference

As you know, pronouns take the place of nouns. When you read, it's important to understand the meaning of pronouns, to know which noun a pronoun refers to. To find the noun that a pronoun refers to, look back in the sentence or in the sentences that come before it.

example: Over 100,000 international students attend graduate school. Most of <u>them</u> are studying business and management. (What does *them* refer to? <u>international students</u>)

exercise   Look back at the reading selection "College Students in the United States Today" to find the meaning of the following pronouns. What does each pronoun refer to?

1. they (paragraph A, line 2) _____

2. they (paragraph A, line 7) _____

3. them (paragraph A, line 15) _____

4. their (paragraph D, line 4) _____

5. their (paragraph E, line 4) _____

Discussing the Reading

activity   In small groups, talk about your answers to these questions.

1. In your country, are there foreign students in colleges and universities? If so, where do they come from? Are there many?

2. In your country, are students today different from students in the past? If so, how are they different?

3. What are the main reasons that students in your country go to college?

4. Do students in your country do volunteer work? If so, what kind?

WHAT DO YOU THINK?

Part of college life in North America these days is discussion of P.C.—political correctness. The reason for P.C. is to make students more sensitive to differences among various groups of people and to teach them to be more careful with their language. Most students and teachers try to be politically correct, but many think that "things have gone too far." What do *you* think?

Here are some words and phrases that people used in the past and the more careful, politically correct words that some people now use, instead. Can you think of reasons why people who use the politically correct words don't like the less politically correct words? Which P.C. words seem good to you? Why? Do any seem strange? If so, why?

LESS POLITICALLY CORRECT	POLITICALLY CORRECT
able-bodied	temporarily able
blind	visually challenged
disabled; handicapped	differently abled
fat people	people of size
mankind	humanity
Orientals	Asians
pets	animal companions
policeman	police officer
remedial classes	basic classes
short people	vertically challenged
Third World countries; underdeveloped countries	developing countries

Synonyms

exercise

Match the words with their meanings. Write the letters on the lines, as in the example.

1. _g_ cooperation
2. _____ method
3. _____ reflect
4. _____ memorize
5. _____ drawback
6. _____ recite
7. _____ discipline
8. _____ majority
9. _____ prepare
10. _____ startled

a. learn and remember
b. disadvantage
c. most; larger number
d. say aloud
e. control
f. surprised
g. working together √
h. way
i. get ready
j. show

Words in Context

exercise

Write the missing words in the blanks here and on the next page. Choose from these words.

| graduate | society | combination | value |
| elementary | demonstrate | major | formal |

1. Children often have art lessons in _elementary_ school.

2. National and religious differences are part of the culture of American

   _____ .

3. In a _____ college classroom, the teacher lectures and the students listen.

4. Some people _____ against the government to express their political opinions.

5. Many students attend college after they _____ from high school.

6. Some societies _____ individualism and original ideas.

7. She plans to _____ in engineering.

8. There are advantages and disadvantages to any educational system; the best system probably uses a _____ of methods.

focus on testing

Reading and Following Instructions

Textbooks, quizzes, and exams often use special words in instructions. It is important to follow these instructions carefully.

exercise 1 Which words show examples of which instructions? Match the instructions on the left with the words on the right. Write the letters of the words on the lines, as in the example. Pay special attention to the verbs.

1. Circle the word. _m_

2. Underline the word. ____

3. Put a box around the word. ____

4. Put a check by the word. ____

5. Cross out the word. ____

6. Count the words and write the number. ____

7. Fill in the blank. ____

8. Complete the word. ____

9. Divide the word; draw lines. ____

10. Write the past tense of the word. ____

11. Match the words; connect them with lines. ____

12. Cross out the mistakes and correct the word. ____

a. attention

b. Canadian

c. √activities

d. politics

e. social — administration
   business — science

f. high, free, popular _3_

g. major in a ____ subject
   consider
   (practical)
   anthropology

h. difficulties

i. study studied

j. an Asian country

k. mem|o|ri|zat|ion

l. ejucashun (education)

13. Choose the correct word and circle it. _____

14. Number the words in alphabetical order. _____

15. Write the words in order. _____

m. (original)

n. __2__ society

__1__ school

__3__ system

o. OFTEN TOGETHER WORK IN SCHOOL STUDENTS

Students often work together after school.

exercise 2 Follow the instructions carefully. The first one is done as an example.

1. Circle the college subjects.

(anthropology)   contrast   (sociology)   (art)   tuition

2. Put a check by the nouns. Underline the verbs.

methods   facts   choose   happen   idea   consider

3. Draw lines to match the words with opposite meanings.

advantage   free   enter   difficult   forget

expensive   disadvantage   remember   easy   graduate

4. Cross out the incorrect words, correct the spelling mistakes, and write the correct words above them.

It's difficult to pass the intrance egzam without ekstra prepareashun.

5. Count the words that name shapes. Write the number here. _____

smaller   circle   identical   triangle   box   relatively

6. Draw lines to separate the words from each other.

Readtheseparagraphsquicklywithoutadictionary.

exercise 3 Write instructions for the groups of words, as in the example.

1. Underline the adjectives and put a check by the adverbs. _____

poor   √ probably   original   basic   √ relatively   √ seriously

2. _____

instructor   university   private school   college   exam

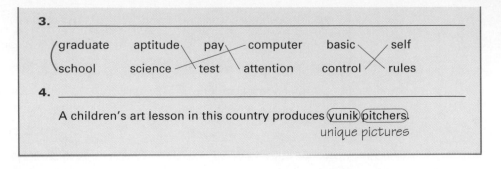

3. _____

graduate   aptitude   pay   computer   basic   self
school   science   test   attention   control rules

4. _____

A children's art lesson in this country produces (yunik)(pitchers).
                                                  unique pictures

PART **four**

Reading in the Real World

Scanning for Information
School Documents

Sometimes you want to find information quickly. In this case, you don't read every sentence. Instead, you *scan* the material—you look quickly for the important words. To do this, have a question in your mind. Then run your finger down the page until the answer "jumps out" at you. Don't read any more than necessary in order to answer your question.

exercise 1

In this section, you will scan an application form from an American school. In the United States, a student from another country needs to have a student visa. This visa is called an F-1. To get an F-1 visa, a student must first fill out an I-20 form. Before you scan the next few pages, quickly look over the following list. It contains vocabulary from the letter on page 18.

community adult school	=	a school where students over 18 can get free education
residents	=	people who have their home in a certain place
Immigration and Naturalization Service	=	a government agency
requirements	=	necessary conditions
a minimum of	=	at least
questionnaire	=	a form that asks questions
submit	=	offer; send; give a paper to a school or government office

sponsor	=	a person who is responsible for an immigrant
transcript	=	a list of all courses that a student has taken and the student's grades in the classes
verification	=	proof; evidence that something is true
financial status	=	a person's "money situation"
recommendation letter	=	a letter that says good things about a person
fees	=	money for something
application	=	a written request to do something
prerequisite	=	something that is necessary before something else can happen
status	=	position
objective	=	purpose; plans
post-	=	after
absence	=	not being in a place
work permits	=	government permission to get jobs

exercise 2 Read the letter on page 18. Find the answers to the questions below, and write them on the lines below.

1. What can students learn at E. Manfred Evans Community Adult School?

_____

2. Who goes to this school? _____

3. How old must a student be to get an I-20 form? _____

4. Which of the following must a student send along with his or her questionnaire? Put checkmarks on the lines.

a. _____ a medical form from a doctor

b. _____ a letter from the student's parents

c. _____ a paper from the student's sponsor

d. _____ four big pictures

e. _____ a $500 check for tuition

f. _____ high school and/or college transcripts

g. _____ information about his or her sponsor's financial situation

h. _____ a list of reasons that the student needs to study English

i. _____ a letter from the student's present school or job

E. Manfred Evans Community Adult School

717 NORTH FIGUEROA ST., LOS ANGELES, CALIFORNIA 90012-2196

TELEPHONE: (213) 626-7151

Date:

Dear Prospective Student:

E. Manfred Evans Community Adult School is a Los Angeles City School specializing in teaching students to communicate in English. Although designed for residents of the Los Angeles area, it has also been approved by the United States Immigration and Naturalization Service for admittance of nonimmigrant F-1 visa students. F-1 visa students' class hours are 1:30-6:40 p.m., Monday through Friday, from September to June.

REQUIREMENTS FOR THE I-20 FORM ARE AS FOLLOWS:

1. Must be a minimum of eighteen years of age.

2. Complete and submit the attached questionnaire.

3. Submit medical form completed, signed, sealed, and dated by a medical doctor. Chest x-ray results must also be included.

4. Submit the signed sponsor statement.

5. Submit one passport-type photograph.

6. Submit copies of transcripts of high school and/or college records in English (for the last three years).

7. Submit verification of sponsor's financial status.

8. Submit a recommendation letter from the school currently attending or from an assigned work unit.

There are no fees involved in obtaining the I-20. There is, however, a voluntary 50¢ student membership card.

The required forms constitute an application to Evans Community Adult School, not an acceptance. After the completed forms reach this school, if all is satisfactory, an I-20 form, a prerequisite for F-1 student visa status, will be issued.

Sincerely,

Counseling Staff

Find the answers to these questions about the application form on page 20. Write the answers on the lines below.

1. What is the student's first name? _____

    The student's last name? _____

2. In what country is he living right now? _____

3. Where was he born? _____ Is he a citizen of that country? _____

4. How much money will he probably spend in one year in the United States?

    _____ Where will he get the money?_____

5. How many years did he spend in elementary school? _____ Did he finish

    high school? _____ Has he gone to college? _____

6. What does he plan to do after he finishes his courses at Evans?

    _____

7. What will his field of study probably be? _____

8. What must he do to stay in school? Check the answers.

    a. _____ go to class at least 25 hours a week

    b. _____ get a job after school

    c. _____ study and get good grades

    d. _____ live with an American family

Going Beyond the Text

 **activity**

Bring to class things to read about college life. Some examples are catalogs, course schedules, school newspapers, orientation information, and so on. Share them with the class. Discuss the important information and learn new vocabulary.

LOS ANGELES UNIFIED SCHOOL DISTRICT

E. Manfred Evans Community Adult School

717 NORTH FIGUEROA ST., LOS ANGELES, CALIFORNIA 90012-2196

TELEPHONE: (213) 626-7151

In Country: _____

Out of Country: ✓

Date: __1/12/96__   Counselor: _____

PERSONAL DATA

__de Menezes__   __Carlos__   __E.__
PRINT - LAST NAME   FIRST   INITIAL

PRESENT ADDRESS: __R. Almirante   32 Saõ Paulo   Brazil__
                              STREET   CITY   COUNTRY

BIRTHDATE: __3 / 19 / 57__   __Portugal__   __Brazil__
                  MONTH DAY YEAR   COUNTRY OF BIRTH   COUNTRY OF CITIZENSHIP

FINANCIAL STATUS: The estimated cost of living in the United States is approximately $6,000 per year. Who will provide your financial support? __Brother__

EDUCATION: Please indicate number of years of school in your country at each level. Elementary: __9__ Secondary: __3__ University or college: __3__ Total: __15__

EDUCATIONAL OBJECTIVE: Do you plan to return to your country as soon as you have completed your English course of studies at Evans? Yes: __X__ No: _____
If your answer is "NO," please indicate your post-Evans educational plans:
Community College: _____ University: _____ Trade School: _____
Business College: _____ Graduate School: _____
Other: _____

What field of study would you like to pursue (example: business, engineering, medicine, education, etc.)? __film direction__

GENERAL INFORMATION:

1. Student MUST be at least 18 years of age.

2. Student will attend assigned F-1 visa classes for a minimum of 25 hours per week. Excessive absence is a cause for dismissal from the F-1 visa program.

3. Work permits are not granted by the Immigration and Naturalization Service to students enrolled in a language school.

4. Students are to exhibit satisfactory academic progress and good citizenship.

5. The status of F-1 visa students is considered to be a contract between student and school. IT IS ESSENTIAL FOR STUDENTS TO FULLY UNDERSTAND THE REQUIREMENTS OF THE F-1 VISA PRIOR TO ACCEPTING THIS STATUS.

6. Class hours are 1:30 p.m. to 6:40 p.m., Monday through Friday, from September through June.

STUDENT ACCEPTANCE:

I have read (or had translated for me) the information on this page, and I agree to follow school requirements.

Student's Signature: __Carlos E. de Menezes__ Date: __1/12/96__

CHAPTER two

City Life

in this chapter

The first reading selection discusses the causes and effects of overcrowding in some of the world's largest cities. Next, you'll read about indoor air pollution—just one example of a problem that occurs in modern cities. Finally, you'll learn how to find information quickly on a city map.

PART one

The Urban Crisis

Before You Read

Getting Started

Look at the graph and the pictures, and discuss them.

1. Where do you think the pictures take place?
2. What might be some of the problems in these cities?
3. How many people now live in cities in Nigeria? In Indonesia? In India?
4. How many people will be living in cities in these countries by the year 2025?

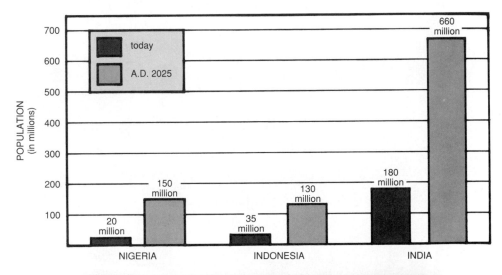

Preparing to Read

As you read the following selection, think about the answer to this question: What are some problems of (and solutions to) overpopulation?

Read the following selection quickly. Do not use a dictionary. Then do the exercises that follow the reading.

A

The Urban Crisis

One goal of many Americans and Canadians is to move out of a busy urban area such as New York, Los Angeles, or Toronto. They say that they want to escape from pollution (for example, smog and noise pollution). They want to get away from crime. They're tired of the crowds of people each day on the mass-transit systems—buses, commuter trains, and subways. Or, if they have cars, they would like to avoid the traffic that they get into when they commute daily from their homes to their offices and back. These people believe that life would be better in the suburbs—that is, the areas just outside the city—or even farther away, in the countryside.

B

This dream of a better life in another place is certainly not unique to people living in the United States and Canada. However, this dream may take various forms in different parts of the world. In some areas, there is a movement to the countryside; in contrast, millions of people are moving *away* from rural areas in other countries. In other words, in much of the world there is an exodus from the countryside to the cities. The urban population in most developing countries such as India and Nigeria is increasing very fast.

C The statistics are not pleasant. In 1993, the world population reached 5½ billion. More than 1 billion of these people lived in cities in the developing nations. People who study population growth predict that by the year 2025, the population of the world will be more than 8 billion. These experts say that cities in developing countries—where overpopulation will be especially serious—will be home to almost 4 billion of these people.

D There are several reasons for this enormous population growth. Of course, there is a general increase in the world population because modern medicine and new methods of food production allow adults to live longer and babies to survive, not die soon after birth. In Latin America, where seven out of ten people already live in cities, most future growth will be from this natural increase. But in many other countries millions of people are moving to urban areas because they must find work. "In a poor country like India, they don't come looking for the comforts of city living; they come for jobs," says Rajinder Kuman Takkar, a government official in Delhi. There simply aren't jobs in the countryside. There isn't enough good farmland for large families in rural areas. In addition, farming methods are not always modern. These out-of-date methods cause farms to be unsuccessful. These problems are worsening, not getting better, so more and more people are leaving their homes to find a better life in cities.

E Is life better in cities? Probably not. Many people find that the city of their dreams has become a nightmare. Population growth is causing unbelievable overcrowding. Nairobi, Kenya, for example, has basic services for 200,000 people but will soon have a population of 5 *million.* Mexico City is home to almost 25 million. This overcrowding causes many serious problems: traffic, pollution, sickness, and crime. There isn't enough water, transportation, or housing. There aren't enough sewers; in Sao Paulo, Brazil, for instance, only 40% of the homes are connected to the city sewer system, which carries away dirty water and waste through pipes under the ground. Perhaps most serious of all, there aren't enough jobs. One-third to one-half of the people in many cities in developing nations cannot find work or can find only part-time jobs. Millions of these people are hungry, homeless, sick, and afraid. The crisis is worsening daily; that is, this time of danger and difficulty is becoming more horrible every day. Population experts tell us that by the year 2025, the population in cities in developing nations will increase to *four times* its present size.

F The situation seems hopeless, but perhaps it isn't. The answer to the problem ". . . is to provide jobs for them where they live, where they were born," Takkar says. Beijing, Cairo, New Delhi, and other urban centers are trying to create smaller cities, in the countryside, with jobs and housing. The hope is to slow the exodus of rural people to the already overcrowded cities.

After You Read

Getting the Main Ideas

exercise Write T on the lines before the statements that are true, according to the reading. Write F on the lines before the statements that are false.

1. _____ Many Americans would like to move out of cities.

2. _____ The population of cities in developing nations is getting smaller.

3. _____ Eight billion people will be living in cities by the year 2025.

4. _____ Millions of people in many countries are moving to cities because they need to find work.

5. _____ Overcrowding in many cities is creating terrible problems.

6. _____ There is no hope for the future.

Guessing Meaning from Context

> You do not need to look up the meanings of new words if you can guess them from the context.
> Sometimes there are examples of the meaning of a new vocabulary item in another sentence or sentence part. The words *for example, for instance,* and *such as* or punctuation marks such as parentheses ( ), dashes (—), and commas may introduce examples.

 Find examples of the underlined word(s) in each sentence here and on the next page, and write them on the lines.

example: One goal of many Americans and Canadians is to move out of a busy <u>urban area</u> such as New York, Los Angeles, or Toronto.

New York, Los Angeles, Toronto

1. They want to escape from <u>pollution</u> (for example, smog and noise pollution).

_____

2. They're tired of the crowds of people each day on the <u>mass-transit system</u>—buses, commuter trains, and subways.

_____

3. The urban population in most <u>developing countries</u> such as India and Nigeria is increasing very fast.

_____

> Sometimes another word or words in another sentence or sentence part has the opposite meaning from a new vocabulary item.
>
> _example:_   In some areas, there is a movement to the countryside; in contrast, millions of people are moving *away* from rural areas in other countries. In other words, in much of the world there is an <u>exodus</u> from the countryside to the cities. (An <u>exodus</u> is a movement *away* from a place.)

exercise 3   Write the words from each item that have an opposite meaning from the underlined word.

1. Modern medicine and new methods of food production allow adults to live longer and babies to <u>survive</u>, not die soon after birth.

_____

2. Farming methods are not always modern. These <u>out-of-date</u> methods cause farms to be unsuccessful.

_____

3. These problems are <u>worsening</u>, not getting better.

_____

4. Many people find that the city of their dreams has become a <u>nightmare</u>.

_____

> A definition or explanation follows the connecting words *that is* and *in other words.*
>
> _example:_   These people believe that life would be better in the <u>suburbs</u>—that is, the areas just outside the city. (<u>Suburbs</u> are the areas just outside the city.)

1. Millions of people are moving away from <u>rural</u> areas. In other words, in much of the world there is an exodus from the countryside to the cities.

_____

2. The <u>crisis</u> is worsening daily; that is, this time of danger and difficulty is becoming more horrible every day.

_____

Sometimes details about a vocabulary item give clues to its meaning.

 Write the answers to the following questions about the underlined word or words in each item.

1. If they have cars, they would like to avoid the traffic that they get into when they <u>commute</u> daily from their homes to their offices and back.

   a. What part of speech is <u>commute</u> in this sentence (noun, verb, adjective)? _____

   b. What do people who <u>commute</u> want to avoid? _____ What do they have? _____

   c. How often do they <u>commute</u>? _____

   d. Where do they go when they <u>commute</u>? _____

   e. What does <u>commute</u> mean? _____

2. The <u>statistics</u> are not pleasant. In 1993, the world population reached 5½ billion. One billion of these people lived in cities in developing nations. People who study population growth <u>predict</u> that by the year 2025 the population will be over 8 billion, and they say that cities in developing countries will be home to almost 4 billion of these people.

   a. What part of speech is <u>statistics</u>? _____

   b. What is similar about all of the information in these sentences? (In what form are the pieces of information?) _____

   c. What are <u>statistics</u>? _____

   d. What kind of verb is <u>predict</u>? (Does it express action, condition, or speech?) _____

   e. What do people make predictions about? _____

   f. What does <u>predict</u> mean? _____

Understanding Reading Structure

exercise **6** In the reading selection "The Urban Crisis," there are letters next to the six paragraphs. Match each paragraph and its letter with a topic; write the letters on the lines.

1. _____ Predictions about world population growth by the year 2025

2. _____ People who are moving to urban areas

3. _____ Introduction: People who want to escape from the problems of cities

4. _____ Conclusion: A possible solution

5. _____ Reasons for the increase in population in many urban areas

6. _____ Conditions in crowded cities

exercise **7** Here are two lists of information from the reading selection. Which *specific* ideas give support to each *general* idea? Write the letter of the general idea next to each specific idea as in the example.

SPECIFIC IDEAS

1. _b_ People move to cities because they want to find work.

2. _____ They want to escape from pollution, crime, crowds, and traffic.

3. _____ There isn't enough water, housing, or transportation.

4. _____ Nairobi will soon have a population of 5 million but has basic services for only 200,000.

5. _____ They believe life would be better in the suburbs or the countryside.

6. _____ Traffic, pollution, sickness, and crime are the result of overcrowding.

7. _____ There aren't enough jobs in the countryside.

8. _____ There aren't enough sewers to carry away dirty water and waste.

GENERAL IDEAS

a. Many Americans and Canadians want to escape from the problems of city life.

b. In many developing countries, there is a movement of people from the countryside to the cities.

c. Overcrowding causes terrible problems in many cities.

 **exercise 8**   A reading expresses one main idea, which sums up (summarizes) the topics of all the paragraphs in the selection. Circle the number of the main idea of the reading selection "The Urban Crisis."

1. People everywhere want to move to cities.
2. There are many people who can't find work in big cities.
3. The world population is growing fast because of modern medicine and new methods of food production.
4. Overpopulation is causing the beginning of a crisis, especially in cities in developing nations.

exercise 9   Turn back to the Preparing to Read section on page 23 and answer the questions.

Discussing the Reading

 activity   In small groups, talk about your answers to these questions.

1. Do you come from a big city, a suburb, or a rural area?
2. What do you think are some reasons for so many homeless people in many U.S. cities?
3. What solutions do you suggest to urban problems?
4. Do you think that overpopulation will be as bad as people predict? How can we avoid this crisis?

San Francisco

PART two

Sick Building Syndrome

Before You Read

Skimming for Main Ideas

> As you learned in Chapter One, a paragraph usually tells about one topic. Often one sentence, which tells the topic and the main idea of the paragraph, is the topic sentence.

Read these paragraphs quickly. Do not use a dictionary and don't worry about the details. When you finish, write the topic and topic sentence of each paragraph.

Note: For a short vocabulary study of this reading passage, turn to pages 38–39.

Sick Building Syndrome

A **W**hen Oakland High School in California was moved into a new building, the students and teachers noticed a strong smell. Then almost half of the students began to have headaches and sore throats and to be very tired. These three symptoms disappeared on weekends. The reason was a mystery. Experts came to investigate and find the cause of the sickness. Finally, they discovered that the air in the building was not safe to breathe. They were surprised to find that the cause was the shelves in the school library! These shelves were made of particleboard—that is, an inexpensive kind of board made of very small pieces of wood held together with a chemical. This is just one example of a modern problem that is most common in cities—*indoor* air pollution.

Topic: _____

Topic sentence: _____

_____

B   People have worried about smog for many years, and the government has spent billions of dollars to try to clean up the air of big cities. But now we find that there is no escape from unhealthful air. Recent studies have shown that air *inside* many homes, office buildings, and schools is full of pollutants: chemicals, bacteria, smoke, and gases. These pollutants are causing a group of unpleasant and dangerous symptoms that experts call "sick building syndrome." A "sick building" might be a small house in a rural area or an enormous office building in an urban center.

Topic: _____

Topic sentence: _____

_____

C   A recent study reached a surprising conclusion: Indoor air pollution is almost always two to five times worse than outside pollution! This is true even in buildings that are close to factories that produce chemicals. Better ventilation—a system for moving fresh air—can cut indoor pollution to a safe level, but *lack* of ventilation is seldom the main cause of the problem. Experts have found that buildings create their own pollution. Imagine a typical home. The people who live there burn oil, wood, or gas for cooking and heating. They might smoke cigarettes, pipes, or cigars. They use chemicals for cleaning. They use hundreds of products made of plastic or particleboard; these products—such as the bookshelves in Oakland High School—give off chemicals that we can't see but that we *do* breathe in. And in many areas, the ground under the building might send a dangerous gas called *radon* into the home. The people in the house are breathing in a "chemical soup."

Topic: _____

Topic sentence: _____

_____

D

There is a possible solution to the problem of "sick" buildings. A scientist at NASA (National Aeronautical and Space Administration) was trying to find ways to clean the air in space stations. He discovered that *houseplants* actually remove pollutants from the air. Certain plants seem to do this better than others. Spider plants, for example, appear to do the best job. Even defoliated plants (without leaves) worked well! In another study, scientists found that the chemical interaction among soil, roots, and leaves works to remove pollutants.

Topic: _____

Topic sentence: _____

_____

E

This seems like a good solution, but we don't know enough yet. There are many questions. For instance, which pollutants can plants remove? Which *can't* they remove? How many plants are necessary to clean the air in a room—one or two or a whole forest of plants? When we are able to answer these questions, we might find that plants offer an important pollution-control system for the 21st century.

Topic: _____

Topic sentence: _____

_____

After You Read

exercise **1** After you write the topic and topic sentence of each paragraph, exchange your answers with another student. Are your answers the same? Are your topics the same but perhaps in different words? Do you agree about the topic sentences? If you don't agree, give reasons for your answers. One of you might want to change an answer!

Understanding Pronoun Reference

exercise **2** Look back at the reading selection "Sick Building Syndrome" to find the meaning of the following pronouns. What does each pronoun refer to?

1. they (paragraph A, line 6) _____

2. their (paragraph C, line 6) _____

3. they (paragraph C, line 8) _____

4. he (paragraph D, line 3) _____

5. they (paragraph E, line 3) _____

Interactions II • Reading

Discussing the Reading

In small groups, talk about your answers to these questions.

1. Is there a problem with smog in your city? When is it the worst? What are the causes?
2. Have you ever experienced sick building syndrome? If so, what were your symptoms?
3. How many possible pollutants can you find in your home and classroom? Make a list.
4. In your home country, do people usually have houseplants? Why or why not?

WHAT DO YOU THINK?

Classifying and Evaluating

1. What is this person in the cartoon worried about?
2. In your opinion, what is the point (idea) of this cartoon? In other words, what is the writer telling us?
3. Do you worry about any problems in modern life? If so, which ones?
4. Do some people worry too much? If so, what should they do about this?

PART three

Building Vocabulary and Study Skills

Parts of Speech

To guess the meaning of a new word from the context, you may find it helpful to know its "part of speech"; that is, is the word a noun, a verb, an adjective, or a preposition? Many words can be more than one part of speech.

examples: He tried to <u>answer</u> the question. (<u>Answer</u> is a verb; it is part of the infinitive <u>to answer</u>.)

It's difficult to find an <u>answer</u> to the problem. (<u>Answer</u> is a noun.)

In some cases, different parts of speech (usually a noun and a verb) have the same spelling but different pronunciations.

examples: We can <u>contrast</u> the problems of rural and urban areas. (<u>Contrast</u> is a verb; the emphasis—the syllable stress—is on the second syllable, <u>-trast</u>.)

In Latin America, by <u>contrast</u>, there won't be much more of an exodus to urban areas. (<u>Contrast</u> is a noun; it is the object of the preposition <u>by</u>. The emphasis is on the first syllable, <u>con-</u>.)

exercise 1 Study and pronounce the words in this chart.

noun	verb	noun	verb
answer	answer	dream	dream
cause	cause	house	house†
change	change	increase	increase*
contrast	contrast*	study	study
crowd	crowd	worry	worry

*The singular noun ends in a voiceless sound /s/; the verb ends in a voiced sound /z/.
†The noun has the accent on the first syllable; the verb has the accent on the last syllable.

Complete each sentence with words from the chart in Exercise 1. Use the same word for both blanks of each item, and write the part of speech—(n) for *noun* or (v) for *verb*—in the parentheses after each blank as in the example.

1. What <u>causes</u> (v) air pollution? One <u>cause</u> (n) is traffic.

2. Some people avoid subways because of the big _____s ( ) of people who _____ ( ) onto the trains of the mass-transit system twice a day.

3. Can we solve the problem of overcrowding? No one can _____ ( ) this question. We don't have the _____ ( ).

4. In some cities, people without _____s ( ) may have to sleep in the streets. It is difficult to _____ ( ) all the people who need apartments.

5. The cost of housing doesn't go down; it _____s ( ) every year. Often elderly people with little money have to move because of the _____ ( ).

6. A recent _____ ( ) has shown that indoor air pollution is a growing problem. Experts are _____ing ( ) the situation and trying to find solutions.

7. People who live in big cities often _____ ( ) about crime. _____ ( ) can cause illness.

8. The _____ ( ) of some people is to move to a quiet rural area. Other people _____ ( ) of moving to a city.

> Many words are related to one another; they have the same stem (base word) but different endings.
>
> *example:* After they lived in the <u>suburbs</u> for a year or so, they began to see that there are disadvantages as well as advantages to <u>suburban</u> life. (Suburbs is a plural noun; it is the object of the preposition <u>in</u>. Suburban is an adjective; it describes the noun life.)

exercise 3   Study and pronounce the words in this chart.

noun	verb	adjective	adverb
creation	create	creative	creatively
crowd	crowd	crowded	
difference	differ	different	differently
difficulty		difficult	
life	live	livable	
pollution, pollutant	pollute	polluted	
prediction	predict	predictable	predictably
safety	save	safe	safely
solution	solve	solvable	
suburb		suburban	
	worsen	worse	worse

exercise 4   Complete each sentence with the missing words from the chart above. Use forms of the base word (the underlined words to the left of each section) and write the part of speech in the parentheses after each blank—(n) for *noun*, (v) for *verb*, (adj) for *adjective*, and (adv) for *adverb*. The first one is done as an example.

1. <u>solve</u>: They are trying to find a <u>solution</u> (*n*) to the problem of overcrowding, but this is a difficult problem to <u>solve</u> (*v*).

2. <u>pollute</u>: Most people know about air _____ ( ) in big cities, but they're just beginning to learn about the many _____ s ( ) that we have *inside* buildings.

3. <u>crowd</u>: There are _____ s ( ) of people everywhere; the mass transit system is especially _____ ( ).

4. <u>safe</u>: The city is not _____ ( ) because of crime. People can't leave their homes _____ ( ) at night, and the police can't provide for their _____ ( ).

5. <u>live</u>, <u>suburb</u>: Many people prefer to _____ ( ) in the _____ s ( ); they say that _____ ( ) _____ ( ) is more pleasant than city living.

6. <u>predict</u>, <u>worse</u>: Some people _____ ( ) that urban life will get _____ ( ); according to their _____ s ( ), conditions will _____ ( ) every year.

7. <u>differ</u>: The causes of indoor air pollution _____ (   )

from area to area. One reason for the _____ (   ) is that

people heat their homes _____ (   ). People in some

areas burn wood for heat; in other areas, they use something

_____ (   ).

Using the Dictionary to Find Parts of Speech

You know that you don't need to look up every new word in a dictionary because you can often guess the meanings from the context. Sometimes, however, you may want to use a dictionary for other purposes—for instance, to find out the part of speech of a word or to learn related words.

A dictionary will tell you the parts of speech a word can be, usually with these abbreviations: *n.* = *noun, v.* = *verb, adj.* = *adjective, adv.* = *adverb, prep.* = *preposition, conj.* = *conjunction.* The abbreviation appears before the meanings of the word with that part of speech.

example: This dictionary entry shows that the word <u>reason</u> can be a noun (with four meanings) or a verb (with one meaning). A related adjective is <u>reasonable</u>.

rea·son[1] /riy'zən/ *n*   **1** purpose, cause (for a belief or act): *The reason for the error was clear.*   **2** an excuse: *I didn't have any reason for being late.*   **3** the ability to think clearly: *She is normally a person of good reason.*   **4** good judgment: *He has lost all reason!*
reason[2] *v*   to persuade or think in a sensible way: *I tried to reason with him, but he won't listen to me.*
rea'son·a·ble   *adj*   having reason or sense: *She is normally a very reasonable person, but today she's upset.*

If possible, everyone in the class should use the same kind of dictionary for the following exercises. Work quickly. The first student with the correct answers is the winner.

<u>*exercise*</u> **1**   Find these words in your dictionary. Write the part of speech on the lines before each word—(*n*) for *noun*, (*v*) for *verb*, (*adj*) for *adjective*, and (*adv*) for *adverb* as in the examples. Some words, in different contexts, can be more than one part of speech.

1. <u>adj</u> terrible

2. <u>n, v</u> discipline

3. ____ value

4. ____ original

5. ____ pleasant

6. ____ water

7. ____ expert

8. ____ commute

9. ____ farm

10. ____ smog

11. ____ air

12. ____ produce

13. ____ enormous

14. ____ mystery

15. ____ individual

 **exercise 2** Complete the chart. Write the appropriate related words under each heading as in the examples. (X means that no word of that part of speech exists.)

nouns	verbs	adjectives	adverbs
surprise	surprise	surprising	surprisingly
X	X	surprised	X
exactness			exactly
	educate		
	X		X
	believe		
	X	X	X
		formal	
origin			X
	prepare		
consideration			
	survive	survivable	X
	X	X	X

Guessing Meaning from Context

Many standardized exams don't test your vocabulary, but they test how well you can *guess* the meaning of a word or phrase from the context. Often on tests such as the one below, one answer is close but not close enough. One has the correct part of speech but the wrong meaning. Another is simply wrong; perhaps it is the opposite of the correct answer or has the wrong part of speech. Always keep in mind that there is only one correct answer.

exercise Take this practice test. Guess the meaning of the underlined words from the reading selection "Sick Building Syndrome." Circle the letter of the correct answer. Don't use a dictionary, and work as fast as you can.

1. Almost half of the students began to have headaches and <u>sore</u> throats and to be very tired.
    a. painful   **c.** difficult
    b. well   **d.** problem

2. Almost half of the students began to have headaches and sore throats and to be very tired. These three <u>symptoms</u> disappeared on weekends.
    a. syndromes   **c.** signs of a sickness
    b. headaches   **d.** situations on a weekend

3. These pollutants are causing a group of unpleasant and dangerous symptoms that experts call "sick building syndrome."
   a. polluted
   b. problem with a large building
   c. symptom
   d. combination of symptoms

4. They were surprised to find that the cause of the sickness was the shelves in the school library. These shelves were made of particleboard.
   a. plants to remove smoke from the air
   b. books in a library
   c. long, flat pieces of wood to put things on
   d. metal handles on doors and windows

5. The air was full of pollutants: chemicals, bacteria, smoke, and gases.
   a. pollution
   b. chemicals
   c. smog inside a building
   d. things that pollute

PART four

Reading in the Real World

Scanning for Information

City Maps

 You scan city maps to quickly find the information that you need—usually street names. Sometimes maps give other information as well. Before you scan the next few pages, quickly look over the following list. It contains vocabulary from the city map.

boat launching	= a place where you can put your boat into the water
groceries	= things in a food store
produce	= fresh fruit and vegetables
exhibit	= a show; something to see (usually in a museum)
planetarium	= a building where people study the stars
breathtaking	= very beautiful
trail	= a small road for people to walk on

 **exercise 2** Scan the list of "outstanding attractions." Write the answers to the following questions.

1. What city are these attractions in? _____

2. Fill in the blanks in this chart.

PLACE	WHAT IS IT? WHAT DOES IT OFFER?
(A) Stanley Park	a playground with a zoo
(D) _____	_____
(F) _____	_____
(I) _____	_____
(K1) _____	_____
(Q) _____	_____

Outstanding attractions

VANCOUVER

(A) Stanley Park—A 404 hectare playground 10 minutes from downtown includes zoo, with polar bears and penguins. A miniature railroad and children's zoo open during summer months. An aquarium with killer whales and sea otters. ▆▆ Take an 11 STANLEY PARK BUS which may be boarded along the north side of Pender. Returns over the same route to downtown but as 17 OAK BUS.

(A1) The Vancouver Art Gallery—owns the largest collection of works by westcoast artist Emily Carr, and also has a continuing programme of contemporary exhibitions. Located at 1145 W. Georgia St. until early autumn of 1983, thereafter at 800 W. Georgia St. — a magnificent building that was formerly the Court House. For information call 682-5621.

(B) MacMillan Planetarium—Shows feature the nature of the universe. Closed Mon. For information call 736-4431. **Vancouver Museum**—Exhibits of local history, anthropology and natural science with gift shop and restaurant. **Maritime Museum**—Collection of B.C. and naval memorabilia. Home of the **R.C.M.P. St. Roch**, the only vessel to sail the N.W. Passage in both directions. ▆▆ Board 22 MACDONALD BUS on west side of Burrard, alight at Cypress. Walk 4 blocks north. Return to downtown over same route via the 22 KNIGHT BUS.

(C) Robsonstrasse—Section of downtown Robson Street offers European atmosphere in boutiques, restaurants and speciality stores. Within walking distance of downtown.

(D) Chinatown—North America's second largest Chinese community. The commercial centre stretches along three blocks of Pender between Gore and Carrall Streets. Numerous restaurants, curio shops and oriental stores. ▆▆ Take a 19 KINGSWAY or 22 KNIGHT bus going east on Pender. Return on a 15 CAMBIE or 22 MACDONALD.

(E) Gastown—Where Vancouver began, now has antique shops, restaurants, smart stores and lively nightclubs, all with an old-time charm. Open daily. ▆▆ Take a 50 FALSE CREEK bus on the Granville Mall which will loop into Gastown via Cordova, Columbia to Powell, and return to the Granville Mall via Powell, Water and Cordova.

(F) Granville Island Public Market—Located at the south side of False Creek under Granville Street Bridge, Vancouver's Granville Island Public Market offers fresh produce, fresh fish and seafood, meats and other groceries and plants. Several places for snacks or meals, with lots of parking. Open 9 a.m. to 6 p.m. every day, except Mondays. ▆▆ Board 20 GRANVILLE BUS on west side of Granville Mall. Alight at Granville and Broadway and transfer to 51 GRANVILLE ISLAND BUS. Return to downtown via reverse of outbound trip.

(G) Queen Elizabeth Park—A flower lover's delight, in two former stone quarries. Houses the Bloedel Conservatory, a triodetic dome filled with tropical plants. Highest point within the city limits. Bring your camera. ▆▆ Board 15 CAMBIE BUS on west side of Burrard Street, the 15 CAMBIE routes via Burrard Robson, Cambie. Passengers alight at 33rd Avenue for Queen Elizabeth Park. Return to downtown as 19 KINGSWAY BUS.

(H) Van Dusen Gardens—One of the most comprehensive collections of ornamental plants can be found at this attraction. Man made lakes and many large stone sculptures add interest, here too is MacMillan Bloedel Place with exhibits on the forest industry. ▆▆ Take the #17 OAK BUS on Granville Mall heading North. Disembark on Oak St. at 37th Ave. Return to downtown via the 11 STANLEY PARK.

(I) Hastings Mill Store—The first store and post office built in Vancouver is now a small local museum. Open 10-4 daily from June to mid-September and from 1-4 weekends the rest of the year. ▆▆ Board 4 FOURTH BUS on west side of Granville Mall at any stop south of Pender Street. This bus takes you to Alma; disembark. Walk four blocks north to Pt. Grey Road. Return to downtown by the 24 NANAIMO bus.

(J) University of B.C.—Well known for its many beautiful gardens scattered over its 396 hectare campus. Visitors are welcome and Visitinfo booths dispense campus maps and specific information on Nitobe Japanese Memorial Gardens, the Rose Garden, Museum of Anthropology and Fine Arts Gallery. The

Museum of Anthropology— on N.W. Marine Drive at U.B.C., a new building on the water side of Marine Drive housing world famous collection of B.C. Coastal Indian Art and other Artifacts from many cultures. ▄▄ Board a 10 TENTH-U.B.C. BUS anywhere along the Granville Mall southbound. This BUS terminates within the campus area. Return to downtown by the 34 HASTINGS EXPRESS.

(K) Pacific National Exhibition Grounds—Site of Western Canada's largest fair — Many professional sporting events take place here. Coliseum is the home of the Vancouver Canucks Hockey team. The Track has horse racing four times weekly from April to October. B.C. Pavilion has a large three-dimensional map of the province and the B.C. Sports Hall of Fame. Also Playland Amusement Park with the giant Roller-coaster. ▄▄ Board a 14 HASTINGS or 16 RENFREW BUS on Granville Mall northbound, alight on Hastings Street at Renfrew. Return to Downtown as 18 ARBUTUS or 16 RENFREW.

(K1) The Arts, Sciences & Technology Centre—600 Granville St. Vancouver's new "hands-on" museum. Located downtown, Vancouver's transit system provides easy access to this interesting and educational collection of participatory exhibits which demonstrate a fascinating blend of art, science and technology. Many exciting special events take place regularly. Come and discover, explore, and experiment. For more information call 687-8414.

BURNABY

(L) Simon Fraser University—Architecturally outstanding university atop Burnaby Mountain. Student guided tours daily July and August and Saturday and Sunday the rest of the year. ▄▄ Board a 14 HASTINGS BUS on Granville Mall northbound. Transfer at Kootenay Loop to 35 WESTRIDGE SFU BUS for Simon Fraser University. Return to downtown via reverse of outbound trip.
Centennial Park—On Burnaby Mountain below Simon Fraser campus are picnic sites and a restaurant, with a view of the city and Indian Arm.

(M) Heritage Village—Burnaby's recreation of a typical village of the turn of the century, containing an apothecary shop, general store, blacksmith, school house, Garage, log cabin, church and soda parlour. **Burnaby Art Gallery**—Adjacent to Heritage Village at 6344 Gilpin Street. Emphasis on contemporary prints. In the garden, sculptures and 200 varieties of Rhododendrons. ▄▄ Board 820/120 CANADA WAY BUS on Melville Street directly behind the Royal Centre or at designated stops along Hastings Street eastbound. Closest bus stop is Burnaby Municipal Hall. Return to downtown via reverse of outbound trip.

NEW WESTMINSTER

(N) Irving House—A stately old home built in 1882 and preserved, adjacent to Royal City Museum at 302 Royal Avenue. See also the Japanese Friendship Gardens and Queens Park. ▄▄ Board 820/120 CANADA WAY as outlined in **M** above and alight in New Westminster at Columbia and 8th Street. Transfer to eastbound 96 SIXTH STREET BUS and request to alight on Agnes at Merrivale (one block behind Irving House). Return to downtown via reverse of outbound trip.

(O) NORTH SHORE

Capilano Suspension Bridge—One of the world's longest suspension bridges — 137 metres across Capilano Canyon, 70 metres above the river. Illuminated at night during the summer. ▄▄ By SEA-BUS, to Lonsdale Quay. Transfer to 246 HIGH-LANDS BUS. Alight at Ridgewood and walk north approximately 1½ blocks. To return downtown, reverse movement.

(P) Capilano
Salmon Hatchery—
in Capilano Canyon Park. Guided tours available. **Cleveland Dam**—A fine hiking and picnic area with a view of the twin peaks called the Lions. ▄▄ By SEA-BUS, to Lonsdale Quay. Transfer to 246 HIGHLAND BUS to Edgemont at Ridgewood and transfer to 232 QUEENS BUS.

(Q) Grouse Mountain—Take the superskyride to the top of Grouse Mountain for a breathtaking view of Vancouver day or night. 1100 metres above Vancouver. Once at the top visitors can enjoy a walk through the nature trail around Blue Grouse Lake; a ride up the Peak Chair to a 1250 metre viewpoint or relax in our Chalet's Lounge, Restaurant or Cafeteria. For reservations and information call 984-0661. Be sure and visit our Gift Shops at the Chalet. ▄▄ By SEA-BUS, to Lonsdale Quay. Transfer to 246 HIGHLANDS BUS to Edgemont at Ridgewood and transfer to a 232 QUEENS BUS.

(R) Cates Park—On the road to Deep Cove, a 23 hectare wooded waterside park and boat launching site. Swimming and scuba diving. ▄▄ Board 210 MOUNTAIN H'WAY BUS northbound on Burrard north of Smithe, or eastbound on Hastings, to Phibbs Exchange. Transfer to 212 DOLLARTON BUS to Cates Park. Return to downtown via reverse of outbound trip.

(S) The Park & Tilford Gardens—A unique eight garden complex at 1200 Cotton Road. Visitors welcomed year round. Illuminated at night in summer. Permanent displays and special seasonal displays. Free parking. ▄▄ Board 210 MOUNTAIN H'WAY BUS northbound on Burrard north of Smithe, or eastbound on Hastings, to Phibbs Exchange. Transfer to 239 CROSSTOWN BUS ("Park Royal") to Gardens. By SEA-BUS, to Lonsdale Quay. Transfer at Quay to 239 CROSSTOWN BUS ("Phibbs Exchange or Capilano College") to Gardens. Return to downtown via reverse of outbound trip. 987-9321.

3. Now answer these questions here and on the next page about the places on your chart.

   a. How many minutes is Stanley Park from downtown? _____

   b. When is the children's zoo in Stanley Park open? _____

   c. How large is Vancouver's Chinatown? _____

   d. What can you buy at the Granville Island Public Market?

   _____

   _____

e. What hours is the market open? _____

f. What day is it closed? _____

g. Why is the Hastings Mill Store an attraction? _____

h. What is the telephone number of the Arts, Sciences, and Technology

Centre? _____

i. Can you ride to the top of Grouse Mountain in the daytime, at night, or

both? _____

j. Do you need to bring food when you go to Grouse Mountain, or can

you eat there? _____

Now scan the map on the next page, and complete the following exercises.

1. Draw a circle around each of these places on the map.
   (A) Stanley Park   (I) Hastings Mill Store
   (B) MacMillan Planetarium   (Q) Grouse Mountain
   (G) Queen Elizabeth Park   (W) Vancouver International
                                        Airport

2. Scan the explanation of symbols at the bottom of the map. Then write the
   meanings of these symbols.

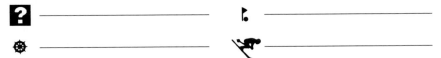

3. Answer these questions.
   a. Is there a visitors' information center at Vancouver International

   Airport? _____

   b. What are two places where you can ski? _____

   _____

   c. What is the name of one boat launching? _____

exercise 4

Now work in pairs. Ask and answer questions, like those above, about the list of
attractions and the map.

Going Beyond the Text

Bring to class maps of cities that show attractions for visitors. Discuss new vocabulary. Then summarize the information on your map for the class; tell about the
interesting things in that city.

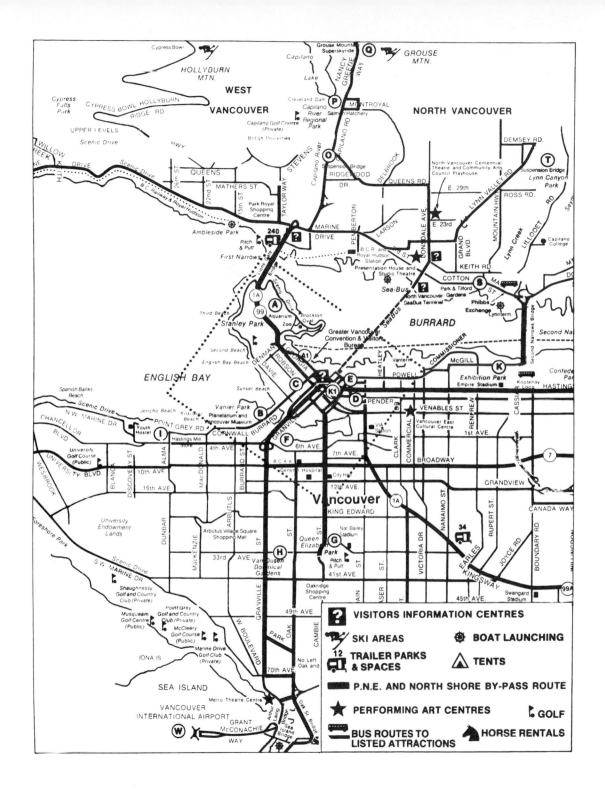

VISITORS INFORMATION CENTRES

SKI AREAS

TRAILER PARKS & SPACES

P.N.E. AND NORTH SHORE BY-PASS ROUTE

PERFORMING ART CENTRES

BUS ROUTES TO LISTED ATTRACTIONS

BOAT LAUNCHING

TENTS

GOLF

HORSE RENTALS

CHAPTER **three**

Business and Money

The first reading selection is an article about how some organizations are helping people escape from poverty. The second reading discusses what our individual money habits say about our beliefs and values. Banking forms, including a credit card bill, are the subject of the last section.

in this chapter

PART one

Banking on the Poor

Before You Read

Getting Started

Look at the pictures and discuss them.

1. The picture at the bottom takes place in a bank. What might the people be doing?
2. How are the people in the other two pictures different from the people in the bank?
3. What might be some problems of the people in the first two pictures?

Preparing to Read

As you read the following selection, think about the answer to this question. How can banks help poor people to change their lives?

Read the following selection quickly. Do not use a dictionary. Then do the exercises that follow the reading.

Banking on the Poor

A   **F**or many people, there seems to be no escape from poverty; in other words, they are poor, and they have no hope that this will ever change. In addition, they have the social problems of poverty. Imagine this situation: A poor woman has an idea for a small business to lift her and her family out of poverty. She needs a little money to begin this business. She goes to a bank to borrow the money, and the banker interviews her. At this bank, as at most banks, the borrower must meet three necessary conditions: *character, capacity,* and *collateral.* That is, if this woman wants to borrow money from the bank, she must show that she (1) is honest (has character), (2) is able to run her business (has capacity), and (3) owns a house, land, or something valuable (collateral) for the bank to take if she can't pay back the money. So what happens to the woman? The bank won't lend her the money because she doesn't have any collateral.

B   One possible solution these days is *microlending.* This is a system of special banks and programs that are loaning money to people in "borrowing groups." For example, an international organization called Good Faith lends small amounts of money to people who want to go into business. Each person must do two things to borrow money: take classes in business and join a borrowing group. This is a group of microentrepreneurs—i.e., people who own and run their own small business. Everyone in the group must approve the loan of every other group member, or Good Faith won't lend the money. To receive a loan from Good Faith, people still must have *character.* They find *capacity* in the business classes. But *collateral* is not necessary any longer. Instead of collateral, there is peer pressure; i.e., group members make sure that each person pays back his or her loan. They want to keep their "good name" and continue doing business with Good Faith.

C Good Faith has had many successes and only a few failures. In Pine Bluff, Arkansas, a small town in the United States, one person was able to open a hair salon, another a plant shop, and another a car decorating business—all with loans from Good Faith. In a developing country such as Bangladesh, a person can begin a small business with only $10 to $15. Because of many small loans from Good Faith, there are now 1.6 *million* new entrepreneurs in Bangladesh. Of course, not all these loans were a success. At first, Good Faith lent half of the money to men and half to women. Unfortunately, most of the Bangladeshi men spent the money on themselves, not the business. Now Good Faith does business mainly with *women's* borrowing groups in that country.

D In any country, women are the poorest of the poor. They produce more than half of the world's food, but they own just one percent of the world's land. They are 51 percent of the world's population, but very, very little money goes to programs to help them. In the late 1980s, Anne Firth Murray took the initiative and began the Global Fund for Women. This fund now has more than $3 million. It has given money to over 400 women's groups in 94 countries. Unlike Good Faith, which helps people begin businesses, the Global Fund for Women helps to solve social problems—e.g., violence and lack of education. For instance, the fund has helped a group of Palestinian and Jewish women who are working together to stop violence against women. It is giving money to a woman in a village in southern India; she has started a literacy program to teach poor women to read.

E Good Faith and the Global Fund for Women have a lesson for banks around the world: It's a "safe bet" to lend money to the poor. With careful planning, education, and cooperation, most people use the money well and then plow the money and knowledge back into their communities. There is hope that they can begin to break the cycle of poverty for themselves, their families, and society.

After You Read

Getting the Main Ideas

exercise 1

Write T on the lines before the statements that are true, according to the reading. Write F before the statements that are false.

1. _____ Poor people can't borrow money from most banks.

2. _____ Good Faith lends money to poor people in borrowing groups.

3. _____ Good Faith has always been successful.

4. _____ The Global Fund for Women is another fund that lends money so that people can start businesses.

5. _____ It's a good idea to lend money to the poor.

Guessing Meaning from Context

> Sometimes certain abbreviations (shortened forms of words) help you understand a new word or phrase. Here are two:
>
> e.g. = for example
> i.e. = that is = in other words

Circle the words that give clues to the meaning of the underlined word(s). Then answer the questions.

1. This is a group of microentrepreneurs—i.e., people who own and run their own small business.

   Who are microentrepreneurs?_____

   _____

2. Instead of collateral, there is peer pressure; i.e., group members make sure that each person pays back his or her loan.

   What happens when there is peer pressure?_____

   _____

3. The Global Fund for Women helps with social problems—e.g., violence and lack of education.

   What are examples of social problems?_____

> Sometimes the context has an explanation of the new word, but in order to think of a synonym, you need to change a part of speech.
>
> example: For many people, there seems to be no escape from poverty; in other words, they are (poor), and they have no hope that this will change.
>
> In this example, you see that *poverty* is close in meaning to *poor,* but the two words are different parts of speech. *Poverty* is a noun, and *poor* is an adjective. (What is *poverty*? "Poorness" or the condition of being poor.)

Circle the words that mean the same or almost the same as the underlined words. Then change those words to the same parts of speech as the underlined words.

If this woman wants to borrow money, she must show that she (1) is honest (has <u>character</u>), (2) is able to run her business (has <u>capacity</u>), and (3) owns a house or land or something valuable.

   a. What part of speech is <u>character</u>? _____

   b. What is <u>character</u>? _____

   c. What part of speech is <u>capacity</u>? _____

   d. What is <u>capacity</u>? _____

Sometimes the context does not give a clear definition or example of a new word. You can't be sure about the *exact* meaning, but you can still make an intelligent guess and not waste time by going to the dictionary. First, figure out the part of speech of the new word. Then imagine in your mind what other word might be logical in that place.

example: Everyone in the group must <u>approve</u> the loan of every other group member, or Good Faith won't lend the money.

     part of speech: verb

     possible meanings: agree to; say OK about; sign

Some of your guesses might be wrong, but that's not a problem. If you see the word again, in a different context, the meaning will become more clear.

---

exercise 4

Make guesses about the underlined words. Don't worry about being "right" or "wrong." Just try to be logical. When you finish, compare your answers with a partner.

1. A poor woman has an idea to <u>lift</u> her and her family out of poverty.

   Part of speech: _____

   Possible meanings: _____

2. The organization has had many successes and, unfortunately, a few <u>failures</u>.

   Part of speech: _____

   Possible meanings: _____

3. She began the Global Fund for Women. This <u>fund</u> now has more than $3 million. It has given money to over 400 women's groups.

   Part of speech: _____

   Possible meanings: _____

4. With careful planning and cooperation, most people use the money well and then <u>plow</u> both money and knowledge back into their communities.

Part of speech: _____

Possible meanings: _____

exercise 5 Now read the selection "Banking on the Poor" again carefully. Try to guess the meanings of new words from the context. Use your dictionary only when absolutely necessary. Check your answers to the "Getting the Main Ideas" exercise. Correct your errors if necessary.

Understanding Reading Structure

exercise 6 Match the paragraphs in the reading selection "Banking on the Poor" with their topics and write the letters of the paragraphs on the lines.

1. ____ Microlending

2. ____ Why most banks don't help poor people

3. ____ A group that helps women to solve social problems

4. ____ Why it's good to lend money to the poor

5. ____ Examples of some successes and one failure of microlending

exercise 7 Circle the number of the *one* main idea of the reading selection.

1. There seems to be no escape from poverty for many people.
2. Microlending is a system of banks and programs that are loaning money to people in borrowing groups.
3. It's possible to break the "cycle of poverty" with planning, education, cooperation, and some money.
4. Good Faith and the Global Fund for Women give money to poor people.

exercise 8 Turn back to the Preparing to Read section on page 47 and answer the question.

Discussing the Reading

activity In small groups, talk about your answers to these questions.

1. In your country, do banks require collateral before they loan money to someone? What kinds of things are used for collateral?
2. In your country, do people sometimes join a cooperative group to borrow money? If so, what are these groups called? How do they work?
3. What are some social problems in your country? What are people doing to solve them?

What idea is the cartoonist expressing? Do you agree?

PART two
The Psychology of Money

Before You Read
Skimming for Main Ideas

exercise Read the following paragraphs quickly. Do not use a dictionary and don't worry about the details. When you finish, write the topic and topic sentence of each paragraph.

The Psychology of Money

A **D**o you enjoy shopping? Do you sometimes buy things that you don't need and can't afford? Do you spend a lot of money on your friends and family? When you're sad, lonely, or upset, do you go shopping to feel better? If you choose Brand X instead of Brand Y of toothpaste (or clothing or a TV set), do you have a good reason for your choice? Your answers to these questions may reflect your personality because, according to psychologists, individual money habits show our values, fears, and beliefs about ourselves.

Topic: _____

Topic sentence: _____

_____

B Experts in psychology believe that for many people, money is an important symbol of strength and influence, love, or guilt. Husbands who complain about their wives' spending habits may be afraid that they are losing power in their marriage. Wives, on the other hand, may waste huge amounts of money because they are angry at their husbands. Many people consider money a symbol of love. They spend it on their family and friends to express love, or they buy themselves expensive presents because they need love. Spending habits can also reflect a person's feelings of guilt. For example, a man who spends most of his time at work might feel ashamed that he has no time for his family. He might buy expensive presents for his wife and children to make him feel less guilty.

Topic: _____

Topic sentence: _____

_____

C   Most successful businesspeople and advertisers have some knowledge of psychology and use it to increase business. They know that all of us have some fears; all of us are dissatisfied with something about ourselves. Advertisers give us hope that we'll be better—more attractive, younger-looking, happier—if we buy their product. They make us worry that we'll be uglier, older-looking, or sadder·if we *don't* buy it.

Topic: _____

Topic sentence: _____

_____

D   People can be addicted to different things—e.g., alcohol, drugs, certain foods, or even television. People who have such an addiction are compulsive; i.e., they have an unusually powerful psychological need that they feel they *must* satisfy. According to psychologists, many people are compulsive spenders; they feel they *must* spend money. This compulsion, like most others, is irrational—impossible to explain reasonably. For example, most people look for sales, low prices, and discounts in order to save money. This is "healthy" bargain hunting. But *compulsive* bargain hunters often buy things that they don't need just because the merchandise is cheap. When they can buy something—*anything*—for less than other people, they feel that they are winning a kind of game. For compulsive spenders who buy on credit, charge accounts are even more exciting than money. In other words, compulsive spenders feel that with credit, they can do anything. Their pleasure in spending enormous amounts is actually greater than the pleasure that they get from the things they buy.

Topic: _____

Topic sentence: _____

_____

E   Psychologists often use a method called "behavior therapy" to help individuals solve their personality problems. In the same way, they can help people who feel that they have problems with money: They give them "assignments." If a person is a compulsive spender, for instance, a therapist might teach him self-discipline in this way: On the first day of his therapy, he must go into a store, stay five minutes, and then leave. On the second day, he should stay for ten minutes and try something on. On the third day, he stays for fifteen minutes and asks the salesclerk a question but does not buy anything. Soon he will learn that nothing bad will happen to him if he doesn't buy anything, and he can solve the problem of his compulsive buying.

Topic: _____

Topic sentence: _____

_____

After You Read

exercise 1

After you write the topic and topic sentence of each paragraph, exchange your answers with another student. Are your answers the same? Are your topics the same but perhaps in different words? Do you agree about the topic sentences? If you don't agree, give reasons for your answers. One of you might want to change an answer!

Understanding Pronoun Reference

Look back at the reading selection "The Psychology of Money" to find the meaning of the following pronouns. What does each pronoun refer to?

1. their (paragraph B, line 3) _____
2. they (paragraph B, line 5) _____
3. he (paragraph B, line 10) _____
4. it (paragraph C, line 2) _____
5. it (paragraph C, line 6) _____
6. they (paragraph D, line 3) _____

Discussing the Reading

activity 1

In small groups, talk about your answers to these questions.

1. Describe your spending habits. (To do this, you might go back to paragraph A and answer the questions.) In your opinion, what do your spending habits show about your personality?
2. Make a list of products that you buy. Do you always buy the same brand of each product? If so, can you give a reason for your choice?

Going Beyond the Text

activity 2

In small groups, choose one of the following products: toothpaste, cars, laundry detergent, or cigarettes. Look through magazines for advertisements on your product. Bring as many ads as you can to your group. Together, study them. What kind of person would be attracted to each ad?

PART three
Building Vocabulary and Study Skills

Related Words

Which word in each group does not belong? Cross it out as in the example. Explain your reasons for your answers.

1. psychologist   scientist   ~~company~~   therapist
2. stores   shops   markets   checks

Interactions II • Reading

3. compulsive	irrational	addicted	valuable
4. cash	credit	center	money
5. comfort	bargain	discount	sale
6. shopping	salesclerk	advertiser	businessperson
7. entrepreneur	lender	borrower	microlending
8. complete	power	influence	strength
9. values	accounts	beliefs	opinions
10. spend	claim	waste	save

Parts of Speech

To guess the meaning of a new word from the context, you might find it helpful to know its part of speech; that is, is the word a noun, a verb, an adjective, an adverb, etc.? Sometimes you can tell the part of speech from the suffix (the word ending). Here are some common suffixes, listed by the parts of speech that they usually indicate.

NOUNS		ADJECTIVES	
-er/-or	-ee	-ive	-ful
-ist	-(i)ty	-able/-ible	-ant/-ent
-sion/-tion	-ance/-ence	-(u)al	-ous
-ment	-ure	-ic(al)	-ar(y)

exercise 1

Are the following words nouns or adjectives? The suffixes will tell you. On the lines, write <u>n</u> or <u>adj</u> as in the examples. (In a few cases, both answers may be correct.)

1. <u>adj.</u> compulsive	**12.** _____ instance	**23.** _____ pleasure
2. <u>n.</u> spender	**13.** _____ transportation	**24.** _____ enormous
3. _____ possible	**14.** _____ violence	**25.** _____ scientist
4. _____ hunter	**15.** _____ computer	**26.** _____ information
5. _____ psychologist	**16.** _____ pressure	**27.** _____ failure
6. _____ personality	**17.** _____ elementary	**28.** _____ special
7. _____ individual	**18.** _____ addition	**29.** _____ consumer
8. _____ important	**19.** _____ expensive	**30.** _____ public
9. _____ influence	**20.** _____ different	**31.** _____ beautiful
10. _____ basic	**21.** _____ poverty	**32.** _____ cultural
11. _____ assignment	**22.** _____ addiction	**33.** _____ culture

Complete each sentence with words related to the underlined words. Then look back at the list of suffixes to check your answers. The first one is done as an example.

1. Every <u>person</u> has his or her own <u>personality</u>   in relation to money. A person's _____ opinions and values form the <u>basis</u> of his or her habits.

2. Bargain _____s are always <u>hunting</u> for discounts and low prices. For some <u>addictive</u> personalities, shopping is a kind of

    _____.

3. Advertising is a kind of _____ that has a strong

    _____ on consumers; it should not only <u>influence</u> people

    to buy products, but also <u>inform</u> them.

4. This organization has been _____ in solving some serious

    <u>social</u> problems in that _____. Their <u>success</u> is due to hard work and the cooperation of many people.

focus on testing

Increasing Reading Speed—Reading in Phrases

You need to read fast during tests to finish within the time limit. Of course, you can benefit from fast reading skills in general because, as a student, you probably have to read a lot of material. Interestingly, fast readers usually understand reading material better than slow readers.

Slow readers often read one word at a time, like this:

According | to | psychologists, | our | individual
money | habits | show | our | beliefs | and | values.

Faster readers don't usually read individual words. Instead, they take in several words at a time, like this:

Experts in psychology | believe that for many people,
money is an important symbol | of strength and influence.

exercise 1 Read these sentences in phrases, as shown.

1. Husbands who complain | about their wives' spending habits
    may be afraid | that they are losing power | in their marriage.

2. Many people | are compulsive | in their addictions—
    i.e., they must satisfy | their needs | to feel comfortable.

Certain words often belong together in phrases. For example, a noun phrase can include adjectives and other words before or after the noun. A verb phrase may include noun objects, adjectives, or adverbs. A prepositional phrase includes an object after a preposition, and an infinitive phrase may include an object after the verb. Examples include:

NOUN PHRASES	VERB PHRASES
money habits	spend money
a symbol of love	ask the clerk a question

PREPOSITIONAL PHRASES	INFINITIVE PHRASES
for their behavior	to save money
on the next day	to feel comfortable

***exercise* 2** Which words belong together in reading? Read the following sentences in phrases and separate the phrases with lines. (There are several correct possibilities.)

1. Most people, even compulsive spenders, keep their money in banks—in checking and savings accounts. To put money into accounts, you write out forms called deposit slips. On these slips of paper, you put down the amount of money you are depositing—the currency (cash in paper bills) and the checks. You add up the amounts, subtract the money that you want to receive in cash, and write the total deposit. You endorse (write your name on the back of) all your checks and bring everything to the teller's window at the bank.

2. Nowadays, to save time, many people bank by mail or use the automatic teller machines (ATMs) outside their banks. They put checks and deposit slips into bank envelopes, which they seal and mail or put into the machines. They can also make payments (for their houses, cars, loans, etc.) in these ways. People who have special cards and numbers can withdraw certain amounts of cash from the instant tellers. The bank statements that they receive at the end of the month will include the amounts that they have deposited or withdrawn by mail or machine.

Reading in the Real World

Scanning for Information
Banking Forms

 **exercise 1** The following vocabulary items often appear on bank forms. Match them with their meanings.

1. _____ deposit
2. _____ withdraw
3. _____ currency
4. _____ due
5. _____ slip
6. _____ endorse
7. _____ previous
8. _____ teller
9. _____ cash

a. a piece of paper; a form
b. from before
c. put money into (a bank account)
d. a person who works at a bank window
e. sign (write your name on)
f. take money out (of a bank account)
g. paper bills
h. payable; owed
i. paper money and coins

 **exercise 2** Scan the banking forms below and on the next page. Write the answers to the questions that follow.

BA BANK OF AMERICA   **Checking Deposit**

ACCOUNT NUMBER
PABLO RAMOS
NAME (PLEASE PRINT)

ADDRESS

CITY   STATE   ZIP CODE

DATE

PLEASE SIGN IN TELLER'S PRESENCE FOR CASH RECEIVED.

LIST CHECKS BY BANK NO	DOLLARS	CENTS
CURRENCY	$50	00
COIN		
CHECKS 16-66	25	00
	107	62
TOTAL OF CHECKS LISTED ON REVERSE		
SUBTOTAL	182	62
◄ LESS: CASH RECEIVED		
TOTAL DEPOSIT	$182	62

R-3 1-83 BANK OF AMERICA NT&SA

⑈510000354⑈

A

B

BANK OF AMERICA		Savings Deposit

ACCOUNT NUMBER					—						

DATE

NAME (PLEASE PRINT): Mohammed El-Gamal

ADDRESS ART 3.8

CITY   STATE   ZIP CODE

NEW PASSBOOK BALANCE

PLEASE SIGN IN TELLER'S PRESENCE FOR CASH RECEIVED

LIST CHECKS BY BANK NO.	DOLLARS	CENTS
CURRENCY		
COIN		
CHECKS 62-20 1	255.	00
16-66 2	100.	00
16-4 3	40.	00
4		
SUBTOTAL	395.	00
◀ LESS. CASH RECEIVED	- 95.	00
TOTAL DEPOSIT	$ 300.	00

S-151 2-83 BANK OF AMERICA NT&SA

⑂:5010⑊0000⑂:

C

BANK OF AMERICA		Savings Withdrawal

NOT NEGOTIABLE

ACCOUNT NUMBER					—						

DATE

RECEIVED FROM BANK OF AMERICA

$ 75.00

Seventy-five and no/100s ————————— DOLLARS

X

PLEASE SIGN IN TELLER'S PRESENCE FOR CASH RECEIVED.

Hon-May Fong

NAME (PLEASE PRINT)

FOR BANK USE ONLY ▼

ACTIVITY CHARGE

NEW P.B. BALANCE

ENTERED BY

CONTRA

ADDRESS

CITY   STATE   ZIP CODE

S-155 1-83 BANK OF AMERICA NT&SA

⑂:5010⑊0000⑂:

---

1. Match the forms with these descriptions. Write the letters of the forms on the lines.

_____ a deposit slip for a savings account

_____ a deposit slip for a checking account

_____ a credit card bill

_____ a form to take money out of a savings account

2. How much money is Pablo Ramos depositing in his

   checking account? _____

   How much of the deposit is in cash? _____

   How many checks is he depositing? _____

   Is he taking any money from the bank with him? _____

3. How much money is Mohammed El-Gamal depositing in his

   savings account? _____

   How much of this is in cash? _____

   How many checks is he depositing? _____

   Is he taking any of this money with him? _____

   If so, how much? _____

4. How much money is Hon-May Fong withdrawing from her savings

   account? _____

   When will she sign the form? _____

5. By what date does Jane Doe need to pay this bill? _____

   What is the minimum that she has to pay? _____

   If she pays this bill off—i.e., pays it completely—how much will

   she pay? _____

   If someone steals Jane Doe's credit card, what should she do?

   _____

Going Beyond the Text

 Bring to class other banking forms and brochures about banking services. Discuss new vocabulary. Then summarize the information for the class.

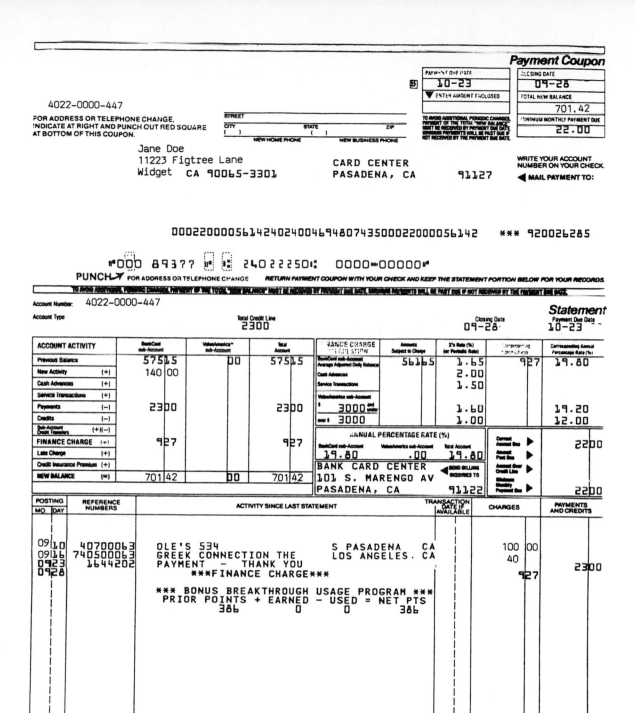

CHAPTER four

Jobs and Professions

in this chapter

The first article discusses the advantages and disadvantages of workaholism, an addiction to work similar to other people's addiction to drugs or alcohol. The second selection is also about workaholism—specifically among the Japanese. The last part of the chapter covers how to quickly find the information you need in classified ads.

PART one
Workaholism

Before You Read

Getting Started

Look at the picture and discuss it.

1. What is this man doing? Why is he doing so many things at the same time?
2. Do you think this man is happy with his life? Why or why not?
3. Do you know anyone similar to this man? Tell about that person.

Preparing to Read

As you read the following selection, think about the answer to this question. What are some advantages and disadvantages of workaholism?

Read the following selection quickly. Do not use a dictionary. Then do the exercises that follow the reading.

Workaholism

A   **M**ost workers spend eight or nine hours on the job. They work because it's unavoidable. They need to make enough money for necessities: food, rent, clothing, transportation, tuition, and so on. They spend about one-third of their lives at work, but they hate it. They complain and count the minutes until quitting time each day—or the days until their next vacation. The situation is even worse for white-collar workers in powerful positions. In many companies, they often put in over sixty hours a week and don't take vacations at all. To keep their jobs or get ahead, they feel they have to put in "face time"—to stay late at the office just to make sure the boss knows they're there.

B   By contrast, there are some people who actually enjoy work—in fact, they *love* to work. They spend many extra hours on the job each week and often take work home with them. These workaholics are as addicted to their jobs as other people are to drugs or alcohol.

C   In some urban centers, workaholism is so common that people do not consider it unusual: They accept the lifestyle as normal. Government workers in Washington, D.C., for example, frequently work sixty to seventy hours a week. They don't do this because they *have* to; they do it because they *want* to. Hundreds of workaholics in New York City tried to go to work even in the famous blackout of 1977. There was no electricity— no air conditioning, elevators, or lights—but many people went to their offices anyway. They sat impatiently on the steps outside their office buildings and did paperwork or had business meetings.

D   Workaholism can be a serious problem. Because true workaholics would rather work than do anything else, they probably don't know how to relax; that is, they might not enjoy movies, sports, or other types of entertainment. Most of all, they hate to sit and do nothing. The lives of workaholics are usually stressful, and this tension and worry can cause health problems such as heart attacks or stomach ulcers. In addition, typical workaholics don't pay much attention to their families. They spend little time with their children, and their marriages may end in divorce.

E   Is workaholism always dangerous? Perhaps not. There are, certainly, people who work well under stress. Some studies show that many work- aholics have great energy and interest in life. Their work is so pleasurable that they are actually very happy. For most workaholics, work and enter- tainment are the same thing. Their jobs provide them with a challenge; this keeps them busy and creative. Other people retire from work at age sixty-five, but workaholics usually prefer not to quit. They are still enthusi- astic about work—and life—in their eighties and nineties.

F   Why do workaholics enjoy their jobs so much? There are several advantages to work. It provides people with paychecks, of course, and this is important. But it offers more than financial security. It provides people with self-confidence; they have a feeling of satisfaction when they've produced a challenging piece of work and are able to say, "I made that." Psychologists claim that work gives people an identity; through participation in work, they get a sense of self and individualism. In addition, most jobs provide people with a socially acceptable way to meet others. Perhaps some people are compulsive about their work, but their addiction seems to be a safe—even an advantageous—one.

G   People who are addicted to work are similar to one another in some ways. Here is a list of ten characteristics of workaholics. Which ones apply to you? Check (√) your answers.

		YES	NO
1.	Do you get up early even if you go to bed late?	☐	☐
2.	Do you read or work while you eat?	☐	☐
3.	Do you make lists of things to do?	☐	☐
4.	Do you find it unpleasant to "do nothing"?	☐	☐
5.	Do you usually have a lot of energy?	☐	☐
6.	Do you work on weekends and on holidays?	☐	☐
7.	Can you work anytime and anywhere?	☐	☐
8.	Do you prefer not to take vacations?	☐	☐
9.	Do you think you probably won't want to retire?	☐	☐
10.	Do you really enjoy your work?	☐	☐

If you answered "yes" to eight or more questions, you might be a workaholic.

After You Read

Getting the Main Ideas

exercise 1

Which statements are *true* about workaholics, according to the reading? Check (√) them.

1. _____ They spend no more than eight to nine hours on the job.

2. _____ They complain a lot about their jobs and watch the clock.

3. _____ They spend a lot of time working at their jobs and at home.

4. _____ They work only because they have to.

5. _____ They would rather work than rest.

6. _____ They may have health problems from their inability to relax.

7. _____ They may be happy because their work provides a lot of pleasure.

8. _____ They retire from their jobs before the age of sixty-five.

9. _____ They probably have a feeling of satisfaction and a sense of identity.

10. _____ They probably meet people through their work.

Guessing Meaning from Context

 Circle the words here and on the next page that give clues to the meanings of the underlined word(s). Then circle the letter of the correct meaning of each underlined word.

1. These <u>workaholics</u> are as addicted to their jobs as other people are to drugs or alcohol.
   a. people who drink too much alcohol
   b. drug addicts
   c. people who work
   d. compulsive workers

2. The lives of workaholics are usually <u>stressful</u>, and this tension and worry can cause health problems such as heart attacks or stomach <u>ulcers</u>.
   stressful:
   a. busy
   b. compulsive and addicted
   c. tense and worried
   d. emphasized
   ulcers:
   a. a break in the skin or area inside the body
   b. food
   c. headaches
   d. difficulty with breathing, especially in certain work situations

3. Hundreds of workaholics in New York City tried to go to work even in the famous <u>blackout</u> of 1977. There was no electricity.
   a. a very dark night
   b. time without electric power
   c. time of dirty streets
   d. increases in crime

4. For most workaholics, their jobs provide a <u>challenge</u>; this keeps them busy and creative.
   a. solution to problems in work situations
   b. advantage
   c. prediction of success
   d. something that requires action and energy

5. Their jobs keep them busy and creative; they are still <u>enthusiastic</u> about work—and life—in their eighties and nineties.
   a. individualistic
   b. wanting a rest
   c. very interested
   d. impatient

6. Work provides people with <u>self-confidence</u>; they have a feeling of satisfaction when they've finished a challenging piece of work and are able to
say, "I made that."
   a. belief in their ability
   b. inability to relax
   c. discipline
   d. ability to memorize

7. Psychologists claim that work gives people an <u>identity</u>; through participation in work, they get a sense of self.
   a. cultural individualism
   b. special creative qualities
   c. values and opinions
   d. ideas about who they are

Read the selection "Workaholism" again carefully. Try to guess the meanings of
new words from the context. Use your dictionary only when absolutely necessary.
Check your answers to the Getting the Main Ideas exercise. Correct your errors if
necessary.

Understanding Reading Structure

exercise 4

Match the paragraphs in the selection "Workaholism" with their topics. Write the
letters of the paragraphs on the lines.

1. _____ The advantages of workaholism

2. _____ Feelings of "normal" workers about their jobs

3. _____ A definition of workaholism

4. _____ A "test" of the characteristics of workaholics

5. _____ Examples of workaholism in big cities

6. _____ Problems of workaholism

7. _____ People for whom workaholism is not dangerous

exercise 5

Circle the number of the one main idea of the reading selection.

1. Workaholism can lead to serious problems, but it can also create a happy
life.
2. Workaholics are usually successful people, but they don't stay married
long.
3. People who enjoy their work usually enjoy movies, sports, and other kinds
of entertainment.
4. People who work even under difficult conditions may be very creative.

 Turn back to the Preparing to Read section on page 66 and answer the question.

Discussing the Reading

 In small groups, talk about your answers to these questions.

1. In your opinion, is workaholism an addiction? What are its advantages? Its disadvantages?
2. Should a workaholic try to change his or her lifestyle? Why or why not? If so, how?
3. People such as the painter Pablo Picasso or the musician Pablo Casals enjoyed working even when they were very old. What were some possible reasons for this?
4. Can you think of other people who never wanted to retire?

PART two

Workaholism: A National Syndrome?

Before You Read
Skimming for Main Ideas

exercise Read these paragraphs quickly. Do not use a dictionary and don't worry about the details. When you finish, write the topic and topic sentence of each paragraph.

A   When an American president takes a vacation, his assistants usually emphasize to news reporters the *work* that he does during his vacation. In contrast, when the prime minister of Japan took a vacation a while ago, his aides emphasized to the press that his purpose was *relaxation*—no work at all. In Japan's newspapers and on radio and TV, the press reported the prime minister's activities during his time off: He went to parties, took walks in the forest, read poetry books, and played golf and tennis.

Topic:_____

Topic sentence:_____

_____

B   Many Japanese do not seem to think that leisure is important; they take their jobs so seriously that they are sometimes considered the world's greatest workaholics. Labor statistics show that the average Japanese

worker puts in about 2,150 hours a year at work. In the United States, the average worker puts in about 1,900 hours a year. In Germany, the figure is about 1,610. In Japan, the six-day work week is common, and many people stay on the job until 10:30 or 11:00 each night. Many people, especially employers, do not take their annual vacations. In most of the world, people believe that leisure time is an important part of life. But for many Japanese "leisure" is not "a time for relaxation, away from work," as it is in most countries; they see it as a waste of time.

Topic:_____

Topic sentence:_____

_____

c   By taking a truly leisurely vacation, the prime minister was basically telling the people of Japan, "It's okay to relax and to enjoy yourselves." This was an important lesson for two main reasons. First, leisure is important for emotional and physical health and for a happy family life. Second, leisure is important for the Japanese economy, which exports more than it imports. If the people of Japan work less and spend more, there will be a better balance of exports and imports.

Topic:_____

Topic sentence:_____

_____

D   To encourage people to relax and use their leisure time, both private companies and the government are taking action. Some companies that produce cars, steel, or textiles are investing millions of dollars in sports and entertainment facilities such as sports centers. In addition, banks and government offices have begun to close for two Saturdays each month instead of just one. Also, some companies are now giving white-collar employees two-day weekends every week.

*Topic:*_____

*Topic sentence:*_____

_____

E   It will be interesting to see if there is a true change in the Japanese attitude to work and leisure. Some people believe that nothing will really change; they say that Japanese workaholics of the future might *seem* to be relaxing when they are actually working, in the same way that they do these days. For example, businessmen of today often spend late nights at nightclubs, where they eat and drink and have a good time; however, the main purpose of these evenings on the town is to discuss business. Another activity that allows businesspeople to appear to relax while they are actually discussing business is *golf*. Some people say that the Japanese seem to work very hard at relaxing!

*Topic:*_____

*Topic sentence:*_____

_____

After You Read

 exercise **1**   After you write the topic and topic sentence of each paragraph, exchange your answers with another student. Are your answers the same? Are your topics the same but perhaps in different words? Do you agree about the topic sentences? If you don't agree, give reasons for your answers. One of you might want to change an answer.

Understanding Pronoun Reference

Look back at the reading selection "Workaholism" to find the meaning of the following pronouns. What does each pronoun refer to?

1. his (paragraph A, line 1)_____
2. his (paragraph A, line 4)_____
3. it (paragraph B, line 11)_____
4. it (paragraph C, line 6)_____
5. they (paragraph E, line 4)_____

Recognizing Sentence Structure

> Sometimes the *parallel structure* of two sentences or clauses can help you understand new words. In parallel structure, there are often synonyms, corresponding words, or opposites.

Use the parallel structure of these sentences to help you answer the questions about the underlined words.

When an American president takes a vacation, his assistants usually emphasize to news reporters the work that he does during his vacation. In contrast, when the prime minister of Japan recently took a vacation, his aides emphasized to the press that his purpose was relaxation—no work at all.

1. What person has a position that corresponds to an *American president*?

_____

2. What is a synonym for *assistants*? _____
3. What is a synonym for *news reporters*? _____
4. What is the opposite of *work*? _____

Discussing the Reading

In small groups, talk about your answers to these questions.

1. What is the average work week in your country? (In the United States, it's 40 hours per week.) How many days are in a typical work week: 4? 5? 5½? 6?

2. Is workaholism a problem in your country? If so, is this because people truly enjoy working, or are they just putting in "face time"?
3. What "fun" activities do employers in your country expect employees to do as part of their job?

WHAT DO YOU THINK?

Understanding Proverbs and Quotations

Here are two English proverbs and three quotations about work. In small groups, discuss your answers to these questions about each of them.

1. What does the proverb (or quotation) mean? (You might need to use a dictionary for a few words.)
2. Do you agree with it?
3. What are some proverbs about work in your language? Translate them into English and explain them.

PROVERBS AND QUOTATIONS

- All work and no play makes Jack a dull boy. (proverb)

- Ninety percent of inspiration is perspiration. (proverb)

- Work expands to fill the time available. —*C. Northcote Parkinson*

- Laziness travels so slowly that poverty soon overtakes him. —*Benjamin Franklin*

- It is neither wealth nor splendor, but tranquility and occupation, which give happiness. —*Thomas Jefferson*

PART three

Building Vocabulary and Study Skills

Adjective and Noun Phrases

> Some words often appear together in phrases. In some phrases, there is a hyphen (-).
>
> *example:* The situation is bad for white-collar workers.
>
> The last word of a phrase is usually a noun or an adjective. The first word may be a noun, an adjective, or an adverb.
>
> *examples:* city life (= noun + noun)
> social sciences (= adjective + noun)
> especially interesting (adverb + adjective)

exercise  Complete each sentence with the missing words as in the example. Choose from the following:

financial	air	city
self	specialty	mass
socially	quitting	shopping
business	office	traffic

1. Most workers work only for <u>financial</u> security, and they count the hours until _____ time.

2. People who enjoy their work may have a lot of _____-confidence. They might spend a lot of time at work because it is a _____ acceptable way to meet people.

3. During the famous New York blackout, when there was no _____-conditioning in their _____ buildings, many people had _____ meetings outside.

4. Some advantages of _____ life are the _____ centers with their interesting _____ shops and their _____ transportation systems. A disadvantage is the _____ jams.

exercise 2 Match the pairs of words by writing the letters on the lines as in the example.

1. _d_ high
2. _____ business
3. _____ drinking
4. _____ public
5. _____ bargain
6. _____ charge
7. _____ behavior
8. _____ self-

a. administration
b. hunting
c. therapy
d. school
e. transportation
f. discipline
g. account
h. water

Compound Words

Some words belong together in "compounds" (long words that consist of smaller words).

examples: I talked to a salesclerk at the supermarket.

exercise 1 Draw a line between the two words of each compound. Then match the words with the definitions by writing letters on the lines. The first one is done as an example.

1. _h_ black/board
2. _____ teenage
3. _____ overcrowding
4. _____ classroom
5. _____ yardwork
6. _____ downtown
7. _____ videotape
8. _____ paperwork
9. _____ paycheck
10. _____ nightclub

a. room in a school
b. the center of a city
c. a recording with television pictures
d. money for work
e. between the ages of thirteen and nineteen
f. jobs that require reading and writing
g. a place where people eat, drink, and dance
h. a surface on the wall to write on
i. jobs in the garden
j. too many people in one place

How many compound words or phrases can you make from these words, in any order? Work as fast as you can for five minutes. Write them on the lines and then check them in your dictionary. The student with the most correct words or phrases is the winner.

high	work
net	exam
office	public
college	police
self	tuition
science	school
transportation	service
life	city
planning	
confidence	

1. high school _____

2. _____

3. _____

4. _____

5. _____

6. _____

7. _____

8. _____

9. _____

10. _____

11. _____

12. _____

13. _____

14. _____

15. _____

16. _____

Increasing Reading Speed—Left-to-Right Eye Movements

Slow readers look at the same words several times. Their eyes move back and forth over each sentence. Fast readers usually move their eyes from left to right one time for each line. They don't look back very often. A fast left-to-right eye movement increases reading speed. The following exercises will help you improve your reading speed. You will feel less nervous during tests if you can read quickly.

exercise Your teacher will tell you when to begin each section. Look at the underlined word at the left of each line. Read across the line, from left to right, as fast as you can. Some words in the line are the same as the underlined word. Circle them. At the end of each section, write down your time (the number of seconds it took you to finish). Try to read faster with each section.

<u>banking</u>	banks	banking	bank	banking	banking
<u>loan</u>	loans	lend	alone	loaning	loan
<u>savings</u>	savings	save	savings	saving	saver
<u>benefit</u>	benefits	benefit	benefited	benefit	beneficial
<u>employer</u>	employ	employee	employer	employed	employment
				Time: _____	

<u>experience</u>	experience	experienced	expertise	experience
<u>opening</u>	opening	opening	opened	opening
<u>excellent</u>	excel	excelled	excellent	excellent
<u>tellers</u>	retell	tellers	teller	telling
<u>account</u>	account	accounts	account	accounting
			Time: _____	

<u>part-time</u>	part-time	part-time	full-time	part-timer
<u>position</u>	possible	position	positive	position
<u>public</u>	public	private	publicity	publicize
<u>appointment</u>	appoint	appointed	appointment	appointment
<u>insurance</u>	insurance	insure	assurance	insurance
			Time: _____	

<u>salary</u>	salary	celery	salaries	salaried	sales
<u>typing</u>	typing	typed	type	typing	typing
<u>skills</u>	skilled	skill	skills	skills	skillful
<u>apply</u>	applied	apply	apply	apply	application
<u>ability</u>	ability	able	capable	ability	capability
				Time: _____	

Reading in the Real World

Scanning for Information
Classified Ads

> When you scan something (such as classified ads) for specific information, there will be other information that you *don't* need and *aren't* looking for. You need to learn to ignore it; pay no attention to it. Instead, remember to keep a question in your mind as you run your finger down the center of the page or column and let the answer "jump out" at you.

exercise 1   Here are some common abbreviations (shortened forms of words) from advertisements. Match them with their meanings. Write the letters on the lines as in the example.

1. _f___ co
2. _____ exp
3. _____ hr
4. _____ min (or mini)
5. _____ mo (or mos)
6. _____ ofc
7. _____ S&L
8. _____ wk
9. _____ wpm
10. _____ xlnt
11. _____ yr

a. hour
b. office
c. year
d. excellent
e. words per minute (typing speed)
f. company
g. experience
h. minimum (at least)
i. week
j. month(s)
k. savings and loan (similar to a bank)

Scan the following classified ads. The numbers next to the groups of statements refer to the numbers next to the ads (there is *not* a group of statements for every ad). Write T on the lines before the true statements; write F on the lines before the false statements. If the ad does not give enough information, write I *(impossible to know)*.

1.

BANKING

LOAN AGENTS

Aggressive S & L is looking for experienced loan agents, S/F.V. South Bay & other prime territories. We are a direct lender offering 17 day processing & 24 hr. approval for FHA, VA & conventional loans. Our commissions, incentive & benefit programs are tops in the industry. For interview call Tom Smith National S & L, 800/647-0747 or 800/425-6000.
Equal Oppty Employer

2.

BANKING

LOAN PROCESSOR

Fast growing S & L has immediate opening for that person with 2 yrs. min. experience with conventional & govt loan processing. We are looking for someone with current experience. We offer xlnt benefits, pleasant working conditions & opportunity for growth. Contact: Judy at First International S & L, 818/647-0600 or 800/224-4200.
Equal Oppty Employer

2. a. ____ This job is at a savings and loan company.

   b. ____ It requires three years' experience.

   c. ____ Men and women can apply.

3.

★ **BANKING/TELLERS** ★

We have 18 open positions with major banks & S&L's. We need 14 Tellers & 4 New Accounts people. Minimum 1 yr experience, xlnt benefits & future. Call Today!

THE DAVIS AGENCY

26400 Fair Oaks Enc.
464-5000
Eves & wknds by appt.

3. a. ____ This job is for a loan officer.

   b. ____ It requires a college degree.

   c. ____ It offers good benefits.

4.

COMPUTER OPERATOR
Burbank entertainment co seeks detail-oriented individual with 6 mos operating experience &/or education. Good communication skills & ability to work any shift a must. Xlnt benefits & working environment. Please call Janet 921-2700. Equal Oppty Employer M-F-H

4. a. ____ This job is with an entertainment company.

   b. ____ It requires one-half year of experience.

   c. ____ The person who gets this job will use a computer.

5.

Computer Operator IBM/SYSTEM 23
Printing corp is seeking an operator with bookkeeping background + 1 yr experience on IBM/SYSTEM 23 or equivalent. Salary commensurate with experience + full benefits pkg. (No phone calls please) Send resume: A.L. Johnson & Son., 9612 Beverly Dr. No. Hollywood 91605 Att. Louis Johnson

6.

CLERICAL

COLLECTION ACCOUNT REPRESENTATIVE

We are looking for a few outgoing individuals interested in working part-time. Your work hours would be 2:00 p.m. to 4:00 p.m. Monday-Friday. This position involves public relations, heavy use of phone, as well as some door to door contact (this is done by previously scheduled appointments).

We require light typing and good communication skills, a good driving record and proof of insurance. We offer good salary and mileage reimbursement. Please apply in person or call for more information (647-4000).

College Students
Encouraged to Apply

6. a. _____ This is a full-time job.

   b. _____ It requires some typing.

   c. _____ It may be a good job for college students.

7.

ENGINEER - ELECTRICAL DESIGN
Min. of 10 yrs experience in power/lighting design for industrial, commercial & hospitals. Min. of 5 yrs experience in U.S.A. Salary based on experience. XInt benefits. Non smoker. Van Nuys 818/621-7020.

ENGINEER/ELECTRONIC
Wilson Industries   265-0211

7. a. _____ This job is good for a person without much experience.

   b. _____ It is good for a person who doesn't smoke.

   c. _____ The person who gets this job will type and answer phones.

8.

ENGINEER
RF DESIGN ENGINEER
VHF TX RX
Degree optional
Star Industries
Mike Lyndon, 360-2420

9.

ENGINEERING TRAINEE.
Must have good math, neat printing, good mechanical aptitude. Elizabeth, 240-2650.

9. a. _____ This job is good for a person without much experience.

   b. _____ It requires a college degree.

   c. _____ It offers excellent salary and benefits.

10.

SECRETARY/general ofc. Type 60+ wpm, financial statements, for Encino CPA firm. Accounting firm experience required. 240-0577

11.

SECRETARY/Legal Trainee. Dynamic Encino law firm desires bright individual with good office skills. Call Wendy 105-0020.

12.

SECRETARY Part Time Mature non-smoker, typing, dictation required. Property Management Co.-Encino Call Monday 380-9216

13.

SECRETARY / Typist. Busy pool construction office needs take-charge person. Construction scheduling, heavy phones. 501-2530

14.

TEENAGER to do 4-5 hrs of yard work per wk. Sherman Oaks area. $5 hr. 091-2611

10. a. _____ This job requires a typing speed of at least sixty words per minute.

   b. _____ It requires experience.

   c. _____ It is with a bank.

14. a. _____ This job is part time.

   b. _____ It is at a computer company.

   c. _____ It is for people over thirty years old.

**exercise 3** Find the appropriate job for these people. Write the ad number(s) on the line.

1. _____ A man is good at computer work. He wants to meet actors and actresses.

2. _____ A fifty-year-old woman has excellent office skills. She can't work all day. She doesn't smoke.

3. _____ A woman wants to work with money but doesn't want to be a bank teller. She knows about loans.

4. _____ A sixteen-year-old boy wants to earn some extra money. He can't type or use a computer. He likes to be outside.

5. _____ A young man types very fast and takes shorthand. He wants to become a lawyer.

exercise 4 Work in pairs. Ask and answer questions like those above about the classified ads.

Going Beyond the Text

activity Bring to class classified ads for jobs from local newspapers. Discuss new vocabulary and abbreviations. Choose jobs that interest you. Explain them to the class.

CHAPTER five

Lifestyles

in this chapter

The first selection discusses the ways and the reasons our lives are influenced by fashion. The second reading is the journal of an international student who writes about his experiences while living in the United States and Canada and how his impressions changed his opinions about stereotypes. The last part of the chapter looks at advertisements for activities and classes for people with very different lifestyles.

PART one

Our Changing Lifestyles: Trends and Fads

Before You Read

Getting Started

Look at the pictures and discuss them.

1. What are the people in these pictures wearing? What are they doing?
2. What else do you see in each picture? What do you know about these things?
3. About when (what general time) does each picture take place?
4. How are these scenes similar to (or different from) scenes in your country?

Preparing to Read

As you read the following selection, think about the answer to this question. What are fads, and why do people follow them?

Read the following selection quickly. Do not use a dictionary. Then do the exercises that follow the reading.

Our Changing Lifestyles: Trends and Fads

A   These days urban lifestyles seem to change very fast. It is more than just clothing and hairstyles that are in style one year and out of date the next; it's a whole way of living. One year people wear sunglasses on top of their heads and wear jeans and boots; they drink white wine and eat sushi at Japanese restaurants; for exercise they jog several miles a day. However, the next year everything has changed. Women wear long skirts; people drink expensive water from France and eat pasta at Italian restaurants; everyone seems to be exercising at health clubs. Then, suddenly, it has changed again. People wear only natural fabric (safe for the environment); they drink gourmet coffee and eat Thai food; for both leisure and exercise, they go rollerblading.

B   Almost nothing in modern life escapes the influence of fashion; food, music, exercise, books, slang words, movies, furniture, places to visit, even *names* go in and out of fashion. For a while, it seems that all new parents are naming their babies Heather, Dawn, Eric, or Adam. These names are "in." Then, suddenly, these same names are "out," and Tiffany and Jason are "in." It's almost impossible to write about specific fads because these interests that people enthusiastically follow can change very quickly.

C   In the United States, even *people* can be "in" or "out." Like people in any country, Americans enjoy following the lives of celebrities: movie stars, sports heroes, famous artists, politicians, and the like. But Americans also pay a lot of attention to people who have no special ability and have done nothing very special. In 1981, for example, an unknown elderly woman appeared in a TV commercial in which she looked at a very small hamburger and complained loudly, "Where's the beef?" These three words made her famous. Suddenly she appeared in magazines and newspapers and on TV shows. She was immediately popular. She was "in." In 1987, an exterminator in Dallas, Texas, decided that he would be very happy if he could find more customers for his small business; he needed more people to pay him to kill the insects and rats in their houses. He put an unusual advertisement in a Dallas newspaper: He offered to pay

$1,000 to the person who could find the biggest cockroach. This strange offer made him suddenly famous. There were stories about him nationwide—from New York to California. He was "in." However, this kind of fame does not last long. Such people are famous for a very short time.

D

This is the essence, the central quality, of a fad; it doesn't last long. Some fads disappear before we have all even heard of them. How many people remember Green Peace swimsuits? (They changed color to indicate polluted water.) And then there was "Beethoven Bread." Popular in Japan in 1994, it was expensive—$20 for one loaf. It was made while classical music played in the kitchen. The woman who created this bread emphasized that "bread doesn't like rock music."

E

A person who participates in fads should remember that they come and go very fast, and they often come back in style after 10 to 15 years of being "out." It might be a good idea never to throw anything away. Mickey Mouse watches and Nehru jackets may soon be "in" again!

F

What causes such fads to come and go? And why do so many people follow them? Although clothing designers and manufacturers influence fads in fashion because they want to make a profit, this desire for money doesn't explain fads in other areas, such as language. For example, why have teenagers in the past twenty-five years used—at different times—the slang words *groovy, boss, awesome, rad,* or *tubular* instead of simply saying *"wonderful"*? According to Jack Santino, an expert in popular culture, people who follow fads are not irrational; they simply want to be part of something new and creative, and they feel good when they are part of an "in group." Dr. Santino believes that fads are common in any country that has a strong consumer economy—e.g., Britain, Japan, Germany, and the United States. However, in the United States there is an additional reason for fads: Most Americans seem to feel that something is wrong if there isn't frequent change in their lives.

G

Dr. Santino points out that it's sometimes difficult to see the difference between a *fad* and a *trend*. A fad, he says, lasts a very short time and is not very important. A trend lasts much longer. A recent trend is the interest in good health, but many fads come from this trend: aerobic dancing, special diets, cholesterol-counting, organic vegetables, and the like. A trend in the 1980s was the use of personal computers; certain computer games were fads. However, these days we can't really continue to call computers a "trend" because now they have become an essential part of everyday life.

H   An exciting trend began in Europe in the mid-1990s: The cultural borders between countries began to break down. Travelers from other parts of the world noticed that "Eurokids" (under 25 years old) from Lisbon to Stockholm, from London to Athens seemed to be very similar to each other. They had more in common with each other than with older people from their own countries. These young people all followed the same fads in fashion (the colors and designs of Spain), music (*rave* music from Italy, Belgium, and Great Britain), and food *(tapas)*. Barcelona, Spain became the "style capital." These Eurokids had the same lifestyle and values. For example, they were worried about the environment; one report noted, "They are concerned more about rain forests than clothes." Some of the Eurokids' fads will certainly disappear and others will come along, but it will be interesting to see if the trend continues and becomes a true part of European culture.

After You Read
Getting the Main Ideas

Write T on the lines before the statements that are true, according to the reading. Write F on the lines before the statements that are false.

1. _____ Fashion influences many things in addition to clothing and hairstyles.

2. _____ Fads come and go very quickly.

3. _____ People who follow fads are irrational.

4. _____ Trends are the same as fads.

5. _____ When a trend becomes an essential part of everyday life, it isn't called a "trend" any longer.

6. _____ Young people from one European country have a very different lifestyle from young people in another.

Guessing Meaning from Context

Circle the words that give clues to the meaning of each underlined word. Then circle the letter of the correct meaning of the underlined word.

1. Lifestyles seem to change very fast. A lifestyle is more than just clothing and hairstyles that are in fashion one year and out of date the next; it's a whole way of living.
   a. styles of clothes
   b. living habits
   c. costs of living
   d. networks of friends

2. It's almost impossible to write about specific <u>fads</u> because these interests that people enthusiastically follow change very quickly.
   a. clothing styles
   b. famous people
   c. things that people are very interested in
   d. things that people try to write about

3. In 1987 an <u>exterminator</u> in Dallas, Texas, decided that he would be happy if he could find more customers for his small business; he needed more people to pay him to kill the insects and rats in their houses.
   a. customer
   b. person who has a business
   c. person who cleans houses for customers
   d. person who kills small, common, harmful animals

4. There were stories about him <u>nationwide</u>—from New York to California.
   a. everywhere in the country
   b. a big nation
   c. from south to north
   d. in New York

5. Although clothing designers and manufacturers influence fads in fashion because they want to make a <u>profit</u>, this desire for money doesn't explain fads in other areas, such as language.
   a. money that people steal
   b. clothing design
   c. money that people make
   d. new fad

6. Why have teenagers in the past twenty-five years used—at different times—the <u>slang</u> words *groovy, boss, awesome, rad,* or *tubular* in conversation instead of simply saying *wonderful*?
   a. informal
   b. long
   c. formal
   d. nouns

7. It's sometimes difficult to see the difference between a fad and a <u>trend</u>. A fad lasts a very short time and is not very important. A trend lasts a long time and becomes a true part of modern culture.
   a. a fad
   b. a fad that doesn't disappear quickly
   c. modern culture
   d. a modern fad

 *exercise* **3**

Read the selection "Our Changing Lifestyles: Trends and Fads" again carefully. Try to guess the meanings of new words from the context. Use your dictionary only when absolutely necessary.

   Check your answers to the Getting the Main Ideas exercise. Correct your errors if necessary.

Understanding Reading Structure

 Circle the number of the *one* main idea of the reading selection.

1. Trends and fads are the same thing.
2. Fads are common because clothing manufacturers and store owners make a lot of money if styles change every year.
3. Fads usually last a very short time.
4. People follow many different kinds of fads because they like to be part of something new and creative.

Discussing the Reading

 What are some fads these days? Are these fads part of any trend? To help you answer these questions, fill in this chart. Then compare your charts in small groups and discuss your answers.

clothing	hairstyles	food	music	activities

PART two

Breaking Stereotypes: An Inside Look

Before You Read

Skimming for Main Ideas

A paragraph does not always have a topic sentence. When there is no topic sentence, you need to figure out the main idea from the details. For example:

People worldwide believe certain stereotypes about people from other countries. Some stereotypes are positive and some are negative, but all are somewhat dangerous—or untrue—because they are too general. Although stereotypical ideas are partly right, they are also partly wrong. A stereotype often begins with the word *all:* "All people from that country are poor." Sometimes the word *all* is not said, but it is implied (suggested): "The people in this city are impolite." People who believe a certain stereotype usually do so because they lack knowledge. Before going to another country or after being in that country for only a short time, people often carry many stereotypes with them; they believe that they "know" about the country. However, after living there for a *long* time, meeting many people and having many different experiences there, they change their opinions about stereotypes. As people learn more about another culture, they begin to see and appreciate the great variety of customs, educational levels, beliefs, and lifestyles.

(The topic of the paragraph is stereotypes. The details include a definition of the word, the fact that people everywhere believe certain stereotypes, and the information that people change their opinions about stereotypes when they have more knowledge. Therefore, the main idea of the paragraph is that people who don't know much about another culture may have oversimplified ideas—stereotypes—about it.)

exercise   Read the following impressions of one international student in North America. Then circle the number of the sentence that best expresses the main idea.

August
Seattle, Washington

A   **B**efore I came here to travel and later to study, I guess I had a lot of stereotypes about North Americans. I used to think most Americans were rich and had a big house in the suburbs. I was sure they all drove their big

cars to baseball games every weekend, where they drank beer and ate hot dogs. (In fact, I had this idea that hot dogs and hamburgers were the *only* food Americans ate.) I thought it was really important to these people to be fashionable and trendy. I knew a lot of other Americans were very poor and homeless and that nobody cared about them. I was sure that Americans didn't have close families, the way we do in my country. And I thought they were very violent; I was sure every American owned a gun. As I visited people in different parts of the States and Canada, however, many of my ideas changed. I kept a journal to describe my impressions. I discovered that it's difficult to describe a "typical" North American.

1. *People who live in the United States have different lifestyles from people who live in Canada.*
2. *Everyone has a lot of stereotypes about North Americans.*
3. *Although most North Americans are rich and trendy, go to baseball games, and have big cars, others are poor and homeless.*
4. *One student changed some of his ideas about North Americans.*

June
Fort Lee, New Jersey

B   I arrived last Tuesday and have spent this week with some friends of my parents. The Burke family lives in a town in New Jersey which almost seems to be a suburb of New York City. The wife, Anne, is a social worker, so she sees a lot of the problems of modern life: homelessness, drugs, and poverty. She says she's "burned out"—very tired and discouraged by her job. She's thinking of changing professions. Her husband, Ted, is a newspaper reporter who has strange hours and isn't home much. They both wish they could spend more time with their two kids. But the kids, who are teenagers, aren't home much, either. They go to school, of course, but they're also busy with a lot of other activities: school plays, football, and guitar lessons. The big trend for teenagers seems to be "hanging out at the mall." (This was some new English vocabulary for me. It means they spend time with their friends at a big shopping center, just walking around, not really shopping.) Anne and Ted dream of moving to a small town up in the mountains, far away from urban problems ("and shopping centers," adds Ted). They want to cut wood, bake bread, catch fish, read poetry, and "live a simple life." But Anne laughs and says they can't afford a simple life because the kids will need to start college soon. In some ways, the Burkes fit my stereotypical ideas of a North American family.

1. The Burkes fit some of the stereotypes of a "typical" American family.
2. Most Americans and Canadians dislike their lifestyle and want to move to the mountains.
3. The members of the Burke family don't seem to love each other very much because they don't spend much time together.
4. It's interesting to see how people actually live.

July
Denver, Colorado

c   While I was at the Burkes', Anne contacted some friends of hers in Colorado and others in California. They invited me to visit when I traveled west. So I met Libby Monroe and Paul Esquivel. They're a couple who live in Denver in an old house that they're trying to renovate; they can't pay workers to fix up their house, so they're doing most of the renovation work themselves. In fact, it seemed that they were working all the time— and actually enjoying it. They have jobs, of course, but they also do volunteer work in the community and work in their garden on weekends. They're both great cooks, and they fixed some fabulous gourmet meals while I was there. They're vegetarians, and they use a lot of organic fruits and vegetables from their garden. It seemed to me that Libby and Paul didn't exactly fit my stereotypes of Americans.

1. Libby and Paul are a young married couple living in Denver.

2. Libby and Paul are poor, so they can't pay workers to fix up their old house or to do yardwork for them.

3. Libby and Paul seem to work very hard but to enjoy their life.

4. Libby and Paul are workaholics.

July

Los Angeles, California

D   I liked the Burkes and Libby and Paul, but my most interesting visit was yesterday, with the least typical "family" I met on my trip. There were eight elderly people—from seventy to eighty-nine years old—living together in a communal home in L.A. A lot of older people in North America have problems with health and finances and depression; they often feel unsafe, useless, and lonely. But the people I met in *this* group have enormous enthusiasm, energy, and interest in life. Each person contributes to the group. Several of them are good cooks; some enjoy gardening; others provide transportation to the store, the doctor, and so on; and others provide entertainment—they play the piano, sing and dance, or tell stories. Most of them do volunteer work, too, either with the homeless or with literacy programs. Each person feels important and useful, and nobody is lonely. This family helped me break a lot of my stereotypes about Americans.

1. Elderly people who live alone often feel afraid and lonely.

2. The communal lifestyle may provide many advantages to older people who no longer live in the "typical American family."

3. If people have the opportunity, they will choose to live in big family groups rather than in couples or alone.

4. A good place to stay when you travel is in a communal house because there are many people to visit with.

After You Read

Learning to Summarize

You can show your understanding of reading material by *summarizing* it. When you write a summary, you retell the main ideas and the important details in short form. You can use some words from the reading and some of your own words. Following is a summary of the paragraph on page 92:

People worldwide have stereotypes (ideas that are partly right, partly wrong, but always too general) of people from other countries. As people learn more about another culture, their stereotypes begin to disappear.

exercise 1

Work in groups of four. Each person will choose a different paragraph from the reading selection, "Breaking Stereotypes: An Inside Look," and summarize it for the group. In your summary, you might begin with the main idea that you chose; then add a few important details.

Viewpoint

exercise 2

In your opinion, which family did the speaker in the selection in Part Two like the most? The least? Why do you think so? Which family's lifestyle did *you* like the most? Why?

Discussing the Reading

activity

In small groups, talk about answers to these questions.

1. Which lifestyle is most similar to your own? How?
2. Is the traditional family lifestyle changing in your culture? If so, how?
3. Do you have North American friends? If so, in what ways do they fit or break some common stereotypes of them? (*Hint:* If you have trouble answering this, do the What Do You Think? activity on page 97 first, and then return to this question.)

WHAT DO YOU THINK?

Discussing Stereotypes

Stereotypes are almost unavoidable. However, people who live abroad or who have friends from other cultures usually work at overcoming their stereotypes; that is, they fight against having these ideas. They try to keep open to the *variety* of people in the culture.

1. In the chart, make a list of stereotypes of North Americans from paragraph A on pages 92–93. Add to this list any other stereotypes that you know about.
2. Make a list of stereotypes that people from other cultures have about *your* culture.

Interactions II • Reading

3. For each stereotype, write a brief note about it. How, in your opinion, is this stereotype correct, incorrect, or both? If it is incorrect, in what way?
4. In small groups, discuss the information in your charts.

	stereotypes	how these are correct or incorrect
North America		
my culture		

Building Vocabulary and Study Skills

Suffixes and Prefixes

Suffixes (word endings), such as *-er, -sion,* and *-ive,* often indicate the part of speech of a word (see the list on page 57). Here are some more suffixes, listed by the parts of speech that they usually indicate.

NOUNS	VERBS	ADJECTIVE	ADVERB
-ess	*-ate*	*-less*	*-ly*
-ship	*-ize*		
-ism	*-en*		

exercise 1 Write _n___ on the lines before the nouns, _v___ on the lines before verbs, _adj_ before adjectives, and _adv_ before adverbs. In some cases, two answers are correct. (If necessary, refer to the list of suffixes on page 57.)

1. _n___ attention
2. _____ entertainment
3. _____ organization
4. _____ international
5. _____ vacation
6. _____ visitor
7. _____ information
8. _____ hopeless
9. _____ general
10. _____ typical
11. _____ pleasant
12. _____ individualism

13. _____ communal
14. _____ exactly
15. _____ worsen
16. _____ frequently
17. _____ workaholism
18. _____ indicate
19. _____ religious
20. _____ participate
21. _____ hostess
22. _____ experience
23. _____ traveler
24. _____ member

25. _____ enjoyable
26. _____ positive
27. _____ description
28. _____ concentrate
29. _____ renovate
30. _____ socially
31. _____ friendship
32. _____ memorize
33. _____ dangerous
34. _____ impatiently
35. _____ characteristic

The prefix (beginning) of a word sometimes gives a clue to its meaning. Some prefixes create a word with an opposite meaning.

examples: We've <u>discovered</u> many <u>unusual</u> hotels in our travels. (<u>Discover</u> means to "uncover" information—i.e., to find out something that we didn't know before. <u>Unusual</u> means "not usual"—i.e., out of the ordinary.)

The following prefixes can have the meaning "no" or "not."

    un- in- im- dis-

exercise 2

Use one of the prefixes above to change each word into its opposite as in the examples. Use your dictionary, if necessary.

1. _un_ pleasant

2. _im_ patient

3. ____ expensive

4. ____ characteristic

5. ____ avoidable

6. ____ usual

7. ____ safe

8. ____ frequent

9. ____ count

10. ____ advantage

11. ____ possible

12. ____ interesting

Here are some other prefixes with their usual meanings.

con-/com-	= with, together	*pre-*	= first, before
ex-/e-	= out of, from	*re-*	= again, back
inter-	= between, among	*trans-*	= across
mis-	= wrong		

exercise 3

The definitions on the right are based on the meanings of prefixes. Match them with the words on the left by writing the letters on the lines as in the example.

1. _g_ reflect

2. ____ contact

3. ____ transit

4. ____ international

5. ____ preparation

6. ____ experience

7. ____ replace

8. ____ prevent

9. ____ combination

10. ____ concentrate

a. among different countries
b. get knowledge from life (not books)
c. moving people or things across places
d. stop something before it happens
e. provide something again
f. put together in one place
g. throw back; give back an image of
h. joining together of people or things
i. get together and talk with
j. getting ready for something to happen

Dictionary Entries

Some words have only one meaning. You can find the meaning in a dictionary entry, which sometimes includes an example.

 Read these two dictionary entries and answer the questions about them.

> **fad** /fæd/ *n* a short-lived interest or practice: *Her interest in photography is only a passing fad.*
> **ren-o-vate** /ˈrɛnəˌveᵞt/ *v* **-vated -vating** to repair: put back into good condition: to *renovate an old house* **-renovation** /ˌrɛnəˈveᵞʃən/ *n*

1. What part of speech is *fad*? _____

2. What is the dictionary definition of the word? _____

   _____

   _____

3. What part of speech is *renovate*? _____

4. What is the dictionary definition of the word? _____

   _____

   _____

5. What word is related to it? _____

Most words, however, have more than one meaning. Often the same word can be more than one part of speech, and each part of speech can have different meanings.

example: The word <u>style</u> is most commonly a noun. In the first dictionary entry, it has five meanings; the last meaning is part of a hyphenated phrase. <u>Style</u> can also be a verb, with two other forms.

> **style**¹ /stail/ *n* **1** a general way of doing something: *the modern style of building|a formal style of writing* **2** fashion, esp. in clothes: *the style of the 30's* **3** a type or sort, esp. of goods: *They sell every style of mirror|a hair style* **4** high quality of social behavior, appearance, or manners: *She gives dinner parties* **in style** (= in a grand way), *with the best food and wine.* **5** **-style** in the manner of a certain person, place, etc.: *He wears his hair short, military-style.*
> **style**² *v* **styled, styling** to form in a certain pattern, shape, etc.: *The dress is carefully styled.*

 Refer to the dictionary entries above to answer these questions on the next page.

Interactions II • Reading

1. What part of speech is the word *style* when it means "fashion, especially in clothes"? _____ Give an example of this use of the word in a phrase. _____

2. How many meanings does the word *style* have as a noun? _____ As a verb? _____

3. Write the part of speech of the word *style* in each of these sentences.

   When they travel, they go in *style*. _____

   The couple preferred a modern *style* of life. _____

   All the people in the house *styled* their own hair. _____

4. Write the dictionary definition of the word *style* in each of these sentences.

   When they travel, they go in *style*. _____

   _____

   _____

   The couple preferred a modern *style* of life. _____

   _____

   _____

   All the people in the house *styled* their own hair. _____

   _____

   _____

   In my travels, I saw many *styles* of furniture, clothing, etc._____

   _____

   _____

 **exercise 3**   Read the following dictionary entries, paying close attention to the parts of speech, the different meanings, and the examples for each meaning. Then write the part of speech and the meaning of the underlined word in each sentence as in the example.

1. There have been travelers' organizations for many years; they are not a <u>novel</u> idea.

   nov-el¹ /ˈnɑvəl/ *n* a long written story dealing with invented people and events: *"War and Peace," the great novel by Leo Tolstoy*
   novel² *adj* new; not like anything known before; *a novel suggestion, something we hadn't tried before*

   adjective – new _____

   Are you going to write a <u>novel</u> about all your experiences?

   _____

   _____

2. It's easier to get a job if you have the right <u>contacts</u>.

_____

_____

_____

Before you arrive, you have to <u>contact</u> your host by telephone.

_____

_____

_____

I've lost <u>contact</u> with the friends I made during my travels.

_____

_____

_____

3. I very much <u>value</u> the friendships I made on my travels.

_____

_____

_____

That hotel has comfortable rooms for the money; it is an excellent <u>value</u>.

_____

_____

_____

What is the present <u>value</u> of the house where you live?

_____

_____

_____

con-tact[1] /'kantækt/ n 1 the condition of meeting, touching, or receiving information from: _Have you been in contact with your sister recently?|to make contact with the ship by radio|She has lost all contact with reality._ 2 _infml_ a social or business connection; person one knows who can help one: _I've got a contact in the tax office. She can help us._ 3 an electrical part that can be moved to touch another part to complete an electrical circuit

contact[2] v to get in touch with (someone); reach (someone) by telephone, etc.

value[1] /'vælyu^w/ n 1 [U] the degree of usefulness of something: _You'll find this map of great value/of little value in helping you to get around the city.|The government sets a higher value on defense_ (= considers it more important) _than on education._ 2 [C;U] the worth of something in money or as compared with other goods for which it might be changed: _Because of continual price increases, the value of the dollar has fallen in recent years.|I bought this old painting for $50, but its real value must be about $500.|The thieves took some clothes and a few books, but nothing of great value._ 3 [U] worth compared with the amount paid: _We offer the best value in the city: only three dollars for lunch with coffee and dessert.|You always get value for your money at that store._ (= the goods are always worth the price charged) -see also VALUES; WORTHLESS (USAGE) **-valueless** _adj_

value[2] v **-ued, -uing** [T] 1 to calculate the value, price, or worth of (something): _He valued the house and its contents at $75,000._ 2 to consider to be of great worth: _I've always valued your friendship very highly._

Using Analogies

A common activity in the vocabulary section of standardized tests is *analogy*. An analogy involves finding relationships and making comparisons. On a test, you show both your knowledge of vocabulary and your use of logic when you complete an analogy. An analogy on such a test has three words; the first two are related in some way. You need to: (1) figure out the relationship between the two words and (2) add a fourth word that has the same relationship to the third word. Look at this analogy:

failure:success::guilt:innocence

This means "*Failure* is related to *success* in the same way that *guilt* is related to *innocence*." (They are opposites.) On a test, you would need to supply the fourth word, *innocence.* Here are some other examples.

analogy to complete	relationship of words in each pair	possible answers
1. ability:capacity::salary:	synonyms	pay; wages
2. poverty:poor::wealth:	noun to adjective	rich; wealthy
3. loaf:bread::ear:	quantity of food	corn

exercise   Complete these analogies with words of your own. Try to do this without a dictionary. (On a test, you will not be able to use a dictionary.) When you finish, compare your answers with those of your classmates. Explain the relationship in each analogy.

1. beautiful:ugly::cheap: _____

2. the press:reporters::aides: _____

3. addicted:addiction::compulsive: _____

4. employer:employee::teacher: _____

5. city:urban::countryside: _____

6. enormous:big::tiny: _____

7. smog:pollution::radon: _____

8. Spain:Europe::Canada: _____

9. nightclub:dance::store: _____

10. drawback:disadvantage::startled: _____

PART four

Reading in the Real World

Scanning for Information

Advertisements

 **exercise 1** Read the following explanation and study the vocabulary.

Most cities offer a lot of activities for people with different lifestyles. Also, there are many activities and classes for people who are trying to change their lifestyles. The advertisements in this section are from an urban newspaper.

turn of the century = a time around the year 1900 or 2000
inn = a small hotel
word processing = use of a computer to write letters, papers, etc.
career = job; profession
meditation = deep, peaceful thinking
voter turnout = the number of people who vote in an election
pamphlet (or brochure) = a small book that explains or describes something

exercise 2 On pages 105 and 106, which advertisements might the following people call for information? Write the number(s) of the advertisements on the lines. In some cases, more than one answer is possible.

A middle-aged woman has been working as an urban planner for over twenty years. She's a workaholic who hasn't taken a vacation in almost ten years. In the past five years she's begun to hate her job. Where might she go to:

a. _____ relax for a few days in a quiet, beautiful place?

b. _____ get some advice about a change of career?

A police officer has recently quit his job and become a novelist. He loves to write, but he has two problems: He doesn't type well and he hasn't made any money since he quit the police force. Which advertisements might he call about if he wants:

a. _____ a secretary to type his novel?

b. _____ someone to tell him about his financial future?

A high-school student is having some serious problems. He doesn't have many friends because he gets angry very easily, and he doesn't express himself well. What can he try that might help him to:

a. _____ control his anger?

b. _____ express his ideas and feelings?

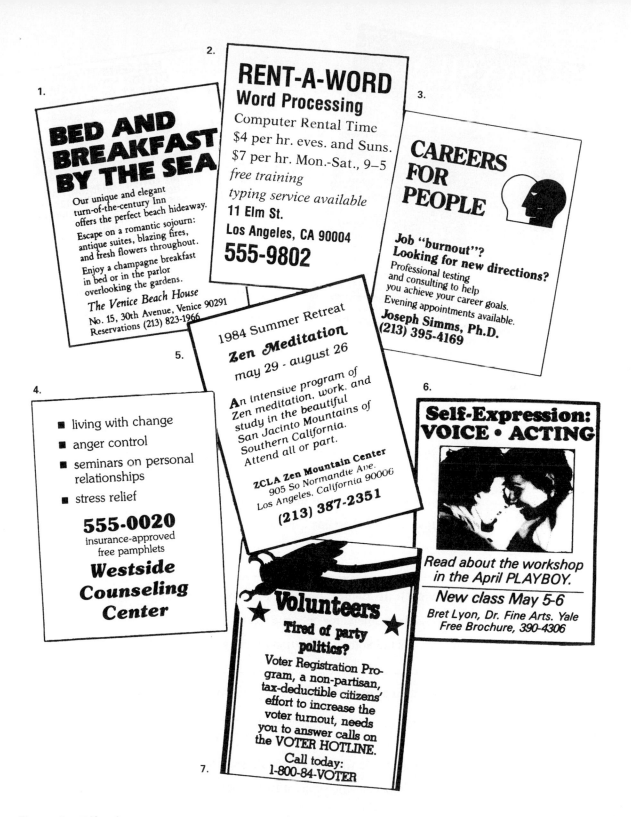

9.

ELYSIUM
cafe

Join us for...
Classic Movies Nightly
Gourmet Sandwiches
& Salads
Desserts
and the Best
Coffee in Town

*in an atmosphere
like home...*

15138 Ventura Blvd.
East of Sepulveda
Sherman Oaks • 818 380 0181
Everyday 8am-1am • and always Free Parking in Rear

100% CERTIFIED ORGANIC
COTTON FUTONS AVAILABLE
ONLY AT BEDFELLOWS

ALL COTTON MATTRESSES ARE
NOT THE SAME. ONLY 100%
ORGANIC COTTON IS GROWN
WITHOUT PESTICIDES OR
CHEMICALS, WHICH IS BETTER
FOR YOU AND THE ENVIRONMENT.

ALSO AVAILABLE:
NATURALLY GROWN WOOL FUTONS
AND PILLOWS CHEMICAL FREE
COTTON SHEETS AND BLANKETS.

Bedfellows
12250 VENTURA BLVD · STUDIO CITY (818) 985-0500

10.

exercise 3 Answer the following questions about the ads.

1. At the Venice Beach House, where do they serve breakfast? _____
   _____

2. How much do you have to pay to use the terminal at Rent-a-Word on a
   Sunday or an evening? ____ How much does it cost on a Wednesday
   morning? ____ What is the fee for training? ____

3. How does the Westside Counseling Center help people? _____
   _____
   _____

4. When is the summer retreat in the San Jacinto Mountains open? ____ Is it
   possible to attend for only one week? ____

5. What is the Voter Registration Program trying to do? _____
   _____

6. What kinds of classes does Dr. Bret Lyon offer? _____
   _____

7. What fads or trends might these people be following:
   • someone who goes to the Elysium Cafe? _____
   • someone who shops at Bedfellows? _____

CHAPTER six

The Global Village

in this chapter

The first reading selection discusses a worldwide crisis: refugees. The second selection looks at some recent exciting changes in global travel. Finally, the last part of the chapter presents valuable tips for reading difficult material.

Before You Read
Getting Started

Look at the pictures and discuss them.

1. What do the people in these pictures have in common; that is, how are they similar?
2. What may have caused the people in each photo to leave their homeland?
3. What do you know about the problems in each of these countries at the time the photo was taken?

Muslim refugees in Bosnia, 1993

Rwandan refugees crossing border into Tanzania, 1994

Bangladesh after April, 1991 cyclone

Preparing to Read

As you read the following selection, think about the answer to this question: What are the main causes of the refugee problem today?

Refugees

A **W**e can see them almost every night on the TV news—thousands of refugees who have chosen to cross international borders to save their lives. They are Afghans, Mozambicans, Guatemalans, Cambodians. They come from Cuba, Rwanda, Bosnia, Ethiopia. Some flee on dangerous, homemade boats. Others escape on foot, carrying a few precious possessions. They often end up in overcrowded refugee camps in terrible conditions. They stare into the camera with eyes that look unnaturally large in their thin faces. Now, at the end of the 20th century and beginning of the 21st, this syndrome of "stay and die or leave and suffer" has become a global crisis.

B It's difficult to say how many refugees there are worldwide; it depends on the definition of the word *refugee.* The United Nations defines *refugee* as a person "outside the country of his nationality" because of fear for reasons of race, religion, nationality, or political opinion. But this definition may be too narrow; it doesn't count the millions of people who have escaped from their countries for economic and environmental reasons. And it doesn't count over 25,000,000 people who have fled violence but have stayed in their own nations. If we include all groups, there are about 50 million refugees in the world today.

C What is causing these enormous floods of refugees? The answer is threefold. First, millions of people are trying to escape from political violence. In many parts of the world, ethnic or religious minorities—such as the Kurdish people in Iraq or the Eritreans in Ethiopia—have reason to fear the government and flee for their lives. Second, hunger is driving millions more from their homeland, especially in northern and eastern Africa. And third, there are over ten million environmental refugees. These people can no longer live on their own land because of drought (not enough rain), floods (too much rain), or other environmental problems.

D In today's world, larger numbers of people than ever before are asking for political asylum in other countries. They feel that they are in danger in their own homeland because they are of the "wrong" race, religion, nationality, or political opinion. One reason for this is the bad economic situation in much of the world. In bad times, people often point to minority groups as the cause of their troubles. Another reason, surprisingly, is the end of the Cold War. Until the late 1980s, communist governments in eastern Europe and the USSR did not approve of religious or political expression, and they did not allow racial or national conflicts. But as communism fell and the former Soviet Union broke up, old ethnic anger and hatred began to appear and then to explode. Fighting broke out in Armenia, Georgia, and Yugoslavia. Some countries in other parts of the world, such as Africa, also exploded in ethnic, religious, or political violence. These countries had been "under the wing" of the Soviet Union during the Cold War. Without the Soviet influence, they, too, became battlegrounds, and minority groups faced danger if they stayed in their own countries.

E Although hunger drives thousands—sometimes millions—of people from their homeland each year, some experts point out that for the first time in human history, there is no *natural* reason for famine. We now have technology to preserve, keep, and transport food over long distances. Kurt Jonassohn, of the Montreal Institute for Genocide and Human Rights Studies, gives the example of Kenya and Ethiopia in the 1980s. There was a serious drought in East Africa at that time. Because of this lack of rain, the farmers in both countries had terrible crop failures. However, there was no famine condition in Kenya because the government imported food and distributed it to the people. The TV news in most countries paid no attention to crop failures in Kenya because they did not result in famine. On the other hand, tens of thousands of Ethiopians died of hunger at that same time because the government there did not take action to import and distribute food to its people. Jonassohn strongly believes that ". . . the famine in Ethiopia was man-made." He says that in today's world, governments of some countries are using *hunger* against certain ethnic groups. Therefore, the millions of famine victims in many refugee camps are probably, in truth, *political* refugees, also.

F In most cases, environmental problems, too, are man-made. For example, we humans cut down forests for wood and farmland. Then, when heavy rains come, there is no system of tree roots to absorb the water. The result is a flood that washes away homes, crops growing in the field, and whole towns. The homeless people become refugees in a new land, where they have to cut down the trees for firewood. And the cycle begins again.

G If the roots of the refugee problem are man-made, the key to the solution is people's desire to end it. Volunteer organizations such as CARE, Save the Children, and Médecins Sans Frontières can provide help in a crisis. However, they can't make much of a change if governments don't want to protect their own people—*all* of them.

After You Read

Getting the Main Ideas

exercise 1

Write T on the lines before the statements that are true, according to the reading. Write F on the lines before the statements that are false.

1. _____ The United Nations' definition of *refugee* includes all people who have escaped their homes for political, economic, and environmental reasons.

2. _____ Political violence, hunger, and environmental problems cause people to try to escape from their homeland.

3. _____ There are fewer political refugees than in the past.

4. _____ If thousands of people die of hunger, it's a natural crisis and there's nothing we can do about it.

5. _____ Most environmental problems are caused by people.

Guessing Meaning from Context

Many words with one basic, *literal* meaning have other, *figurative* meanings.

example: The woman with the sad <u>face</u> is worried about how to <u>face</u> the future. (Literally, *face* is a noun and means "the front part of the head." However, figuratively, *face* is a verb that means "to meet a difficult situation.")

The underlined words express figurative meanings. For each item, circle the words that give clues to the meaning of the underlined word. Then circle the letter of the appropriate meaning *for this context*.

1. Political violence is <u>driving</u> thousands of frightened people from their country into refugee camps.
   a. guiding and controlling a car, bus, or truck
   b. taking someone in a car, bus, or truck
   c. forcing (someone) to leave
   d. killing

2. <u>Floods</u> of people escaped from Rwanda in 1994. Volunteer organizations didn't know how to help so many people.
   a. too much water, covering a place that is usually dry
   b. a very large number
   c. refugees
   d. families

3. Communism in eastern Europe began to <u>fall</u> in the late 1980s.
   a. lose power
   b. come down from a standing position
   c. become lower in level or quantity
   d. be killed in a battle

4. The <u>roots</u> of the refugee problem are man-made.
   a. feelings of belonging to one place
   b. parts of a plant that grow in the soil
   c. part of a tooth or hair that holds it to the rest of the body
   d. causes

5. Education is one <u>key</u> to the solution.
   a. a metal instrument to unlock a door
   b. something that helps to find an answer
   c. important
   d. part of a piano or typewriter

6. The terrible flood <u>washed away</u> crops, homes, and whole towns.
 a. cleaned with water
 b. watered
 c. rained on
 d. caused to be carried off by water

7. In bad times, people often <u>point to</u> minority groups as the cause of their troubles.
 a. hold out a finger to show direction
 b. accuse or blame
 c. aim at or direct
 d. look at

exercise **3**   Find words in the reading selection "Refugees" with the following meanings and write the words on the lines. The letters in parentheses indicate the paragraphs in which the words appear.

1. things that people own (A): _____

2. people who leave their homes and look for safety in another place (A):

_____

3. small parts of a population that are different from the rest in race, religion, etc. (C): _____

4. related to a racial or national group (C): _____

5. run away or try to escape (C): _____

6. a long period without enough rain (C): _____

7. protection that one country gives to people who have left another for political reasons (D): _____

8. disagreements or wars (D): _____

9. places where people fight wars (D): _____

10. a situation in which many, many people die of hunger (E):

_____

11. plants that farmers grow (E): _____

12. gave out (E): _____

13. people who suffer (E): _____

14. take in liquid (F): _____

exercise **4**   Read the selection again carefully. Try to guess the meanings of new words from the context. Use your dictionary only when absolutely necessary. Then go back to the Preparing to Read section and answer the question. Compare your answer with that of other students.

Understanding Reading Structure

Many reading selections follow an *outline.* The outline is the plan, or the organization, of the material. It shows the relationship of the topics and ideas. You can outline reading material to help yourself see clearly the relationship of ideas; you can also write an outline when you organize your ideas for a composition. In an outline, the *general* ideas begin on the left. The more *specific* ideas are indented to the right.

example:

REFUGEES

    I. Introduction: refugee problem—a global crisis
    II. Refugees worldwide
        A. The U.N. definition of *refugee*
            1. "Person outside the country of his nationality"
            2. Person in fear for reasons of race, religion, nationality, or political opinion
        B. Other types of refugees
            1. Economic refugees
            2. Environmental refugees
            3. Refugees in their own countries
    III. Causes of the refugee problem
        A. Political violence
        B. Hunger
        C. Environmental problems
    IV. Reasons for large numbers of political refugees
        A. Bad economic situation
        B. End of the Cold War
    V. Famine: man-made
        A. Kenya
        B. Ethiopia
    VI. Environmental problems: also man-made
    VII. Conclusion: refugee problem
        A. Roots
        B. Solution

 **exercise 5** Answer these questions about the outline.

    1. What is the topic of the whole outline? _____

    2. What are the two parts of the U.N. definition of *refugee*? _____

_____

3. What are three other types of refugees? _____

_____

4. What are three causes of the refugee problem? _____

_____

5. What are two reasons for the large numbers of political refugees in the world today?

_____

_____

 *exercise 6* Now circle the number of the *one* main idea of the reading selection "Refugees."

1. The United Nations' definition of *refugee* is too narrow because it doesn't include people who have escaped their homes but haven't crossed an international border.

2. Larger numbers of people than ever before are asking for political asylum.

3. Two reasons why people flee from their homeland—famine and environmental problems—arc usually man-made, not natural crises.

4. The roots of the refugee problem—political violence, famine, and environmental problems—are man-made, so the solution depends on people's desire to end it.

Discussing the Reading

 activity In small groups, talk about your answers to these questions.

1. What countries are people fleeing from today? For what reasons?

2. In what countries are there refugee camps today?

3. In the past year, what environmental crises have been in the news? (Drought? Floods? etc.) Where have these been?

---

focus on testing

Making Inferences

On tests and in general reading, it's important to be able to make inferences. A reading selection often gives information from which a reader can *infer* (figure out) other information.

example: The refugees are Afghans, Mozambicans, Guatemalans, and Cambodians. They come from Cuba, Rwanda, Bosnia, and Ethiopia.

These sentences do not say, but they *imply,* or suggest, that the refugees come from all over the world, not just one continent.

exercise Complete each sentence by circling the letters of *all* the information that the reading selection "Refugees" on pages 109 to 111 states directly or implies.

1. The U.N. definition of *refugee* _____.
   a. includes people who have fled their countries for political reasons
   b. includes economic refugees
   c. does not include a lot of people who actually seem to be refugees
   d. includes about 50 million people

2. Refugees _____.
   a. are often members of minority groups
   b. always come from poor countries
   c. are against their government
   d. are in greater numbers than ever before

3. The causes of the refugee problem are _____.
   a. ethnic conflicts
   b. hunger
   c. floods
   d. man-made

4. The drought in east Africa in the 1980s _____.
   a. caused famine in Kenya
   b. caused famine in Ethiopia
   c. caused crop failures
   d. was man-made

PART two
The New World of Travel

Before You Read
Skimming for Main Ideas

exercise Read the following paragraphs quickly, without using a dictionary. After each paragraph, circle the number of the sentence that best expresses the main idea.

The New World of Travel

A

When many people think of global travel, they think of expensive cruise ships and hotels or sightseeing tours to famous places. However, global travel has changed a lot in recent years. Now, not all travel is expensive, so lack of money doesn't have to hold people back. And these days there is an enormous variety of possibilities for people of all interests. Are you looking for adventure? Education? Fun? Do you like to travel with a group? Do you prefer to travel on your own? Would you like to get "inside" another culture and understand the people better? Would you prefer to volunteer to help others? Are you in the market for something strange and different? There is something for almost everybody.

1. Global travel doesn't have to be expensive.
2. Global travel is different now from what it was in past years.
3. Global travel includes cruise ships, hotels, and sightseeing.
4. There are now group tours for people with a variety of interests.

B

Train travel used to be simply a means of getting from one place to another. Now, for people with money, it can also offer education or adventure. The Trans-Siberian Special, for example, is a one-week tour that runs from Mongolia to Moscow. The train stops in big cities and small villages so that passengers can go sightseeing, and there is a daily lecture on board the train, in which everyone learns about history and culture. For people who are looking for fun and adventure, there is the Mystery

Cruise passengers on a ship's sun deck

Express, which runs from New York to Montreal, Canada. This trip interests people who love Sherlock Holmes, Hercule Poirot, and Miss Marple. It's for people who have always secretly dreamed of being a private eye and solving mysteries. The passengers on board have the opportunity to solve a murder mystery right there on the train. In the middle of the night, for instance, there might be a gunshot; soon everyone learns that there has been a "murder," and they spend the rest of the trip playing detective. They track down clues, exchange this information and their opinions, and solve the whodunit by the time the train has pulled into Montreal. Of course, no *real* crime takes place. The "murderer" and several passengers are actually actors. The trip is a very creative weekend game.

1. *The Mystery Express allows passengers to solve a murder on the train.*
2. *The Trans-Siberian Special is a tour that offers sightseeing and lectures.*
3. *The Trans-Siberian Special and Mystery Express are expensive.*
4. *Train travel can offer education and adventure, in addition to transportation.*

C   Many people don't realize that the world's largest industry is tourism. Clearly, tourists have a big impact on the environment. Perhaps, then, it's fortunate that there is growing interest in *ecotourism;* by 2000, 34% of all international travel will be nature travel. Serious ecotourists are interested in preserving the environment and learning about wildlife. Most also want

Hiking in Alaska

Student volunteers at an archeological dig in Israel

to experience a new culture. Although it's possible to be very comfortable on an ecotour, many travelers choose to rough it; they don't expect hot showers, clean sheets, gourmet food, or air-conditioned tour buses. They live as villagers do. They get around on bicycle, on foot (by hiking or trekking), or on the water (on a sailboat or river raft).

1. *An increasingly popular form of travel—ecotourism—is for people who are interested in nature.*
2. *Ecotours are not usually comfortable.*
3. *Ecotourists live as villagers do and do not travel by train, bus, or car.*
4. *The world's largest industry, tourism, is changing.*

D   For people who want a valuable experience abroad, there are exciting opportunities to study or volunteer. You can study cooking (for one day or eleven weeks) at Le Cordon Bleu in Paris or painting at the Aegean Center for the Fine Arts in Greece. There are classes in art collecting at Sotheby's in London or Indonesian music at the Naropa Institute in Bali. There is marine biology in Jamaica, archaeology in Israel, meditation in Nepal, film in Sweden. But for those who don't have a lot of money for tuition, volunteering for a few weeks can also offer a rich learning experience. Scientists in Costa Rica need volunteers to help count sea turtles and check their health. Archaeologists from Ireland to Grenada (West Indies) need people to help them with excavations. College-age volunteers can sign up for a summer in India. The opportunities change from year to year, but all offer the chance to learn while helping out.

1. *There are exciting opportunities for people who want to study abroad.*
2. *Scientists in several fields need volunteers to help them.*
3. *It's possible to have a valuable experience by studying or volunteering in another country.*
4. *Volunteering can offer a rich learning experience for people who can't afford tuition for classes.*

E   Volunteering is a good way to experience another country without paying for expensive hotels or tuition. But how can a person *get* to another country cheaply? One possibility is courier travel. For a low fee (about $35), a person can join an association that sends information about monthly courier opportunities. The passenger agrees to become a courier (i.e., carry materials for a business in his or her luggage) and can then receive huge discounts on airfare—e.g., $400 Miami-Buenos Aires round trip or $300 L.A.-Tokyo round trip. People who enjoy ocean travel but don't have money for a cruise ship might try a freighter. Although freighters carry cargo from country to country, most also carry eight to twelve passengers. For people who want to take their time, it's a relaxing way to travel and is less expensive than taking a crowded cruise ship.

1. *It's possible to travel cheaply.*
2. *Courier flights and freighters are two ways to get to another country cheaply.*
3. *On a courier flight, a passenger carries something in exchange for cheap airfare.*
4. *A trip on a freighter is both cheap and relaxing.*

After You Read

Understanding Idioms

An idiom is a phrase that means something different from the individual words in it. Idioms are most common in informal English but are found everywhere. The reading selections in this chapter contain several.

example: Many countries in Eastern Europe, Asia, and Africa had been <u>under the wing</u> of the Soviet Union during the Cold War. Then the Cold War ended, and without the Soviet influence, some of these countries became battlegrounds.

You can often guess the meaning of an idiom from the context. Sometimes, as in the example above, it also helps to visualize ("see" in your mind) the *literal* meaning of the expression.

From the context and your knowledge of the word <u>wing</u>, you can guess that <u>under the wing</u> means "protected by or influenced by."

exercise 1

For each of the following items, find an idiom in the reading selection "The New World of Travel" that has a similar meaning and write it on the line. The letters in parentheses indicate the paragraphs where the idioms appear.

1. cause to stay in one place (A):_____

2. alone; not with a group (A):_____

3. looking for; hoping to find (A):_____

4. travels; goes (B):_____

5. on a train (B):_____

6. detective (B):_____

7. look for and find (B):_____

8. mystery (B):_____

9. arrived in (B):_____

10. travel in a simple and not comfortable way (C):_____

11. go from place to place (C):_____

12. agree to participate in (D):_____

13. travel slowly (E):_____

Making Inferences

 *exercise* **2** Turn back to "The New World of Travel" to answer this question: What can you infer from each paragraph? On the short lines, put a check mark next to each statement that you can infer from the paragraph. Do not check the other statements, even if you think they are true. On the line after each statement you check, write the phrases from which you inferred the information. The first one is done as an example.

PARAGRAPH A

1. __✓__ You don't have to be rich in order to travel. <u>not all travel is</u>

   <u>expensive</u>

2. _____ It costs a lot of money to take a cruise. _____

   _____

3. _____ There is greater variety today in types of travel than there used to be.

   _____

4. _____ It's better to travel on your own than in a group. _____

   _____

PARAGRAPH B

1. _____ Today, train travel is more than just a way to get from place to place.

   _____

2. _____ The Trans-Siberian Special is a lot of fun. _____

   _____

3. _____ The Mystery Express is expensive. _____

   _____

4. _____ The Mystery Express is fun. _____

   _____

PARAGRAPH C

1. _____ Ecotourism is becoming more popular. _____

   _____

2. _____ Ecotours are often not very comfortable. _____

   _____

3. _____ Serious ecotourists care about animals. _____

   _____

4. ____ Ecotourists don't enjoy comfortable hotels._____

_____

1. ____ It's more expensive to study film in Sweden than meditation in Nepal. _____

_____

2. ____ There is a variety of subjects that people can study in different countries. _____

_____

3. ____ Rich people prefer to take courses, and people without money prefer to volunteer. _____

_____

4. ____ Volunteering can be a very good learning experience._____

_____

PARAGRAPH E

1. ____ Cruise ships are expensive._____

_____

2. ____ A freighter is a kind of ship._____

_____

3. ____ Freighters are as exciting as cruise ships._____

_____

4. ____ Travel by freighter is probably not good for people who are in a hurry._____

_____

Discussing the Reading

activity

In small groups, talk about your answers to these questions.

1. What kinds of travel are most interesting to you? Why?

2. Is tourism important in your country? If so, what kind of tourism?

3. Think of one trip that you've taken. (It could have been fun, exciting, boring, terrible, etc.) Tell your classmates about it.

Building Vocabulary and Study Skills

Expressions and Idioms

exercise Complete each sentence with the missing words. Choose from these expressions.

under the wing	private eye
end up	in the market
break out	on board
break up	track down
whodunit	pull into
hold back	rough it
on your own	get around

1. At the end of the Cold War, the former USSR began to _____.

2. We're going to fly to Europe. Then, while we're there, we'll_____ by train.

3. I love to read mystery novels. Someday maybe I'll become a_____ and solve crimes myself.

4. She spent hours in the library, but she wasn't able to_____ the information that she needed.

5. His old car breaks down all the time, so he's _____ for a new car.

6. I don't enjoy camping trips. I've never liked to _____.

7. After her parents died, she was _____ of her aunt and uncle.

8. Everyone is afraid that war might _____ again in that country.

Increasing Reading Speed

exercise The following exercise will help you to improve your left-to-right eye movements and to increase your reading speed. Your teacher will tell you when to begin each section. Look at the underlined phrases to the left of each line. Read across the line, from left to right. Quickly underline the phrases that are the same as the underlined phrase. At the end of each section, write down your time (the number of seconds it took you to finish). Try to read faster with each section.

break up	break out breakfast	break up break off	break into break up
under the wing	under the weather under the wing	under the water underworld	under the wing undercover
pulled into	pulled into pulled up	pulled over pulled for	pulled out pulled into
in a hurry	hurry up in a hurry	no hurry hurry over	in a hurry in a hurry
private eye	private eye private eye	private life private car	private school private eye

Time: _____

by train	train track by train	by train in the rain	by train buy a train
take your time	take much time take some time	take your time take your time	time after time behind the times
see the sights	see the sights keep sight of	sightseeing see the sights	eyesight sight something
in the market	on the market to the market	in a market at the market	in the market in the market
get around	get around get over	get over get under	get up to get around

Time: _____

political asylum	political refugee political asylum	political problems political asylum	political asylum political leaders
on your own	on the town on your own	of your own in your town	your own on your own
sign up for	sign over sign away	sign in sign up for	sign up for sign for
above board	above board overboard	on board above board	across the board above board
hold back	hold over hold down	hold up hold out	hold back hold onto

Time: _____

global crisis	global travel global crisis	global crisis global crime	global warming global crisis
point out	point out point at	point to point out	point out point toward
take place	take part take place	take place take parts	take turns take over
social order	social studies social order	social work social order	social science social organization
child care	child care child care	child's play child care	childhood childbirth

Time: _____

Reading in the Real World

Scanning for Information

Difficult Reading Material

> Often, as a student, you'll need to read material that seems too difficult.
> As with all reading, it will help if you remember the following suggestions.
>
> 1. Consider what you already know about the topic before you read.
> 2. Have questions in mind as you read. When you *scan* for specific
>   information, have a pencil or felt-tip marking pen in hand and your
>   questions in mind. Mark the information as soon as you find it.
> 3. Try not to worry about new words. You may see some of them
>   several times in the same reading selection. Each time you see one,
>   it will probably add to your ability to guess the meaning.

 **exercise 1** Consider these questions before you read.

1. What are some countries with a lot of crime (high-crime cultures)? What are some low-crime cultures?

2. Why do you think some cultures have more crime than others?

3. Which might have more crime—a homogeneous country (with one main ethnic group) or a heterogeneous one (with many ethnic groups)?

exercise 2 As you read, scan for information to help you fill in the chart. Mark the information when you find it. When you finish reading, complete the chart. (*Note:* This reading selection will probably seem very difficult, but *don't worry* about what you don't understand. If you can fill in the chart when you finish, it means that you understand the main ideas.)

	characteristics of high-crime cultures	characteristics of low-crime cultures
Culture		
Parenting		
Wealth		
Social Order		

The Global Crime Wave

Crime is increasing worldwide, and there is every reason to believe the trend will continue through the 1990s and into the early years of the twenty-first century.

5 Crime rates have always been high in multicultural, industrialized, democratic societies such as the United States, but a new phenomenon has appeared on the world scene—rapidly rising crime rates in nations 10 that previously reported few offenses. Street crimes such as murder, assaults, rape, robbery, and auto theft are clearly rising, particularly in some formerly communist countries such as Hungary and in western 15 European nations such as Scandinavia and the United Kingdom.

What is driving this crime explosion? There are no simple answers. Still, there are certain conditions associated with rising 20 crime: increasing heterogeneity of populations, greater cultural pluralism, higher immigration, changing national borders, democratization of governments, greater economic growth, and the rise of anomie— 25 the lack of accepted social ideas of "right" and "wrong."

These conditions are increasingly observable around the world. For instance, cultures that were previously isolated and 30 homogeneous, such as Japan, Denmark, China, and Greece, are now facing the sort of cultural variety that has been common in the United States for most of its history.

Multiculturalism can be a rewarding, 35 enriching experience, but it can also lead to a clash of values. Heterogeneity in societies will be the rule in the twenty-first century, and failure to recognize and plan for such diversity can lead to serious crime problems.

40 The connection between crime and culture cannot be overemphasized: There are high-crime and low-crime cultures around the world. In the years ahead, many low-crime cultures may become high-crime 45 cultures because of changing world populations and politicoeconomic systems. In general, heterogeneous populations in which people have lots of economic choice (capitalism) are prime candidates for crime. 50 Why? The very nature of crime is culturally defined. What is legal and desirable in one culture may be viewed as a serious crime in another.

A culture in which the citizens are very 55 similar—sharing similar ethnicity, religious beliefs, income levels and values, such as Denmark—is more likely to have laws that represent the wishes and desires of a large majority of its people than is a culture where 60 citizens come from diverse backgrounds. For this reason, homogeneous cultures normally have a lower level of law violation than heterogeneous cultures.

In addition, some cultures have a 65 tradition of discipline—a belief that laws ought to be obeyed. In cultures where individualism is strong, and belief and respect for law is low, laws are often broken. Usually these are heterogeneous cultures, 70 where citizens disagree about the laws and are poorly socialized to obey them.

Critical to crime rates in any culture are the parenting and child-care philosophies and methods. Most street crimes such as 75 burglaries and robberies in all societies occur among adolescents and young adults. In some societies, parents are seen as primarily responsible for their children, but all citizens share in that responsibility. In 80 other societies the child is treated as chattel—the property of the parents. The first type of society assures that parents receive preparation for infant care and provides support for parents in caring for their children. In the second type, no such support system exists. In these societies, nothing is required to be a parent—no knowledge, no skills, no income—and the parent is on his or her own to care for the child. It is not difficult to determine which system is more likely to produce a law-abiding young adult.

The disparity between the richest and poorest citizens is narrow in some cultures. People may be poor by world standards, but the little available wealth is shared fairly equally. In other societies, the differences between the wealthy and the poor are enormous: the people at the top may have hundreds, even thousands, of times more wealth than those at the bottom. This disparity between rich and poor may lead to a high crime rate.

Currently, much of the world is in a state of what French sociologist Emile Durkheim called *anomie*—a situation where people don't have clear ideas about the difference between "right" and "wrong." In most societies, the traditional social order has broken down, and there is a lack of clear-cut, well-established laws and limitations on behavior. Some nations, such as the United States, face widespread anomie due to their lack of restraints on human desires. In the United States, people feel that anyone can become a millionaire or president. With the fall of communism, dictatorships, and colonialism and the beginning of democracy in different forms around the world, many peoples are now experiencing huge expectations. Cultural differences increase this anomie. Moving from an authoritative society to a democracy also creates anomie because old rules and ideas are abandoned before new laws and ideas have become accepted.

Anomie results from a breakdown in the "bonding" process (which holds people in a society together). The individual who is closely in agreement with social expectations over a long period of time probably won't commit a serious crime because he or she has developed a "bond" with society.

The United States was the first industrialized, democratic, heterogeneous nation and thus the first to face the crime problems associated with anomie. We can imagine that crime will be a growth industry in many countries as they find themselves gripped by the same social forces that have long affected the United States.

Gene Stephens
The Futurist
July-August 1994

activity After you finish filling in the chart on page 127, compare your chart with those of other students. Were your answers the same? Were they similar (but perhaps in different words)?

WHAT DO YOU THINK?

Applying the Death Penalty

Some countries and some states in the United States have *capital punishment* (the death penalty), and others do not. Capital punishment means that if a person has been found guilty of a very serious crime, such as murder, he or she might receive death as a punishment. People often argue about this. Some believe that capital punishment is necessary to keep the crime rate down. Others disagree and say that it does not result in less crime. What's your opinion—and *why*?

CHAPTER seven

North America: The Land and the People

in this chapter

The first reading selection discusses Native Americans (American Indians) and how their culture has changed. The second selection discusses some regional customs in the United States. The final reading is a chapter from a book by a Native American, in which he remembers an important event that happened when he was sixteen. From his story, you will learn a lot about Native American beliefs.

PART one

North American Indians— Then and Now

Before You Read

Getting Started

Look at the pictures here and on the following page and discuss them.

1. When you think of American Indians, what image (picture) comes to your mind? Why?
2. What do you already know about North American Indians? Do you know something about any of these photos?

Chilkat Indians in dancing costumes, Alaska

A member of the Sioux tribe

Canadian Indians demonstrating in Ottawa

Indians at pow-wow at Stanford University, California

Preparing to Read

As you read the following selection, think about the answer to this question. How is North American Indian culture today different from the culture of the past?

Read the following selection quickly. Do not use a dictionary. Then do the exercises that follow the reading.

A

North American Indians—

The first people to live in North America were the American Indians, or Native Americans. According to the religious and folk stories of many Indian groups, their earliest ancestors arrived in North America from the inside of the earth. Modern scientists, however, believe that the first

Native Americans came from Asia 15,000 to 30,000 years ago across the Bering Strait from Siberia to Alaska. They were nomads; that is, they did not live in one place, but instead were always on the move as they looked for food. In other words, the first American Indians were hunters who followed the animals—their food source—during times of migration from place to place. Together, the nomadic people and animals slowly migrated toward the south.

B

These early inhabitants spread out all over the North American continent (now Canada, the United States, and Mexico). There was a great variety of languages, religious beliefs, and customs among the many tribes, or groups, of Indians. By the time the first Europeans arrived, the Indians were living in several different "culture areas." The way of life in each of these culture areas was determined by the environment in that area. The members of various tribes in each center of culture had frequent contact with one another and shared similar characteristics, but they didn't have much in common with tribes in other culture areas. For example, the Pima and Tohono O'odham tribes of the desert had similar customs, but their lifestyle was completely different from that of the Natchez, who lived on the Gulf Coast; the Apaches, who lived in the Southwest; the Lakota, on the plains; and the Tlingit and Makah, on the Northwest Coast. The lifestyle of each culture area reflected the geography of that area.

C

Many people do not know about this great diversity of cultures. When they think of an "American Indian," just one image comes to mind: a man on a horse, with feathers in his hair; behind him is his home, a *tipi* made of buffalo skin. This stereotype of the "typical" Native American comes to us from early Hollywood movies, which depicted mainly one group—the Plains Indians—during one brief period in history, the 18th and 19th centuries. (It was only after the arrival of the Europeans that Native Americans had the horse, brought to the Americas by Spanish farmers.) The Indians of the eastern plains had an agricultural society; they lived in farming communities and raised crops of corn, beans, squash, and tobacco. Because there were so few trees on the flatlands, their houses were made of earth. While the crops were growing, the people stayed in their villages. After the harvest, when they had brought in the crops, they moved west to hunt buffalo. During the months of the buffalo hunt, their lifestyle was similar to that of the nomadic tribes of the western plains. To these Plains Indians—both eastern and western—the buffalo was very important. It provided most of the necessities for everyday life in addition to meat: skin for tipis, bags, and clothing, bone for tools, knives, and snow shoes, and fur for blankets and beds. The buffalo hunt was also central to most artistic, social, and religious activities.

D

Hollywood moviemakers never considered most other Native American cultures in their films. For example, they did not explore life along the Northwest Coast (now British Columbia, Canada). For hundreds of years, the people there lived by hunting and fishing. They didn't need to lead a nomadic life because their environment was so rich in resources. The forests were full of animal life—deer, elk, and bear, as well as smaller animals. In the forests, the inhabitants could also find berries to eat and wood for boats, houses, and furniture. The oceans and rivers provided salmon, halibut, and many other fish. In the Makah language, in fact, the word for *fish* is the word for *food*. But of all the ocean's creatures, the gray whale was the most important. It provided meat, oil, and huge bones for tools and weapons. The dangerous whale hunt shaped Northwest Coast society as the buffalo hunt shaped Plains society. Geography influenced other areas of life, too. Hunting was seasonal work, best in the summer. Because the people were able to preserve food—by smoking fish, for example—they didn't have a lack of food in the winter, so they had time for creative activities such as storytelling or woodworking.

Totem pole in Sitka National Historical Park, Alaska

E　　When Europeans arrived on the North American continent several hundred years ago, the Native Americans' old way of life began to change. The appearance of Europeans led to disaster for the Indians. They lost their land, their sense of identity, and their lives to the newcomers. As the whites moved west, they took over more and more of the land for themselves and destroyed much of what they took. In European culture, people thought it was important to have as much wealth and own as much private land as possible. This idea was in contrast to Native Americans' great respect for nature and their belief that air, sun, water, and land were common to all people, so nobody could "own" them. When whites hunted the buffalo almost to extinction, when the government moved whole Indian nations to reservations on strange new land or sent Indian children away to school and didn't let them speak their native language, the Native Americans lost their sense of identity. Thousands and thousands also lost their lives—in widespread wars and in epidemics of disease such as smallpox, measles, and tuberculosis, which were nonexistent in North America before the Europeans came.

F　　Today there are about 2 million North American Indians—members of over 500 tribes. Many live in urban areas, but approximately 35% live on reservations. After a long history of conflict, broken promises, and disastrous decisions by the government, many of these people live in terrible conditions. Native Americans have the shortest lives, the highest death rate of babies, and the highest dropout rate of high school students of any U.S. ethnic group. The rates of heart disease, alcoholism, and poverty are way above the national average. The poorest county in the United States, for example, is the one that includes the Pine Ridge Reservation of the Oglala Sioux, in South Dakota; 63% of the people there live below the poverty line.

G　　Nevertheless, in recent years, many Native Americans have experienced a newfound pride in their rich cultural roots. Young people who don't know much about their ancestors' way of life are taking a new interest in learning the traditions. In some cases, where a tribe's language has been almost lost as the people learned English, the younger tribe members are studying the language from the last elderly person who remembers it. Many urban Indians try to return to "the res" whenever possible to spend time with their families and to keep in touch with their traditions.

H　　In both the United States and Canada, native peoples are having "wars" once again—this time in court, where they have succeeded in several legal battles. They are fighting to win back their land, water rights, fishing and hunting rights, and, perhaps most important, the right to self-government. In the United States, in 1971, Congress agreed to give $962 million and 40 million acres to the 60,000 native peoples of Alaska. In 1988 Congress finally kept an 1854 agreement and gave $66 million and 300 acres of valuable land to the Puyallup Indians of Tacoma, Washington. A major victory has occurred in Canada, where the government in Ottawa has turned *one-fifth* of Canada's territory over to 17,500 Inuit ("Eskimos").

A startling change is taking place on many U.S. reservations after a 1988 law and a series of court decisions. Tribes can now be largely self-governing, and many have decided to open gambling casinos. The White Mountain Apaches of Arizona have opened a ski resort and other businesses in addition to their casino, and these provide more than 1,000 jobs for tribal members, so they can remain on the reservation instead of moving to a city to find work. The 300 members of the Mashantucket Pequots of Connecticut take in almost $1 *billion* a year from their gambling casino. This gives them housing, health care, education, and political power. Some people say that the "hunting ground" of today is the gambling casino!

After You Read

Getting the Main Ideas

exercise **1** Write T on the lines before the statements that are true, according to the reading. Write F on the lines before the statements that are false. Write I before the statements that are impossible to know from the reading.

1. _____ The first people to live in North America came from Europe.

2. _____ Indian stories about the first Americans are different from the theories of scientists.

3. _____ The geography of the area where each group lived influenced the culture of that group.

4. _____ The people from different culture areas didn't have much in common with each other, and this led to conflict and war.

5. _____ The arrival of Europeans changed the lives of the people in North America.

6. _____ Today, most Native Americans are rich because of the gambling casinos on their land.

Guessing Meaning from Context

> The following exercises present a summary of ways in which the context of a reading can give clues to the meanings of new vocabulary items.
>
> There can be a definition of the item in the text—usually after the verb *be*—between commas, dashes (—), or parentheses ( ); or after connecting expressions such as *in other words, that is (i.e.),* and so on.

On the lines, write the words and expressions from the reading selection "North America: The Land and the People" that fit these definitions. The letters in parentheses refer to the paragraphs of the reading where the items appear. The first one is done as an example.

1. the first people to live in North America (A): American Indians
   (Native Americans)

2. people who are always on the move (A): _____

3. the area that is now Canada, the United States, and Mexico (B): _____
   _____

4. groups of Indians (B): _____

> Sometimes synonyms (words with similar meanings) or explanations of new vocabulary items give further information.

Circle the words that explain the missing items. Then fill in each blank with a word from the appropriate paragraph of the reading (shown in parentheses). The first one is done as an example.

1. The ⟨earliest people⟩ to live in North America were the
   ancestors _____ of Indian groups today. (A)

2. Indians who killed animals for food were _____. (A)

3. During times of _____ , the Indians were always on the move. (A)

4. The Indians who lived in farming communities had an
   _____ society. (C)

5. Because there were so few trees on the flatlands, the tribes of the eastern
   _____ made their houses out of earth instead of wood. (C)

6. After they had brought in the crops at _____ time, the Indians rode west to hunt buffalo. (C)

7. The Plains Indians hunted _____ for the necessities of life: meat, skin for houses and clothing, etc. (C)

8. Geography influenced the lives of the people who lived in each area: The _____ of the Northwest Coast lived by hunting and fishing. (D)

9. Many modern Indians are having "wars" once again; they are fighting legal _____ in _____ . (H)

There can be words in a text that express the opposite of a new vocabulary item—usually in a negative clause or after words that show contrast (e.g., *but, yet, however, on the other hand, by contrast, although*).

 On the lines, write words or expressions from the appropriate paragraphs of the reading (in parentheses) that express the opposites of these words. The first one is done as an example.

1. people who live in one place (A): nomads _____

2. share (characteristics, interests, etc.) (B): _____

_____

3. widespread (E): _____

4. young (G): _____

Examples can offer clues to meaning—sometimes after connecting words (*for example, for instance, such as,* etc.) or with certain punctuation (commas, dashes, parentheses, a colon).

exercise 5 Write examples from the appropriate paragraphs of the reading (in parentheses) for these categories as in the example.

1. names of geographical places (A): Asia; Bering Strait _____

_____

2. names of geographical places (B): _____

_____

3. fish (D): _____

4. forest animals (D): _____

5. diseases (E): _____

exercise 6

On each line, write the category that the items are examples of. The letter in parentheses refers to the paragraph where the category appears. The first one is done as an example.

1. Pima, Apaches, Natchez (B): _Indian tribes_
2. oceans, rivers, forests (D): _____
3. summer (D): _____
4. corn, squash (C): _____
5. meat, clothing (C): _____

> Some words have two or more very different meanings.

exercise 7

On each line, write a word from the reading that fits both definitions as in the example.

1. the world in which we live; the ground where crops grow: _earth_
2. part of a plant; original culture: _____
3. a light color; a person with light skin: _____
4. short fights in a war; disagreements: _____
5. correct; a legal advantage that people can claim: _____

> If you understand the meaning of a word, it's usually easy to understand a different part of speech of that same word.

exercise 8

For each word, write a related word as in the example.

1. nomad (noun): _nomadic_ (A) (adjective)
2. hunt (noun, verb): _____ (A) (noun)
3. farming (noun, adjective): _____ (C) (noun)
4. art (noun): _____ (C) (adjective)
5. season (noun): _____ (D) (adjective)
6. social (adjective): _____ (D) (noun)
7. culture (noun): _____ (G) (adjective)
8. tribe (noun): _____ (I) (adjective)

exercise 9 Reread the selection "North American Indians—Then and Now" carefully. Try to guess the meanings of new words from the context. Use your dictionary only when absolutely necessary. Check your answers to the Getting the Main Ideas exercise. Correct your errors if necessary.

Understanding Reading Structure

exercise 10 The following outline shows one possible organization of the information in the reading selection. Notice that the more general topics are on the left, and the more specific topics are indented to the right. Some topics have been left blank. Go back to the reading selection, find these topics, and add them to the lines.

NORTH AMERICAN INDIANS—THEN AND NOW

I. The First People in North America

II. Culture Areas

III. Native Americans in the Past

    A. Plains Indians

        1. stereotype

        2. agriculture

        3. _____

    B. _____

        1. forests

        2. ocean and rivers

            a. _____

            b. gray whale

IV. The Effect of Europeans on Native Americans

    A. loss of land

    B. _____

    C. _____

V. Native Americans Today

    A. terrible conditions

        1. health problems

            a. short lives

            b. _____

            c. _____

            d. _____

2. social problems

    a. _____

    b. _____

B. a return to cultural roots

C. legal battles

1. land

2. _____

3. fishing and hunting rights

4. _____

D. gambling casinos on reservations

1. _____

2. Mashantucket Pequots

Discussing the Reading

activity

In small groups, talk about your answers to these questions.

1. Do you know any Native Americans? If so, tell about them. Have you ever visited an Indian reservation? If so, tell about your experience.
2. What movies have you seen that depict Native Americans? Which tribes were depicted in these movies? Were the people stereotyped, or was the depiction realistic?
3. Who were the first inhabitants of your country? Tell something about their history and culture.

Foxwoods Casino, Mashantucket, Pequot Indian Reservation, Connecticut

Living with Gambling

People who live in the small town near the Mashantucket Pequot reservation in Connecticut are not happy about the success of the gambling casino on the reservation. They say that the thousands and thousands of people who come to gamble are ruining the quiet atmosphere of the town. Also, the townspeople are worried that the crowds of people and cars are destroying the environment. The Mashantucket Pequots believe that the townspeople want them to remain poor, as they were before the casino was built. What do you think?

PART two
Regional Customs

Before You Read

Skimming for Main Ideas

exercise

Read each paragraph quickly, without using a dictionary. After each, circle the number of the sentence that best expresses the main idea.

Regional Customs

A   **A**lthough the modern lifestyles of people in all areas of the United States and Canada are relatively similar, certain customs exist in only one region or another. By and large, these regional customs, which are popular forms of entertainment, have to do with the geography as well as the history of each region. Perhaps they also give the natives, along with sightseers from other areas, a sense of nostalgia for the past.

1. *The modern inhabitants of some areas of North America have held on to the regional customs of their ancestors.*
2. *Sightseers may travel to areas other than their own to enjoy old regional customs.*
3. *Geography has influenced modern people as well as the American Indians.*
4. *It is a good idea to remember the customs of the past.*

B   In late winter or early spring, when the sap begins to run in the maple trees of New England (the northeastern region of the United States), a favorite activity among country folk is a maple sugaring-off party. Sap is the clear liquid inside maple trees—and the source of the sweet, golden syrup that North Americans pour over their pancakes at breakfast time. At a sugaring off, the hosts and hostesses heat up the syrup in big pots on the stove. Meanwhile, guests help by setting a long table with spoons, forks, knives, and coffee cups, and by filling huge bowls with fresh, clean snow. They also make sure that there are enough cake doughnuts and sour pickles. When the maple syrup is ready, someone pours it into small bowls at each table setting, and all the guests take seats in front of the bowls of snow. Then they pour spoonfuls of hot maple syrup onto the snow, where it hardens and cools immediately; they take the syrup from the snow, put it onto their doughnuts, and eat the combination. Every bite of doughnut requires a new spoonful of syrup, and it goes without saying

that the doughnut tastes very, very sweet. After just one, many participants are ready to quit. But at that moment, the hosts or hostesses offer them *sour pickles!* Soon they feel like eating more doughnuts with maple syrup.

1. *Natives of the New England region of the United States like to eat very, very sweet things.*
2. *The sour taste of pickles provides a contrast to the sweet taste of doughnuts with maple syrup.*
3. *A seasonal custom of the northeastern region of the United States is a maple sugaring-off party.*
4. *When hot, sweet syrup hits cold snow, it gets hard.*

c A unique seasonal activity on the southern California coast is the grunion hunt. Grunion are small fish that come up onto the beach to lay their eggs on certain summer nights. Newspapers usually predict the time of their arrival, and the adventure of a grunion hunt begins several hours in advance. People sit impatiently around a fire on the beach and tell stories or barbecue hot dogs and roast marshmallows. Then, all of a sudden, the participants who are waiting down near the ocean shout, "Grunion!" On a good night, the beach is soon so crowded with the fish that it turns silver. Enthusiastically, all the people head toward the water to try to catch the grunion with their hands, the only legal method of doing so (according to California law). Because the fish are very slippery to the touch, however, people soon discover that following this rule isn't easy. After a successful grunion hunt, participants cook their "harvest" in butter and have a wonderful meal.

1. *Because grunion are hard to catch with the hands, people don't like the California law for hunting them.*
2. *If people read newspapers, they will probably be able to participate in grunion hunts.*
3. *A meal of grunion with butter tastes especially good on the beach at night.*
4. *The grunion hunt is an exciting Southern California custom that takes place in the summer.*

D   Every so often, when the weather begins to turn cool in the fall, inhabitants of the city who grew up in the country feel nostalgic for a special autumn custom: a hayride. After the fall harvest, farmers in the American Midwest often provide a wagon full of hay (the dry grass that farm animals eat) and horses to pull the wagon. Participants in the hayride dress warmly and sit in the hay as the horses pull the wagon on country roads and through forests. All along the way and then around the fire later on, people sing folk songs. But the best part of hayrides, according to the people who have had a lot of experience with them, is the ride home in the clear night air. As the wagon heads back, people keep warm by sitting very close to someone special.

1. *People in the Midwest roast hot dogs and marshmallows around fires just like people at beach parties in the West.*
2. *The hayride is a custom that reflects the seasons of the midwestern region of the United States.*
3. *The hayride is mainly for city people who want to enjoy a country custom.*
4. *Because it gets cool in the fall in the Midwest, people wear clothes different from those that people who live in the South wear.*

After You Read

Understanding Idioms

For each item, find an idiom or expression in the reading selection that has a similar meaning and write it on the line.

PARAGRAPH A

1. or a different one: *or another* _____

2. generally: _____

3. are related to: _____

4. and also: (two possibilities) _____

PARAGRAPH B

1. putting plates, bowls, spoons, etc. on a table: _____

2. sit down: _____

3. it is obvious (clear): _____

4. want to: _____

PARAGRAPH C

1. produce eggs: _____

2. before in time: _____

3. unexpectedly; suddenly: _____

4. go toward: _____

5. when you feel (something): _____

PARAGRAPH D

1. become colder: _____

2. some time after that: _____

3. return: _____

Making Inferences

exercise 2 Read each section carefully. On the short lines, put a check mark by the statements that you can infer (figure out) from other information. Do not check the other statements, even if you think they are true. On the line after each statement that you check, write the phrases in the section from which you inferred the information.

1. In late winter or early spring, when the sap begins to run in the maple trees of New England (the northeastern region of the United States), a favorite activity among country folk is a maple sugaring-off party. Sap is the clear liquid inside maple trees—and the source of the sweet, golden syrup that North Americans pour over their pancakes at breakfast time.

   a. _√_ A sugaring-off party is a seasonal activity in the northern part of the United States. _in late winter or early spring/_ _the northeastern region of the United States_

   b. ____ There is sap inside all kinds of trees. _____ _____

   c. ____ Syrup tastes good. _____ _____

2. At a sugaring-off party, the participants pour spoonfuls of hot maple syrup onto snow, where it hardens and cools immediately; they take the syrup from the snow, put it onto their doughnuts, and eat the combination. Every bite of doughnut requires a new spoonful of syrup, and it goes without saying that the doughnut tastes very, very sweet. After just one, many participants are ready to quit. But at that moment, the hosts or hostesses offer them *sour pickles!* Soon they feel like eating more doughnuts with maple syrup.

   a. ____ Hot syrup is in liquid form; it becomes hard when it gets cold. _____

   b. ____ Doughnuts and maple syrup are sweet. _____ _____

   c. ____ Participants will feel very sick after a sugaring-off party. _____ _____

   d. ____ If you eat something sour, you may feel like eating something sweet next. _____ _____

3. A unique seasonal activity on the southern California coast is the grunion hunt. Grunion are small fish that come up onto the beach to lay their eggs on certain summer nights. Newspapers usually predict the time of their arrival, and the adventure of a grunion hunt begins several hours in advance. People sit impatiently around a fire on the beach and tell stories or barbecue hot dogs and roast marshmallows. Then, all of a sudden, the participants who are waiting down near the ocean shout, "Grunion!"

a. _____ People hunt grunion only in Southern California in the

summer. _____

_____

b. _____ The newspaper always tells the exact time that the grunion will

come up onto the beach. _____

_____

c. _____ Grunion taste especially good with marshmallows. _____

_____

d. _____ In a grunion hunt, some people wait down near the water for

the first fish to arrive on the beach. _____

_____

4. On a good night, the beach is soon so crowded with the fish that it turns silver. Enthusiastically, all the people head toward the water to try to catch the grunion with their hands, the only legal method of doing so (according to California law). Because the fish are very slippery to the touch, however, they soon discover that following this rule isn't easy. After a successful grunion hunt, participants cook their "harvest" in butter and have a wonderful meal.

a. _____ The color of grunion is silver. _____

_____

b. _____ It is against the law to catch grunion with nets. _____

_____

c. _____ It is difficult to hold onto grunion. _____

_____

d. _____ You can't buy grunion in the supermarket. _____

_____

5. Every so often, when the weather begins to turn cool in the fall, inhabitants of the city who grew up in the country feel nostalgic for a special autumn custom: a hayride. After the fall harvest, farmers in the American Midwest often provide a wagon full of hay (the dry grass that farm animals eat) and horses to pull the wagon. Participants in the hayride dress warmly and sit in the hay as the horses pull the wagon on country roads and through forests. All along the way and then around the fire later on, people sing folk songs. But the best part of hayrides, according to the people who have had a lot of experience with them, is the ride home in the clear night air. As the wagon heads back, people keep warm by sitting very close to someone special.

a. _____ Hayrides are an activity that happened only in the past. _____

_____

_____

b. _____ It's so comfortable to sit in hay that some participants fall

asleep. _____

_____

c. _____ People sing folk songs only in the American Midwest. _____

_____

d. _____ A hayride can be a romantic activity. _____

_____

Viewpoint

exercise **3**

In your opinion, does the author of the reading selection like the entertainment of

regional customs? _____ Why or why not? _____

_____

Discussing the Reading

activity **1**

In small groups, talk about your answers to these questions.

1. Which of the regional customs in the reading seems the most fun to you? Why?
2. Do you know about any other regional customs or activities of the United States or Canada? Describe them.
3. Describe some regional customs or activities from your country.
4. In your opinion, what is the purpose of regional customs? Why do people hold on to them?

Going Beyond the Text

activity 2

Bring to class city and regional magazines and newspapers with lists of activities. In small groups, discuss new vocabulary. Summarize the most interesting information. Which places would you like to visit? Which events would you like to attend? When? Why?

PART three
Building Vocabulary and Study Skills

Categories

exercise

On the lines, write the categories for the numbered groups of words. Then compare your answers with those of another student.

1. <u>fruits and vegetables</u>: berries, beans, squash, corn

2. _____: deer, elk, bear, buffalo

3. _____: desert, plains, coast, ocean

4. _____: community, society, tribe

5. _____: hunting, sightseeing, hayrides, barbecues

6. _____: doughnuts, syrup, sugar, marshmallows

7. _____: summer, winter, spring, autumn

8. _____: inhabitant, participant, native, guest

9. _____: bowl, fork, cup, plate

10. _____: geography, history, art, agriculture

Prefixes and Suffixes

Here is a summary of word prefixes and suffixes and their approximate meanings.

prefixes	meanings	
com-/con-	together; with	
im-/in-/un-/dis-	not	
inter-	between; among	
mis-	wrong	
pre-	before; first	
re-	again; back	

suffixes	parts of speech	meanings
-al	adjective	having the quality of
-ar	adjective	of or relating to; resembling
-(i)an	noun	belonging to; characteristic of
-ed	adjective	passive participle
-en	verb	to make; to become
-ence/-ance	noun	state; quality
-ent/-ant	adjective	having the quality of
-er	adjective	comparative form
-er/-or/-ist	noun	a person who
-ess	noun	a person (female)
-est	adjective	superlative form
-ful	adjective	full of
-ible/-able	adjective	having the quality of; able to be
-ic	adjective	having the quality of; affected by
-ing	noun, adjective	active participle; gerund
-ion	noun	state; condition
-ive	adjective	having the quality of; relating to
-ly	adverb	manner (how)
-ment/-ness/-ship	noun	state; condition; quality
-(i)ous	adjective	full of
-ure	noun	state; result
-y	adjective	having the quality of; full of

In the parentheses after each word, here and on the next page, write the part of speech (n. = noun; v. = verb; adj. = adj.; adv. = adverb). Then complete the sentences that follow with the appropriate words.

1. advantage (n.), advantageous (adj.), disadvantage (n.)

Nature provided certain _advantage_ s to some American Indian tribes. An area of rich forests was _advantageous_ to life. Groups that lived in cold areas were at a _disadvantage_ .

2. member (   ), membership (   ), remember (   )

_____s of modern Indian tribes often

_____ the language and customs of their ancestors.

_____ in their group is important to them.

3. illegally (   ), legal (   ), legality (   )

Nowadays Indians sometimes fight in court for their

_____ rights. They claim that the Europeans took away

their ancestors' lands _____. The courts decide on the

_____ of their claims.

4. farm (   ), farm (   ), farming (   ), farmer (   )

Some Indians stayed in one place to _____ the land.

These_____ s raised different kinds of crops on

their_____ s. _____ was their way of life.

5. ancestor (   ), ancestry (   ), ancestral (   )

Some Indians try to keep to the customs of their_____ s.

They know all about their_____ and consider their

_____ lands special.

6. similar (   ), dissimilar (   ), similarity (   ), similarly (   )

Groups that lived in different areas were _____ in their

cultures, but tribes that lived in the same cultural area had

_____ customs and lifestyles. Because of the

_____ of geography, they lived _____.

7. succeed (   ), success (   ), successfully (   ), unsuccessful (   )

   It is difficult to hold on to a grunion_____ . If grunion

   hunters are_____ in their attempts, they try again. When

   they_____ , they put the fish in buckets. Then they have a

   barbecue to celebrate their_____ .

8. hard (   ), harden (   ), harder (   ), hardest (   )

   Maple syrup_____ s when it gets cool. It becomes even

   _____ when it touches cold snow. It is

   _____ to eat many of the very sweet doughnuts with syrup

   at a sugaring-off party. The _____ thing of all, however, is

   to get up from the table after the party.

9. serve (   ), reserve (   ), reserved (   ), reservation (   )

   After the hayride, the group is going to go to a restaurant where they

   _____ hot food. If the restaurant

   takes_____ s, they'll _____ their tables in

   advance. The group will sit together at the _____ tables.

Word Roots

> Here are some word roots (also called "stems") that can combine with
> prefixes and suffixes to make words.
>
> psych   sent   ist   fine   nat   dict

exercise 1

The words in each horizontal row are missing the same word root. Choose from
those above, make necessary spelling changes, and complete the words. Use your
dictionary, if necessary.

NOUN	VERB	ADJECTIVE	ADVERB
de_fin_ition	de_fine_	de_fin_ite	de_fin_itely
pre____ation	pre____	pre____able	pre____ly
____ure	____uralize	____ural	____urally
ex____ence	ex____	ex____ent	
____ology		____ological	____ologically
pre____ion	pre____	pre____able	pre____ably

Write sentences that show the meanings of some of the words in the chart above. Leave blanks for the words. Then exchange papers with a classmate. Write the appropriate words in the blanks. Exchange papers, make corrections, and discuss the vocabulary.

Learning New Vocabulary

While you are reading, you need to understand vocabulary, but you do not need to learn it actively. Sometimes, however, you may want to remember new vocabulary for use in conversation and writing. These steps may prove useful:

1. Divide a sheet of paper into three columns. Write new words or expressions in the left-hand column. Write the pronunciation under each word or expression. In the middle column, write the definitions. In the right-hand column, write sentences that illustrate the meanings of the items.
2. Look up and write related words, with their definitions and examples, on the same piece of paper.
3. Pronounce the words to yourself. Try to fix their spelling in your mind as you learn them. Repeat the examples to yourself and make up other examples.
4. Cover the words and examples and try to remember them when you read the definitions.
5. Review your list regularly.
6. If desired, put only items that begin with the same letter on each sheet of paper, or write items on separate index cards.

word	definition	example
nostalgia nos·tal′·jə	(N.) homesickness; longing for the past	A train whistle gives me a feeling of <u>nostalgia</u>.
nostalgic	(ADJ.) feeling homesick or longing for the past	The romantic couple had a <u>nostalgic</u> look in their eyes.
nostalgically	(ADV.)	
necessity ne·sess′·ə·ti	(N.) need; condition that makes something necessary	He was forced by economic <u>necessity</u> to steal.
necessitate ne·sess′·ə·tāt	(V.) make necessary	The cool weather <u>necessitated</u> wearing heavy coats.
necessarily	(ADV.)	

List vocabulary items from this book. Use your dictionary to find related words. Discuss the meanings of the prefixes, the suffixes, and the words themselves. Use the words in sentences. Then list and learn the words you have discussed as described above.

Repeat Exercise 1 above with words you have read or heard in other situations.

focus on testing

Comprehension Questions on Reading Tests

Standardized tests often give a reading passage followed by questions about it. You'll be able to answer some from memory, after one quick reading. You'll need to look back and scan for the answers to others. The items are usually in the same order that they appear in the selection, so look for the answer to 1 near the beginning. Some questions ask about information that the passage *states* (says directly). Others ask about information that the passage *implies*. These questions will be harder. Hint: It usually helps to look over the questions before reading.

PART four

Reading in the Real World

Scanning for Information

Literature

The following passage is from the first chapter of a book called *Lame Deer, Seeker of Visions* by John (Fire) Lame Deer and Richard Erdoes. In this passage, Lame Deer (a Native American of the Sioux nation) describes a ritual that he went through when he was sixteen.

First, read the questions (pages 159 to 160) that follow the passage. Then read the first half of the passage (pages 157 to 159) and answer the questions, circling the letter of the best answer for each item. Don't worry if you don't understand every word in the passage. Work as quickly as possible, as you would on a test.

Alone on the Hilltop

I was all alone on the hilltop. I sat there in the vision pit, a hole dug into the hill, my arms hugging my knees as I watched old man Chest, the medicine man who had brought me there, disappear far down in the valley. He was just a moving black dot among the pines, and soon he was gone altogether.

Now I was all by myself, left on the hilltop for four days and nights without food or water until he came back for me. You know, we Indians are not like some white folks—a man and a wife, two children, and one baby sitter who watches the TV set while the parents are out visiting somewhere.

Indian children are never alone. They are always surrounded by grandparents, uncles, cousins, relatives of all kinds, who fondle the kids, sing to them, tell them stories. If the parents go someplace, the kids go along.

But here I was, crouched in my vision pit, left alone by myself for the first time in my life. I was sixteen then, still had my boy's name and, let me tell you, I was scared. I was shivering and not only from the cold. The nearest human being was many miles away, and four days and nights is a long, long time. Of course, when it was all over, I would no longer be a boy, but a man. I would have had my vision. I would be given a man's name.

Sioux men are not afraid to endure hunger, thirst and loneliness, and I was only ninety-six hours away from being a man. The thought was comforting. Comforting, too, was the warmth of the star blanket which old man Chest had wrapped around me to cover my nakedness. My grandmother had made it especially for this, my first *hanblechia,* my first vision-seeking. It was a beautifully designed quilt, white with a large morning star made of many pieces of brightly colored cloth. That star was so big it covered most of the blanket. If Wakan Tanka, the Great Spirit, would give me the vision and the power, I would become a medicine man and perform many ceremonies wrapped in that quilt. I am an old man now and many times a grandfather, but I still have that star blanket my grandmother made for me. I treasure it; someday I shall be buried in it.

The medicine man had also left a peace pipe with me, together with a bag of *kinnickinnick*—our kind of tobacco made of red willow bark. This pipe was even more of a friend to me than my star blanket. To us the pipe is like an open Bible. White people need a church house, a preacher and a pipe organ to get into a praying mood. There are so many things to distract you: who else is in the church, whether the other people notice that you have come, the pictures on the wall, the sermon, how much money you should give and did you bring it with you. We think you can't have a vision that way.

For us Indians there is just the pipe, the earth we sit on and the open sky. The spirit is everywhere. Sometimes it shows itself through an animal, a bird or some trees and hills. Sometimes it speaks from the Badlands, a stone, or even from the water. That smoke from the peace pipe, it goes straight up to the spirit world. But this is a two-way thing. Power flows down to us through that smoke, through the pipe stem. You feel that power as you hold your pipe; it moves from the pipe right into your body. It makes your hair stand up. That pipe is not just a thing; it is alive. Smoking this pipe would make me feel good and help me to get rid of my fears.

As I ran my fingers along its bowl of smooth red pipestone, red like the blood of my people, I no longer felt scared. That pipe had belonged to my father and to his father before him. It would someday pass to my son and, through him, to my grandchildren. As long as we had the pipe there would be a Sioux nation. As I fingered the pipe, touched it, felt its smoothness that came from long use, I sensed that my forefathers who had once smoked this pipe were with me on the hill, right in the vision pit. I was no longer alone.

Besides the pipe the medicine man had also given me a gourd. In it were forty small squares of flesh which my grandmother had cut from her arm with a razor blade. I had seen her do it. Blood had been streaming down from her shoulder to her elbow as she carefully put down each piece of skin on a handkerchief, anxious not to lose a single one. It would have made those anthropologists mad. Imagine, performing such an ancient ceremony with a razor blade instead of a flint knife! To me it did not matter. Someone dear to me had undergone pain, given me something of herself, part of her body, to help me pray and make me stronghearted. How could I be afraid with so many people—living and dead—helping me?

One thing still worried me. I wanted to become a medicine man, a *yuwipi,* a healer carrying on the ancient ways of the Sioux nation. But you cannot learn to be a medicine man like a white man going to medical school. An old holy man can teach you about herbs and the right ways to perform a ceremony where everything must be in its proper place, where every move, every word has its own, special meaning. These things you can learn—like spelling, like training a horse. But by themselves these things mean nothing. Without the vision and the power this learning will do no good. It would not make me a medicine man.

80 What if I failed, if I had no vision? Or if I dreamed of the Thunder
Beings, or lightning struck the hill? That would make me at once into a
heyoka, a contrarywise, an upside-down man, a clown. "You'll know it, if
you get the power," my Uncle Chest had told me. "If you are not given it,
you won't lie about it, you won't pretend. That would kill you, or kill
85 somebody close to you, somebody you love."

Night was coming on. I was still lightheaded and dizzy from my first
sweat bath in which I had purified myself before going up the hill. I had
never been in a sweat lodge before. I had sat in the little beehive-shaped
hut made of bent willow branches and covered with blankets to keep the
90 heat in. Old Chest and three other medicine men had been in the lodge
with me. I had my back against the wall, edging as far away as I could
from the red-hot stones glowing in the center. As Chest poured water over
the rocks, hissing white steam enveloped me and filled my lungs. I
thought the heat would kill me, burn the eyelids off my face! But right in
95 the middle of all this swirling steam I heard Chest singing. So it couldn't
be all that bad. I did not cry out "All my relatives!"—which would have
made him open the flap of the sweat lodge to let in some cool air—and I
was proud of this. I heard him praying for me: "Oh, holy rocks, we receive
your white breath, the steam. It is the breath of life. Let this young boy
100 inhale it. Make him strong."

questions

1. The writer mentions white children to show that they
   a. come from small families
   b. have parents who go out visiting
   c. are different from Indian children, who are never alone
   d. have a babysitter and enjoy watching TV

2. You can infer that in Sioux society, people's names
   a. are more important than in white society
   b. change when a person becomes an adult
   c. all come from names of animals
   d. are given by their parents

3. The writer says about the peace pipe, ". . . this is a two-way thing." He
   means that
   a. smoke goes up and down
   b. you can use a peace pipe in two ways
   c. there are two kinds of smoke and two kinds of pipes
   d. smoke goes up to the spirit world, and power comes down

4. To become a Sioux medicine man, it's necessary to have three things. One
   is *learning;* the other two are
   a. ancient ways and medical school
   b. vision and power
   c. herbs and a ceremony
   d. everything in its proper place and words with special meaning

159

5. If a young Sioux man is in a sweat bath, feels too uncomfortably hot, and wants some cool air, he should
   a. say loudly, "All my relatives!"
   b. pour water over the rocks
   c. pray
   d. open the door

6. Lame Deer had his first sweat bath in order to
   a. become lightheaded and dizzy
   b. get clean
   c. sing and pray with his uncle
   d. become purified and strong

Synthesizing Information

 exercise **2**   Now read the second half of the chapter from Lame Deer's book. It's possible to learn a lot about Sioux society and beliefs from this. Some of this information is stated directly, and some is implied.

The sweat bath had prepared me for my vision-seeking. Even now, an hour later, my skin still tingled. But it seemed to have made my brains empty. Maybe that was good, plenty of room for new insights.

Darkness had fallen upon the hill. I knew that *hanhepiwi* had risen, the
5 night sun, which is what we call the moon. Huddled in my narrow cave, I did not see it. Blackness was wrapped around me like a velvet cloth. It seemed to cut me off from the outside world, even from my own body. It made me listen to the voices within me. I thought of my forefathers who had crouched on this hill before me, because the medicine men in my
10 family had chosen this spot for a place of meditation and vision-seeking ever since the day they had crossed the Missouri to hunt for buffalo in the White River country some two hundred years ago. I thought that I could sense their presence right through the earth I was leaning against. I could feel them entering my body, feel them stirring in my mind and heart.

15 Sounds came to me through the darkness: the cries of the wind, the whisper of the trees, the voices of nature, animal sounds, the hooting of an owl. Suddenly I felt an overwhelming presence. Down there with me in my cramped hole was a big bird. The pit was only as wide as myself, and I was a skinny boy, but that huge bird was flying around me as if he had
20 the whole sky to himself. I could hear his cries, sometimes near and sometimes far, far away. I felt feathers or a wing touching my back and head. This feeling was so overwhelming that it was just too much for me. I trembled and my bones turned to ice. I grasped the rattle with the forty pieces of my grandmother's flesh. It also had many little stones in it, tiny
25 fossils picked up from an ant heap. Ants collect them. Nobody knows why.

These little stones are supposed to have a power in them. I shook the rattle and it made a soothing sound, like rain falling on rock. It was talking to me, but it did not calm my fears. I took the sacred pipe in my other hand and began to sing and pray: "Tunkashila, grandfather spirit, help me." But this did not help. I don't know what got into me, but I was no longer myself. I started to cry. Crying, even my voice was different. I sounded like an older man, I couldn't even recognize this strange voice. I used long-ago words in my prayer, words no longer used nowadays. I tried to wipe away my tears, but they wouldn't stop. In the end I just pulled that quilt over me, rolled myself up in it. Still I felt the bird wings touching me.

Slowly I perceived that a voice was trying to tell me something. It was a bird cry, but I tell you, I began to understand some of it. That happens sometimes. I know a lady who had a butterfly sitting on her shoulder. That butterfly told her things. This made her become a great medicine woman.

I heard a human voice too, strange and high-pitched, a voice which could not come from an ordinary, living being. All at once I was way up there with the birds. The hill with the vision pit was way above everything. I could look down even on the stars, and the moon was close to my left side. It seemed as though the earth and the stars were moving below me. A voice said, "You are sacrificing yourself here to be a medicine man. In time you will be one. You will teach other medicine men. We are the fowl people, the winged ones, the eagles and the owls. We are a nation and you shall be our brother. You will never kill or harm any one of us. You are going to understand us whenever you come to seek a vision here on this hill. You will learn about herbs and roots, and you will heal people. You will ask them for nothing in return. A man's life is short. Make yours a worthy one."

I felt that these voices were good, and slowly my fear left me. I had lost all sense of time. I did not know whether it was day or night. I was asleep, yet wide awake. Then I saw a shape before me. It rose from the darkness and the swirling fog which penetrated my earth hole. I saw that this was my great-grandfather, Tahca Ushte, Lame Deer, old man chief of the Minneconjou. I could see the blood dripping from my great-grandfather's chest where a white soldier had shot him. I understood that my great-grandfather wished me to take his name. This made me glad beyond words.

We Sioux believe that there is something within us that controls us, something like a second person almost. We call it *nagi,* what other people might call soul, spirit or essence. One can't see it, feel it or taste it, but that time on the hill—and only that once—I knew it was there inside of me. Then I felt the power surge through me like a flood. I cannot describe it, but it filled all of me. Now I knew for sure that I would become a *wicasa wakan,* a medicine man. Again I wept, this time with happiness.

I didn't know how long I had been up there on that hill—one minute or a lifetime. I felt a hand on my shoulder gently shaking me. It was old man Chest, who had come for me. He told me that I had been in the vision pit four days and four nights and that it was time to come down. He would give me something to eat and water to drink and then I was to tell him everything that had happened to me during my *hanblechia.* He would interpret my visions for me. He told me that the vision pit had changed me in a way that I would not be able to understand at that time. He told me also that I was no longer a boy, that I was a man now. I was Lame Deer.

75

80

activity

Work in groups of five students. Each student will choose *one* topic from the items below. Look through *both* parts of the reading passage from Lame Deer's book and mark all information about your topic. Write notes summarizing what you have learned about your topic. Then share this information with the other members of your group.

1. Names in Sioux society and how people receive them:

_____

_____

_____

2. Vocabulary words in the Sioux language and their meaning:

_____

_____

_____

3. Items that a young man has with him in the vision pit and their meaning:

_____

_____

_____

4. Reasons for the ritual that Lame Deer describes:

_____

_____

5. The voice and vision that Lame Deer experienced in the pit:

_____

_____

CHAPTER eight

Tastes and Preferences

in this chapter

The first reading selection discusses art history and what we can learn about people from their art. The second selection describes things that people do in different societies to make themselves more attractive. The last selection is a newspaper article about the sense of smell and the many ways it can affect our everyday lives.

Before You Read

Getting Started

Look at the pictures on this page and pages 165 and 166 and discuss them.

1. What kinds of pictures are these? Where might you see them?
2. Describe each picture. If you can, talk about the people and the activities.
3. Compare the pictures. What are the similarities? What are the differences?
4. Which picture do you like the best? Why?

José Clemente Orozco, *Hispano América,* 1932-1934

Pablo Picasso, *Guernica,* 1937

Francisco Goya, *The Third of May, 1808,* 1814

Chiwara dancers with headdresses, Bambara people, Bamako area, Mali

Statue for the front of a canoe, Melanesia

Islamic bowl with decoration of arabesques and Kufic writing

Preparing to Read

As you read the selection on pages 166 to 169, think about the answer to this question: What can we learn from *art* history that we can't usually learn in a general history class?

Read the following selection quickly. Do not use a dictionary. Then do the exercises that follow the reading.

A

What Can We Learn from Art?

A study of art history might be a good way to learn more about a culture than is possible to learn in general history classes. Most typical history courses concentrate on politics, economics, and war. But *art*

history focuses on much more than this because art reflects not only the political values of a people, but also religious beliefs, emotions, and psychology. In addition, information about the daily activities of our ancestors—or of people very different from our own—can be provided by art. In short, art expresses the essential qualities of a time and a place, and a study of it clearly offers us a deeper understanding than can be found in most history books.

B   In history books, objective information about the political life of a country is presented; that is, facts about politics are given, but opinions are not expressed. Art, on the other hand, is subjective: It reflects emotions and opinions. The great Spanish painter Francisco Goya was perhaps the first truly "political" artist. In his well-known painting *The Third of May, 1808,* he depicted soldiers shooting a group of simple people. This depiction of faceless soldiers and their victims has become a symbol of the enormous power—and the misuse of this power—that a government can have over its people. Over a hundred years later, symbolic images were used in Pablo Picasso's *Guernica* to express the horror of war. Meanwhile, on another continent, the powerful paintings of Diego Rivera, José Clemente Orozco, and David Alfaro Siqueiros—as well as the works of Alfredo Ramos Martínez—depicted these Mexican artists' deep anger and sadness about social problems. In summary, a personal and emotional view of history can be presented through art.

C   In the same way, art can reflect a culture's religious beliefs. For hundreds of years in Europe, religious art was almost the *only* type of art that existed. Churches and other religious buildings were filled with paintings that depicted people and stories from the Bible, the Jewish and Christian holy book. Although most people couldn't read, they could still understand biblical stories in the pictures on church walls. By contrast, one of the main characteristics of art in the Middle East was (and still is) its *absence* of human and animal images. This reflects the Islamic belief (from the Koran, the book of Islam) that statues are unholy. By Islamic law, artists are not allowed to copy human or animal figures except on small items for daily use (for example, rugs and bowls). Thus, on palaces, mosques, and other buildings, Islamic artists have created unique decoration of great beauty with images of flowers and geometric forms (for example, circles, squares, and triangles). They have also shown great creativity and discipline in their use of Arabic writing as an art form.

D   Art also reflects the religious beliefs of traditional cultures in Africa and the Pacific Islands. In fact, religion is the *purpose* for this art and is, therefore, absolutely essential to it. However, unlike Christian art—which influences people to have religious feelings—the goal of traditional art in Africa and the Pacific is to influence spiritual powers—gods—to enter people's lives. Each tribe or village has special ceremonies with songs and dances to make sure that crops, animals, and tribal members are healthy and increase in number. The dancers in these ceremonies wear unique masks, headdresses, and costumes that they believe are necessary to influence the gods. These masks and headdresses are a very important part of the art.

E   In traditional tribal cultures, art objects—masks, headdresses, statues, etc.—are not created simply for beauty. They are also essential to both religion and daily life. It is impossible to separate art and religion from everyday activities: hunting, war, travel, farming, childbirth, and so on. In the Solomon Islands of Melanesia, for example, the artistic characteristics of common everyday objects are considered to be essential to the successful use of the items. A small figure on a hunter's or soldier's spear is believed to help the spear reach its target (that is, the hunted animal or the enemy in war); a small statue on the front of a boat is supposed to help the boat reach its destination. Another example of the function of traditional art is the use of headdresses in ceremonies of the Bambara people of Mali, in Africa. These headdresses are certainly decorative, but beauty is not the reason they are made. Their purpose is to help the crops grow: They were worn by the Bambara at planting time in dances to celebrate the birth of agriculture. Likewise, among the Bakongo people, there is a rich variety of functional wooden figures: Small statues of ancestors foretell the future, and images of a mother and child give protection to a woman as she gives birth to a baby. To sum up, art in many cultures is believed to serve essential, practical functions.

F   As we've seen, art depends on culture. Similarly, the way that people view art also depends on their cultural background. For most Europeans and Americans, art serves mainly as decoration. It is something on a museum wall or in a glass case. It makes homes more attractive. People look at it and admire it: "Oh, what a beautiful painting!" they might say. "I love the lines and colors." In addition to decoration, ideas are often expressed in this art. "This is a wonderful statue," an admirer might say. "It makes such a strong anti-war statement." However, in much of the rest of the world, art is not considered to be separate from everyday existence. It has a function. A person in a tribal society might look at a mask and say, "Oh, this is a good mask. It will keep my house safe." In brief, the way in which people enjoy art depends on their culture.

G   In conclusion, art is a reflection of various cultures. But art also reflects the *changes* in society that take place when different cultures influence one another. As people from tribal societies move to urban areas, their values and beliefs change, and their ancient art forms begin to lose their function. For example, when most Bambara people turned to Islam, they gave up their ceremonies to make the crops grow; their new religion taught them that their headdresses were unholy, so they stopped using them. Now Bambara artists make these headdresses only for foreign tourists; the headdresses have no function. On the other hand, urban artists learn a lot from traditional art: African masks and figures had a great effect on Pablo Picasso, and Paul Gauguin was deeply influenced by South Pacific culture; many American and Canadian artists study the simplicity of Japanese painting. The result is that as the world gets "smaller," the art of each culture becomes more international.

After You Read

Getting the Main Ideas

exercise 1

Write W on the lines before the statements about Western political art; CH before the statements about Christian art; IS before the statements about Islamic art; and T before the statements about traditional art.

1. _____ Some of these paintings show the horror of war or express anger about social problems.

2. _____ According to the tribespeople, these decorative headdresses help their crops grow.

3. _____ Artistic figures on spears or boats are believed to help them reach their destinations.

4. _____ People learned about the Bible from the stories in this art.

5. _____ Tribe members believe that wooden figures predict the future and protect women in childbirth.

6. _____ Because of religious law, artists decorate buildings with flowered and geometric designs but no human or animal forms.

7. _____ There are no images of living things (people or animals) except on small items for daily use.

8. _____ This art serves a practical, everyday function.

Guessing Meaning from Context

 **exercise 2**   Circle the words that give clues to the meanings of underlined words. Then answer the questions and write a definition for each word. When you finish, check your definitions in a dictionary.

1. In his well-known painting *The Third of May, 1808,* the Spanish artist Goya <u>depicted</u> soldiers shooting a group of simple people.

   What part of speech is <u>depicted</u> (noun, verb, adjective)? _____

   What kind of person might depict something? _____

   What does <u>depicted</u> mean? _____

2. In history books, <u>objective</u> information about the political life of a country is presented; that is, facts about politics are given, but opinions are not expressed. Art, on the other hand, is <u>subjective</u>; it reflects emotions and opinions.

   What part of speech is <u>objective</u>? _____

   Where might you find objective information? _____

   What is *not* part of objective information? _____

   What does <u>objective</u> mean? _____

   What part of speech is <u>subjective</u>? _____

   What does art reflect? _____

   What is the opposite of <u>subjective</u>? _____

3. Thus, on palaces, <u>mosques</u>, and other buildings, Islamic artists have created a unique decoration of great beauty with images of flowers and <u>geometric</u> forms (for example, circles, squares, and triangles).

   What part of speech is <u>mosques</u>? _____

   Mosques are a kind of _____

   What kind of artists decorate mosques? _____

   What does <u>mosques</u> mean? _____

   What part of speech is <u>geometric</u>? _____

   What are examples of geometric forms? _____

   What does <u>geometric</u> mean? _____

Sometimes you need to see a word in several different forms or contexts before you can guess the meaning.

examples: One of the main characteristics of art in the Middle East is its absence of human and animal <u>images</u>.

There is rich variety of functional wooden figures: Small statues of ancestors foretell the future, and <u>images</u> of a mother and child give protection to a woman as she gives birth.

(<u>Images</u> are pictures or figures that represent people or animals.)

exercise **3**

Circle the words that give clues to the meanings of the underlined words. Then write a definition on each line. When you finish, check your definitions in a dictionary.

1. This reflects the Islamic belief (from the Koran, the book of Islam) that statues are <u>unholy</u>.

Churches and other religious buildings were filled with paintings that depicted people and stories from the Bible, the Jewish and Christian <u>holy</u> book.

Their new religion taught them that their headdresses were <u>unholy</u>, so they stopped using them.

What does <u>holy</u> mean? _____

2. These headdresses are certainly <u>decorative</u>, but beauty is not the reason they are made.

For most Europeans and Americans, art serves mainly as <u>decoration</u>. It is something on a museum wall or in a glass case. It makes homes more attractive.

What does <u>decoration</u> mean? _____

exercise **4**

On the lines, write the words from the reading selection that fit these definitions. The letters in parentheses refer to the paragraphs where the words appear.

1. very important; necessary (A): _____

2. object produced by painting, etc. (B): _____

3. wrong or inappropriate use (B): _____

4. way of looking at (B): _____

5. not being present (C): _____

6. formal actions for making an important social or religious event (D):

_____

7. a long pole with a sharp point; a kind of weapon (E): _____

8. the object that someone is trying to shoot at or reach (two possibilities) (E):

_____

9. decorative head coverings (E): _____

10. made for practical use (E): _____

11. tell in advance; predict (E): _____

12. figures (E): _____

13. have a good opinion of; respect and like (F): _____

14. influence (noun) (G): _____

Reread the selection "What Can We Learn from Art?" carefully. Try to guess the meanings of new words from the context. Use your dictionary only when absolutely necessary. Check your answers to the Getting the Main Ideas exercise. Correct your errors if necessary.

Understanding Reading Structure

exercise **6**

As you have seen in Chapters Six and Seven, an outline shows the organization of a composition. On page 173 there is a possible outline for the reading selection "What Can We Learn from Art?" The *general* topics are filled in. But the reading also contains many subtopics that serve as supporting material. Write these *specific* topics in the correct places as in the example. (You'll need to look back at the reading to make sure where they belong.) Use the following list of subtopics.

1. decoration
2. ceremonies to influence spiritual powers
3. Christian images in churches
4. function
5. Picasso's *Guernica*
6. tribal people moving to urban areas
√ **7.** art serving a practical function
√ **8.** Goya's painting *The Third of May, 1808*
9. Islamic designs and Arabic writing
10. people from the Solomon Islands (figures on spears and boats to guide them)
11. the influence of traditional art on Picasso and Gauguin
12. Bambara people (headdresses to help crops grow)
13. Mexican social art
14. the effect of Japanese painting
15. Bakongo people (statues for prediction and protection)

WHAT CAN WE LEARN FROM ART?

I. Introduction: The Study of Art History

II. Art as an Expression of Political Views

A. *Goya's painting The Third of May, 1808* _____

B. _____

C. _____

III. Art as a Reflection of Religious Beliefs

A. _____

B. _____

IV. Traditional Art in Africa and the Pacific Islands

A. *art serving a practical function* _____

B. _____

    1. _____

    2. _____

    3. _____

V. The Way People View Art

A. _____

B. _____

VI. Art as a Reflection of Change in Society

A. _____

B. _____

C. _____

Here are some common connecting words that indicate a summary of material will follow.

in short	in summary
in brief	thus/therefore
the result is	to sum up
in conclusion	as we've seen

exercise 7 Copy the sentences from the reading selection that begin with these connecting words. Then circle the number of the sentence that best expresses the main idea of the entire reading.

1. In short, _____

_____

_____

2. In summary, _____

_____

3. Thus, _____

_____

_____

4. To sum up, _____

_____

5. As we've seen, _____

6. In brief, _____

_____

7. In conclusion, _____

_____

8. The result is _____

_____

Making Inferences

Complete each sentence by circling the letters of *all* the information that the reading selection states or implies.

1. _____ expressed political opinions with pictures of people.
  a. the Spanish painter Goya
  b. Picasso
  c. various Mexican artists
  d. Islamic painters

2. There are examples of religious images _____.
  a. on churches in Europe
  b. on Arab rugs and bowls
  c. in tribal ceremonies
  d. on headdresses

3. Traditional art might be used to _____ .
   a. cover walls of large buildings
   b. help hunters and soldiers
   c. improve agriculture
   d. protect women and children

exercise 9

Turn back to the Preparing to Read section on page 166 and answer the question.

Discussing the Reading

activity

In small groups, talk about your answers to these questions.

1. Tell about art in your culture. Describe typical works of art (paintings, statues, decorations on buildings, etc.). What is the function of art in your country? How do people view art?
2. Compare art in your culture with North American art. What are the similarities? The differences?
3. What kind of art do you prefer? Why?

PART two

Fashion: The Art of the Body

Before You Read
Skimming for Main Ideas

The main idea is not always clearly expressed in a paragraph. Instead, the details may *imply* the main idea, which sums up all the information in the paragraph.

example: For various reasons, clothing of some type has been worn by human beings since the beginning of time. The Eskimos wear animal fur to protect them against the cold winter weather. Nomadic desert people wear long, loose clothing for protection against the sun and wind of the Sahara. But is clothing really essential for protection? Perhaps not. Scientists point out the absence of clothing among certain Indians of southern Chile, where the temperature is usually 43° F (7° C) and often colder. Similarly, the tribal people of Australia, where the weather is like that of the Sahara Desert, wear almost no clothing.

exercise

Read each paragraph quickly, without using a dictionary. To help you figure out the main idea, circle the letters of *all* the correct answers to the questions that follow. The first three questions are done as examples.

Fashion: The Art of the Body

A

The enormous and fascinating variety of clothing may express a person's status or social position. Several hundred years ago in Europe, Japan, and China, there were many highly detailed sumptuary laws—i.e., strict regulations concerning how each social class could dress. In Europe, for example, only royal families could wear fur, purple silk, or gold cloth. In Japan, a farmer could breed silkworms, but he couldn't wear silk. In many societies, a lack of clothing indicated an absence of status. In ancient Egypt, for instance, children—who had no social status—wore no clothes until they were about twelve. These days, in most societies (especially in the West), rank or status is exhibited through regulation of dress only in the military, where the appearance or absence of certain metal buttons or stars signifies the dividing line between ranks. With this exception of the military, the divisions between different classes of society are becoming less clear. The clientele of a Paris café, for example, might include both working-class people and members of the highest society, but how can one tell the difference when everyone is wearing denim jeans?

1. What is the one main topic of the paragraph?
   a. the military
   b. sumptuary laws
   c. uniforms
   d. status

2. What details about the topic does the paragraph provide?
   a. Strict laws in some countries used to regulate what people of each social class could wear.
   b. Rich people wear more beautiful clothing than poor people do.
   c. In many societies, the absence of clothing indicated an absence of status.
   d. Today, the divisions between social classes are becoming less clear from the clothing that people wear.

An outdoor café in Paris

3. *Which idea do all the circled answers have in common—that is, what is the main idea of the paragraph?*
   a. *Today, the differences between various social classes can be seen only in military uniforms.*
   b. *Laws used to regulate how people could dress.*
   c. *Clothing (or its absence) has usually indicated status or rank, but this is less true in today's world.*
   d. *Clothing has been worn for different reasons since the beginning of history.*

B   Two common types of body decoration in tribal societies are tattooing and scarification. A tattoo is a design or mark made by putting a kind of dye (usually dark blue) into a cut in the skin. In scarification, dirt or ashes are put into the cuts instead of dye. In both of these cases, the result is a design that is unique to the person's tribe. Three lines on each side of a man's face identify him as a member of the Yoruba tribe of Nigeria. A complex geometric design on a woman's back identifies her as Nuba—and also makes her more beautiful in the eyes of her people.

1. *What is the one main topic of the paragraph?*
   a. *the Yoruba people*
   b. *geometric designs*
   c. *dirt and ashes*
   d. *body decoration*   **177**

Young woman tattooing another woman's back, Papua, New Guinea

2. What details about the topic does the paragraph provide?
   a. Tattoos are more beautiful than scarification.
   b. Tattoos and scarification indicate a person's tribe.
   c. The dye for tattooing comes from special plants.
   d. Designs on a person's face or body are considered beautiful.

3. Which idea includes all the details circled above—in other words, what is the main idea of the paragraph?
   a. Everyone who wants to be beautiful should get a tattoo.
   b. People decorate their bodies for the purposes of identification and beauty.
   c. A tattoo is a design made by putting dark blue dye into cuts in the skin.
   d. Men more often decorate their faces; women often decorate their backs.

Nigerian man with facial scarification

C   In some societies, women overeat to become plump because large women are considered beautiful, while skinny ones are regarded as ugly. A woman's plumpness is also an indication of her family's wealth. In other societies, by contrast, a fat person is considered unattractive, so men and women eat little and try to remain slim. In many parts of the world, people lie in the sun for hours to darken their skin, while in other places light, soft skin is seen as attractive. People with gray hair often dye it black, whereas those with naturally dark hair often change its color to blond.

1. *What is the one main topic of the paragraph?*
   a. *hair*
   b. *skin*
   c. *body shape*
   d. *body changes*
2. *What details about the topic does the paragraph provide?*
   a. *It is unhealthy to lose or gain too much weight.*
   b. *Some societies consider large people attractive; others, slim ones.*
   c. *Some people prefer dark hair or skin; others, light.*
   d. *Most wealthy people try to stay thin.*
3. *What is the main idea of the paragraph?*
   a. *Individuals and groups of people have different ideas about physical attractiveness.*
   b. *Lying in the sun darkens the skin.*
   c. *In some societies, thinness is an indication that a family is poor.*
   d. *Dark-skinned people usually have dark hair.*

D   In the West, most people visit a dentist regularly for both hygiene and beauty. They use toothpaste and dental floss daily to keep their teeth clean. They have their teeth straightened, whitened, and crowned to make them more attractive to others in their culture. However, "attractive" has quite a different meaning in other cultures. In the past, in Japan, it was the custom for women to blacken, not whiten, the teeth. People in some areas of Africa and central Australia have the custom of filing the teeth to sharp points. And among the Makololo people of Malawi, the women wear a very large ring—a *pelele*—in their upper lip. As their chief once explained about *peleles*: "They are the only beautiful things women have. Men have beards. Women have none. What kind of person would she be without the *pelele*? She would not be a woman at all."

1. *What is the one main topic of the paragraph?*
   a. *dentistry*
   b. *blackening or whitening the teeth*
   c. *changes to the human mouth*
   d. *peleles and beards*

2. *What details about the topic does the paragraph provide?*
   a. *White teeth are attractive to all cultures.*
   b. *In the West, people visit dentists and have their teeth straightened, whitened, and crowned.*
   c. *In some cultures, people blacken their teeth or file them to sharp points.*
   d. *Makololo women wear a large ring in their upper lip.*

3. *What is the main idea of the paragraph?*
   a. *People can easily change the color or shape of their teeth.*
   b. *The word attractive has different meanings.*
   c. *The human mouth suffers change and abuse in many societies.*
   d. *Some methods of changing the appearance of the mouth are dangerous, but others are safe.*

E Body paint or face paint is used mostly by *men* in pre-literate societies in order to attract good health or to ward off disease. It is a form of magic protection against the dangers of the world outside the village, where men have to go for the hunt or for war. When it is used as warpaint, it also serves to frighten the enemy, distinguish members of one's own group from the enemy, and give the men a sense of identity, of belonging to the group. Women have less need of body or face paint because they usually stay in the safety of the village. In modern societies, though, cosmetics are used mostly by *women,* who often feel naked, unclothed, without makeup when out in public—like a tribal hunter without his warpaint. One exception that serves to prove this rule is Victorian society in England and the United States, when women were excluded from public life. In this period, women wore little or no makeup.

1. *What is the one main topic of the paragraph?*
   a. *body and face paint*
   b. *men's warpaint*
   c. *modern women's cosmetics*
   d. *magic protection*

2. What details about the topic does the paragraph provide?
   a. Body or face paint is usually worn by men in tribal societies.
   b. People wear body or face paint to make them more attractive.
   c. Makeup ("face paint") is usually worn by women in modern societies.
   d. When women are excluded from public life, they wear little or no makeup.
3. What is the main idea of the paragraph?
   a. Body paint gives men a sense of identity.
   b. Women in modern times wear makeup to be more beautiful.
   c. In the past, men wore face paint, but in modern times, women wear it.
   d. Body or face paint may be worn as a sort of protection by people who leave the home or village.

Tribal men in body paint

Modern woman in "face paint"

After You Read
Making Inferences

exercise

On the short lines, put a check mark by the statements that you can infer from the example and the reading selection "Fashion: The Art of the Body." Do not check the other statements, even if you think they are true. On the line after each statement that you check, write the phrases from the section from which you inferred the information.

1. _____ All people wear clothing to keep warm. _____

_____

2. _____ Fur provides warmth, while long, loose clothing is useful in hot weather.

_____

3. _____ Rich people wear more clothing than poor people do. _____

_____

4. _____ Social status might be less important now than it was in the past.

_____

5. _____ Some methods of body beautification may be uncomfortable or painful.

_____

6. _____ Body or face paint may make people feel protected. _____

_____

7. _____ Women are more interested in looking good than men are.

_____

Discussing the Reading

activity 1

In small groups, talk about your answers to these questions.

1. Why are people often unhappy with their bodies? Do you agree with their reasons for changing them?
2. What do you think of the methods of body beautification that are described in the reading selection? Why?
3. What methods are common in your culture? (Makeup? Tattoos? Ear piercing? Hair dyeing? etc.) What do you think of them?

Going Beyond the Text

activity 2

Bring to class advertisements about beauty treatments and methods (hairstyling salons, makeup, etc.). Discuss new vocabulary. Tell the class about the most interesting ads and your opinions of them.

Judging Art and Beauty

Here are some quotations about art and beauty. Discuss your answers to each of these questions.

1. What does the quotation mean? (You might need to use a dictionary.)
2. Do you agree with it?
3. What are some proverbs or quotations about art or beauty in your language? Translate them into English and explain them.

- Less is more. —*Robert Browning*
- Beauty is in the eye of the beholder. —*Margaret Hungerford*
- Alas, after a certain age, every man is responsible for his own face. —*Albert Camus*
- Remember that the most beautiful things in the world are the most useless: peacocks and lilies, for instance. —*John Ruskin*
- Form follows function. —*motto of the Bauhaus* (a German school of design)
- Great artists have no country. —*Alfred de Musset*

PART three

Building Vocabulary and Study Skills

Words with Similar Meanings

Although words with similar meanings can often be substituted for one another, they may have somewhat different definitions.

examples: I'm taking a geography <u>course</u>. The <u>class</u> meets twice a week and there is a different <u>lesson</u> at each meeting. (course = series of lessons on a subject; class = a meeting of a course or the students who are taking a course; lesson = a separate piece of material on a subject or the amount of teaching at one time)

The words in each of the following groups have similar meanings, but they are not exactly the same. Match the words with their definitions by writing the letters on the lines as in the examples. If necessary, check your answers in a dictionary.

1. _b_ study
2. _a_ learn
3. _c_ memorize

   a. gain knowledge or skill in a subject
   b. make an effort to learn
   c. learn to know from memory

4. _____ provide
5. _____ present
6. _____ offer

   a. show; introduce
   b. present (something) so that it may be accepted
   c. give

7. _____ depict
8. _____ indicate
9. _____ express

   a. show in the form of a picture
   b. point out; make known
   c. put (thoughts, etc.) into words

10. _____ target
11. _____ goal
12. _____ destination

   a. objective; purpose
   b. the place where someone is going
   c. an object or mark someone tries to reach or hit

13. _____ merchandise
14. _____ products
15. _____ items

   a. things that are made
   b. things that are bought and sold
   c. individual things

In some cases, the meaning of one word *includes* the meanings of many others.

examples: Beautiful art can be found in different kinds of structures: churches, mosques, and palaces. (Churches and mosques are religious buildings, and palaces are buildings for royalty. The word structures can mean buildings, so it includes the meanings of the three other words.)

In each of the following items, circle the one word that includes the meanings of the others. The first one is done as an example.

1. (art) statue painting
2. painter designer artist
3. actor entertainer musician

                                                     Interactions II • Reading

4. traveler   tourist   passenger

5. bus   subway   transportation

6. royalty   prince   king

7. Christianity   religion   Islam

8. murder   crime   theft

Sometimes words with similar meanings have different connotations (implied meanings: "feelings").

examples: In some societies, women overeat to become <u>plump</u> because <u>large</u> women are considered beautiful. In other cultures, a <u>fat</u> person is considered ugly. (The words <u>plump</u>, <u>large</u>, and <u>fat</u> all mean "over normal weight." To say someone is fat is an insult, however, while plump and <u>large</u> are more polite ways of referring to the same characteristic.)

Some dictionaries provide information on usage of words in different situations and on connotations of words with similar meanings. Read the dictionary entries on this page and complete the following exercises.

 **exercise 3**

Write + before the words with positive connotations and − before the words with negative ones as in the examples.

1. __+__ slim

2. __−__ emaciated

3. _____ skinny

4. _____ slender

5. _____ fat

6. _____ overweight

USAGE 1 **Thin** is a general word to describe people who have little or no fat on their bodies. If someone is **thin** in a pleasant way, we say they are **slim** or (less common) **slender,** but if they are too **thin** they are **skinny** (*infml*), **underweight,** or (worst of all) **emaciated:** *I wish I were as slim as you!* | *She looks very thin/skinny/underweight after her illness.* | *After weeks with little or no food, the prisoners were emaciated.* The opposite of **thin** in this sense is **fat,** but this is not very polite. **Plump, overweight, heavy, chubby** (esp. of babies), and **matronly** (only of older women) are all more polite ways of saying the same things. A person who is very fat is **obese.** 2 Things that are long and **thin,** in the sense of having a short distance from one side to another, are **narrow** (opposite **wide**): *a narrow country road* | *a long narrow room.*

beau·ti·ful /ˈbyuʷtəfəl/ *adj* having beauty **–beautifully** *adv*
USAGE When used to describe a person's appearance, **beautiful** is a very strong word meaning "giving great pleasure to the senses." Its opposite is **ugly** or, even stronger, **hideous. Plain** is a less *derogatory* way of saying **ugly. Pretty, handsome, good-looking,** and **attractive** all mean "pleasant to look at;" but **pretty** is only used of women and children, and **handsome** (usually) only of men. **Good-looking, handsome,** and **plain** are normally only used of people, but the other words can also be used of things: *a pretty garden/a hideous dress.*

 **exercise 4**

Circle the words that have a polite connotation.

1. slim

2. emaciated

3. plump

4. matronly

5. obese

6. heavy

exercise 5 For each pair of words, circle the one with the stronger meaning. The first one is done as an example.

1. (beautiful)/ pretty
2. ugly / hideous
3. attractive / beautiful
4. ugly / plain
5. beautiful / good-looking
6. unattractive / ugly

exercise 6 Circle the letters of *all* the words that are usually appropriate for each sentence.

1. He's a very _____ man.

   a. pretty
   b. handsome
   c. attractive
   d. ugly

2. What a _____ baby!

   a. beautiful
   b. handsome
   c. pretty
   d. good-looking

3. This is a very _____ garden.

   a. good-looking
   b. plain
   c. pretty
   d. attractive

activity  Write words with meanings similar to the following words. Use your dictionary for help. Then write the lists of similar words on the board and discuss with your classmates differences in meanings, connotation, and usage.

1. woman
2. thief
3. talk
4. believe
5. old
6. small

Increasing Reading Speed

The following exercises may help you make your eye movements faster and increase your reading speed.

exercise 1 When your teacher tells you to begin each section, look at the underlined word to the left of each line. Read across the line, from left to right. Circle the one word with the most *similar* meaning to that of the underlined word. At the end of each section, write down your time (the number of seconds it takes you to finish). Try to read faster with each section.

<u>exam</u>	culture	test	custom	identity	way
<u>region</u>	hunt	society	state	area	tribe
<u>example</u>	addition	instance	picture	difficulty	social
<u>education</u>	studies	school	memorize	requirement	hard
<u>pleasure</u>	frequent	luxurious	satisfaction	sickness	enjoy

Time: _____

<u>figure</u>	art	painting	statue	mosque	design
<u>gardening</u>	suburbs	transportation	traffic	plants	yardwork
<u>migrate</u>	move	ancestor	nomadic	language	agriculture
<u>predict</u>	therapist	bargain	tourist	organize	foretell
<u>battle</u>	fight	reservation	land	court	rights

Time: _____

<u>chance</u>	provide	offering	presentation	opportunity	allow
<u>rich</u>	various	forest	expensive	wealthy	characteristic
<u>various</u>	different	kind	exist	groups	general
<u>smog</u>	sickness	problem	theory	downtown	pollution
<u>psychologist</u>	science	prove	therapist	artist	member

Time: _____

<u>form</u>	object	fact	shape	information	express
<u>folk</u>	people	religion	hayride	songs	Indians
<u>show</u>	image	expression	smile	depict	match
<u>discount</u>	merchandise	decoration	bargain	geometric	cheap
<u>power</u>	political	government	war	view	strength

Time: _____

exercise 2 Follow the instructions for Exercise 1 on the previous page, but in each line below, circle the one word with the *opposite* meaning to the underlined word.

wonderful	advantageous	horror	result	terrible	luxurious
cities	suburbs	villages	continent	noise	entertainment
communal	group	desert	individual	absence	house
everyday	typical	essential	beliefs	unusual	quality
generally	specifically	result	therefore	thus	such

Time: _____

modern	marketing	traditional	value	economics	activity
birth	child	figure	anger	death	crime
objective	emotional	facts	sadness	reflect	history
criminal	soldier	faceless	symbol	victim	shoot
private	opinion	public	contrast	holy	image

Time: _____

valuable	beautiful	unique	useless	impossible	successful
elderly	young	people	senior	enthusiastic	ancestor
sour	attractive	pickle	doughnut	sweet	barbecue
worsen	produce	improve	influence	summarize	entire
plains	state	flat	mountains	desert	weather

Time: _____

focus on testing

Taking Multiple-Choice Tests

On some multiple-choice tests, there are five answers to choose from. Sometimes one of these is "none of the above." If you choose this, it means that there is no correct answer offered. Sometimes a possible choice is "all of the above." This means that A, B, C, and D are all correct answers. One of the five might be "A and B" or "B and C." If you choose such an answer, it means that there are two correct answers.

Reading in the Real World

Scanning for Information
Scientific Articles

The following passage is part of an article from the *Los Angeles Times*. It is about recent studies into the sense of smell.

exercise

First, read the questions that follow the article. Then read the article, marking the answers to the questions as you find them. Don't worry if you don't understand every word. Work as quickly as you can, as you would on a test.

Scientists Say Aromas Have Major Effect on Emotions

Perhaps it has always been apparent. As plain as the nose on your face. But nobody was paying much attention.

"From an evolutionary point of view, we
5 typically don't think of the nose as very important," said Dr. Gary Schwartz, professor of psychiatry and psychology at the University of Arizona. "But it is stuck square in the middle of the face. Why would
10 something that was less relevant to normal activities be so prominent? It implies there is something more important there than we may have realized."

Indeed, scientists are learning that
15 fragrance affects us more than previously thought. New research indicates that smells influence our minds, our moods and our bodies.

But smell remains one of the least-
20 understood senses. Although we know a great deal about the eyes and ears, we only partly understand smell. According to

Charles Wysocki, an olfactory scientist at the Monell Chemical Senses Center in
25 Philadelphia, we do know that an odor is first detected by the olfactory epithelium, a sort of receptor sheet located in the nose. This starts a chain of events that leads to an information flow to the olfactory bulb and
30 limbic system of the brain, which plays a key role in regulating body functions and the emotions.

Smell, Wysocki said, is the only sensory system to directly project into the limbic
35 system, making it perhaps our most basic, primitive sense. (Other senses reach the limbic system, but travel first to other brain regions.)

Some of the most significant new findings
40 about smell and scent come from William Dember and Joel Warm at the University of Cincinnati. They recently presented their findings at the annual meeting of the American Assn. for the Advancement of

Science and concluded that scents can keep people more alert and improve performance of a routine task.

Subjects tackled a 40-minute vigilance test, which required them to watch a video screen and press a button whenever a certain line pattern appeared. While performing the task, some were intermittently given a whiff of peppermint or muguet (lily of the valley) through oxygen masks. Dember said that those workers receiving the fragrances performed 25% better than those given only whiffs of pure air. A replication study conducted by Raja Parasuramen at Catholic University, using only peppermint, achieved the same findings.

Although it isn't clear exactly *how* fragrance works, Dember believes his study may soon have practical applications. "Truck drivers, even passenger car drivers, who need to keep alert while traveling long distances, could find it helpful," he said. An industry group, International Flavors and Fragrances, selected the scents and sponsored this study.

In Japan, fragrance is already used in the workplace. Shimizu, Japan's largest architectural, engineering and construction firm, has developed an environmental fragrancing system that uses computerized techniques to deliver scents through air-conditioning ducts. The Japanese have found that scents enhance efficiency and reduce stress among office workers.

In one experiment in Japan, 13 key-punch operators were monitored eight hours a day for a month. When the office air was scented with lavender, errors per hour dropped 21%. They dropped by 33% with a jasmine fragrance, and a stimulating lemon aroma reduced errors by 54%. Junichi Yagi, vice president of Shimizu's Boston subsidiary S.

Technology Center-America, said the key-punchers enjoyed the fragrances. "They reported feeling better than they did without it," he maintains.

Yagi said that fragrances were selected based upon the principles of aromatherapy, an ancient form of herbal medicine. Aromatherapists believe that "essential oils," the distilled "essences" of flowers, herbs and plants, can be used to make people feel better. Oils such as lavender and chamomile are considered relaxing; lemon and jasmine, stimulating; pine and eucalyptus invigorating. Aromatherapy is widely practiced in England, France, Belgium, Germany and Switzerland.

"These ideas have been around for a long time," said Yagi, "and now [we're] applying it in Japan."

Other research is still in the laboratory phase. Peter Badia, a professor at Bowling Green State University, is finding that even when you are sleeping, your nose is wide awake. He's worked with about 100 college subjects in the university sleep lab. Electrodes on test participants monitored brainwave activity, heart rate, respiration and muscle tension.

"What we've determined is that we respond to odors in sleep," Badia said. "Tests clearly showed subjects are able to detect the odors; typically their heart rate would increase slightly and their brain waves quicken slightly."

But Schwartz thinks that while he was at Yale University he may have found a relaxing scent: apple spice. Schwartz conducted the experiments over a five-year period, testing more than 400 subjects.

In 1989, Schwartz published findings that he terms "quite remarkable." "We found spiced apple had relaxing effects as measured in brain waves, within a minute of [a subject's] smelling the fragrance."

130 In a separate study, respiration, muscle tension, heart rate and blood pressure were measured as a group of healthy volunteers were asked a series of stressful questions such as: "The kind of person I find sexually
135 attractive is. . . ?" They received whiffs of spiced apple aroma, while a control group was given bursts of plain air. The spiced apple produced a drop in blood pressure, on average of 5 millimeters per person,
140 Schwartz said.

"It's not a big decrease, but could be the difference between taking medication and not taking medication; or reducing the dosage in medication."

145 Schwartz, now at the University of Arizona, continues his work on scent. In one of his current studies, Schwartz is looking at "subliminal scent," scent below the level of awareness.

150 "I think one of the reasons taking trips to pine forests makes us feel so good is the presence of the mixture of molecules in pine," Schwartz said. "Equally important— if not more important—may be the absence
155 of all these other molecules we're not consciously aware our nose is picking up . . . smog molecules, gasoline, carpet, paint . . . putting a great strain on our nervous system."

160 Schwartz points to so-called "sick" buildings as an example. They inhibit the circulation of fresh air, so people instead breathe a veritable soup of man-made chemicals. "The idea is that the nose can
165 detect those molecules and that that information is fed to the brain and does activate brain centers to make us feel queasy or uncomfortable," Schwartz said. "Yet we wouldn't be able to attribute it to any scent
170 we're aware of it."

It is clear that the study of scent is positively blossoming. "It's definitely on the increase," Wysocki said. "We've learned a lot, but we're a long way from fully under-
175 standing smell. We're still on a great adventure."

Carla Kallan

Complete each sentence by circling the letter of *one* answer.

1. Another word that means *smell* is
   a. odor
   b. scent
   c. fragrance
   d. aroma
   e. all of the above

2. People who deal with scent as an important part of their profession are
   a. olfactory scientists
   b. subjects
   c. aromatherapists
   d. A and B
   e. A and C

3. Smell might be the most basic, primitive sense because it
   a. plays a key role in body functions
   b. influences our moods
   c. reaches the limbic system after traveling first to other brain regions
   d. reaches the limbic system directly, without traveling first to other brain regions
   e. none of the above

4. If people are doing a difficult job in which it's important not to make any errors, it would be *best* for them to smell
   a. spiced apple
   b. lemon aroma
   c. lavender
   d. jasmine
   e. none of the above

5. If people are tense and want to relax, it would be *best* for them to smell
   a. spiced apple
   b. lemon aroma
   c. lily of the valley
   d. jasmine
   e. all of the above

6. Taking a trip to a pine forest might make us feel good because of
   a. the presence of the mixture of molecules in pine
   b. the absence of other molecules from smog, gasoline, carpet, and paint
   c. the strain on our nervous system
   d. A and B
   e. none of the above

The first reading selection explores the human brain and how it works. The second selection discusses exciting new technological changes and the ethical questions about them that people are considering. The last selection is from a psychology textbook. It offers information about how babies begin to acquire language.

in this chapter

The Human Brain—
New Discoveries

Before You Read

Getting Started

Look at the diagram and pictures here and on the next page and answer these questions.

1. Which areas of the brain might a person use to compose music? To throw a ball? To paint a picture?
2. If you feel cold and want to put on a sweater, which area of the brain is probably active?
3. It has been observed that little boys and little girls play, speak, and act differently from each other. Do you think these differences might be caused by differences in the brain?
4. Which person might be in better health—the man in picture A or one of the men in picture C? Why do you think so?

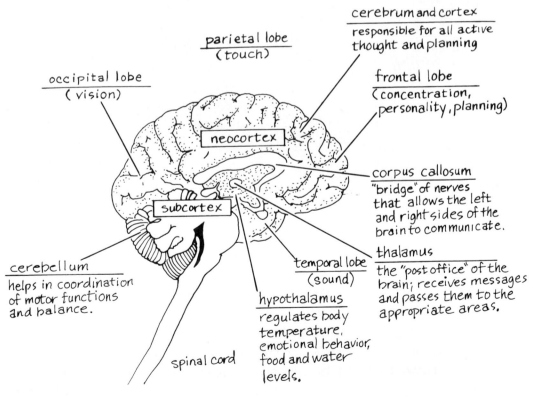

A

B

C

D

Preparing to Read

In academic reading, it often helps to survey (get an overview of) the material before you begin to read it. Pictures or diagrams provide useful first clues to the contents. In addition, some selections contain subheads, or lines that stand out, which give quick information about the reading.

 Survey the first reading selection quickly. Write the subheads here.

_____

_____

_____

_____

_____

Asking yourself questions before and during reading often helps you understand and remember the material.

 Look again at the diagram on page 194 and at the subheads. Then check (√) the questions on the following list that you think, from your surveying, the reading selection might answer.

1. _____ What is the function of different parts of the brain?

2. _____ How are human brains different from animal brains?

3. _____ Why do some people seem to be more creative than others?

4. _____ What is the difference between the left and right side of the brain?

5. _____ Are the happiest memories of most people's lives from their childhood?

6. _____ Is it possible to have a memory of something that never happened?

7. _____ How can we improve our memories?

8. _____ How do men and women communicate with each other?

9. _____ Can the brain cause people to get sick or become well?

The Human Brain—New Discoveries

Parts of the Brain

A

Most of us learn basic facts about the human brain in our middle or high school biology classes. We study the subcortex, the "old brain," which is found in the brains of most animals and is responsible for basic functions such as breathing, eating, drinking, and sleeping. We learn about the neocortex, the "new brain," which is unique to humans and is where complex brain activity takes place. We find that the cerebrum, which is responsible for all active thought, is divided into two parts, or hemispheres. The left hemisphere, generally, manages the right side of the body; it is responsible for logical thinking. The right hemisphere manages the left side of the body; this hemisphere controls emotional, creative, and artistic functions. And we learn that the corpus callosum is the "bridge" that connects the two hemispheres. Memorizing the names for parts of the brain might not seem thrilling to many students, but new discoveries in brain function *are* exciting. Recent research is teaching us a lot about creativity, memory, the differences between men and women, and the relationship between mind and body.

Left Brain/Right Brain: Creativity

B

Psychologists agree that most of us have creative ability that is greater than what we use in daily life. In other words, we can be more creative than we realize! The problem is that we use mainly *one* hemisphere of our brain—the left. From childhood, in school, we're taught reading, writing, and mathematics; we are exposed to very little music or art. Therefore, many of us might not "exercise" our right hemisphere much, except through dreams, symbols, and those wonderful insights in which we suddenly find the answer to a problem that has been bothering us—and do so without the need for logic. Can we be taught to use our right hemisphere more? Many experts believe so. Classes at some schools and books (such as *The Inner Game of Tennis* and *Drawing on the Right Side of the Brain*) claim to help people to "silence" the left hemisphere and give the right a chance to work.

Memory—True or False?

C

In the 1980s in the United States, there were many cases of adults who suddenly remembered, with the help of a psychologist, things that had happened to them in childhood. These memories had been repressed—held back—for many years. Some of these newly discovered memories have sent people to prison. As people remember crimes (such as murder or rape) that they saw or experienced as children, the police have re-opened and investigated old criminal cases. In fact, over 700 cases have been filed that are based on these repressed memories.

However, new studies in the 1990s suggest that many of these might be *false* memories. At a 1994 conference at Harvard Medical School, neuroscientists discussed how memory is believed to work. It is known that small pieces of a memory (sound, sight, feeling, and so on) are kept in different parts of the brain; the limbic system, in the middle of the brain, pulls these pieces together into one complete memory. But it's certain that people can "remember" things that have never happened. Even a small *suggestion* can leave a piece of memory in the brain. Most frightening, according to Dr. Michael Nash of the University of Tennessee, is that "there may be no structural difference" in the brain between a false memory and a true one.

Differences in Male and Female Brains

Watch a group of children as they play. You'll probably notice that the boys and girls play differently, speak differently, and are interested in different things. When they grow into men and women, the differences do not disappear. Many scientists are now studying the origins of these gender differences. Some are searching for an explanation in the human brain. Some of their findings are interesting. For example, they've found that more men than women are lefthanded; this reflects the dominance of the brain's right hemisphere. By contrast, more women listen equally with both ears while men listen mainly with the right ear. Men are better at reading a map without having to rotate it. Women are better at reading the emotions of people in photographs.

One place to look for an explanation of gender differences is in the hypothalamus, just above the brain stem. This controls anger, thirst, hunger, and sexual desire. One recent study shows that there is a region in the hypothalamus that is larger in heterosexual men than it is in women and homosexual men. Another area of study is the corpus callosum, the thick group of nerves that allows the right and left hemispheres of the brain to communicate with each other. The corpus callosum is larger in women than in men. This might explain the mystery of "female intuition," which is supposed to give women greater ability to "read" and understand emotional clues.

The Mystery of the Mind–Body Relationship

There is more and more evidence every day to prove that our minds and bodies are closely connected. Negative emotions, such as loneliness, depression, and helplessness, are believed to cause a higher rate of sickness and death. Similarly, it's possible that positive thinking can help people remain in good physical health or become well faster after an illness. Although some doctors are doubtful about this, most accept the success of new therapies (e.g., relaxation and meditation) that help people with problems such as ulcers, high blood pressure, insomnia (sleeplessness), and migraine headaches.

After You Read
Getting the Main Ideas

exercise 1

Write T on the lines before the statements that are true, according to the reading. Write F on the lines before the statements that are false. Write I on the lines before the statements that are impossible to know from the reading.

1. _____ Different parts of the brain control different activities or parts of the body.

2. _____ Most people probably don't use all their creative ability.

3. _____ Newly discovered memories from childhood are false memories.

4. _____ There is no real difference between the brains of males and those of females.

5. _____ Emotions may affect people's physical health.

Guessing Meaning from Context

On the reading section of standardized exams, there is, of course, no opportunity to use a dictionary. Such exams are testing your ability to guess meaning from the context. Often, you need more than the information in one sentence in order to figure out what a word means. You need to consider the entire paragraph.

exercise Take this practice test. Guess the meaning of the underlined words. You may look back at the reading selection "The Human Brain—New Discoveries," but don't use a dictionary.

1. In paragraph B, "We are <u>exposed</u> to very little music or art" probably means
   a. We are not often in concert halls or museums.
   b. We are taught a little music and art.
   c. Music and art are uncovered.
   d. Music and art are not taught much.

2. In paragraph B, <u>insights</u> are
   a. dreams that we have while we're sleeping
   b. moments when we suddenly understand something
   c. logical moments
   d. vision

3. In paragraph C, the two meanings of the word <u>cases</u> (in lines 1 and 7) are
   a. examples and situations
   b. memories and crimes
   c. examples and events that need police attention
   d. situations and people who murder or rape

4. In paragraph E, <u>gender</u> differences are differences
   a. between males and females
   b. in the way children play
   c. between the left and right hemispheres
   d. in the way men and women speak

5. In paragraph E, <u>rotate</u> probably means
   a. read
   b. look at
   c. understand
   d. turn

6. In paragraph F, <u>intuition</u> is
   a. mystery
   b. the ability to read
   c. the power of understanding without logic
   d. female emotion

Distinguishing Facts from Theories

In affirmative statements, certain words or expressions usually indicate the existence of facts—i.e., information that has been proven accurate. Here are some examples:

know	certain
show	prove
clear	scientific
proof	sure
evidence	positive
fact	objective

Other words can indicate theories—i.e., ideas that are believed by some people but have not been proven to be true. Here are some examples.

think	subjective	scientific
believe	possible	possibly
(dis)agree	likely	doubt
theorize	probably	suggest
claim	may/might	

exercise 2

On the line, write *fact* or *theory* for each statement, according to the presentation of the information in the reading selection "The Human Brain—New Discoveries." (You'll need to look back at the selection for words that indicate fact or theory.)

1. _____ Most of us have creative ability that is greater than what we use in daily life.

2. _____ Many of us don't "exercise" our right hemisphere much.

3. _____ We can be taught to use our right hemisphere more.

4. _____ Some books help people "silence" the left hemisphere and use the right hemisphere.

5. _____ Over 700 cases have been filed that are based on newly discovered memories.

6. _____ Many newly discovered memories are false.

7. _____ Small pieces of memory are kept in different parts of the brain.

8. _____ People "remember" things that have never happened.

9. _____ There is no structural difference between a false memory and a true one.

10. _____ There is a region in the hypothalamus that is larger in heterosexual men than in women and homosexual men.

11. _____ Women have a greater ability to understand emotional clues because they have a larger corpus callosum than men do.

12. _____ Our minds and bodies are closely connected.

13. _____ Negative emotions cause higher rates of sickness.

14. _____ Positive emotions can help people remain in good physical health.

exercise 3 Go back to the Preparing to Read section on page 196 and answer the questions you checked in Exercise 2.

PART two
The Ethics of Change

Before You Read
Skimming for Main Ideas

exercise Read each paragraph quickly, without using a dictionary. To figure out the main idea, circle the letters of all the correct answers to the questions that follow. Then combine the answers to complete a sentence that expresses the main idea. Answers for paragraph A are given as examples.

The Ethics of Change

A   Technology is bringing rapid changes to modern life. Recent discoveries—especially in the areas of communication and medicine—are exciting and can be beneficial, but they also bring with them possible social, moral, and legal problems. In many cases, a new discovery has led to dramatic change before we have a chance to decide if such a change is *right*. These discoveries are causing experts in the fields of philosophy, ethics, and law to consider a number of ethical questions.

1. What is the one main topic of the paragraph?
    a. communication
    b. medicine
    c. the ethics of recent discoveries
    d. dramatic changes in society

2. What details about the topic does the paragraph provide?
    a. The areas of communication and medicine are important these days.
    b. Technology is bringing rapid change.
    c. Recent discoveries bring possible social, moral, and legal problems.
    d. A number of ethical questions are being considered.

3. The main idea of the paragraph is that recent discoveries in technology are bringing up ethical questions.

B   For years, police departments, the FBI, and the CIA have used polygraphs (lie detectors) to check the truth of what someone is saying. These machines record changes in a person's blood pressure, breathing, and the skin's electrical conductivity; these are responses that indicate that a person is lying. Recent technological advances, however, have taken this concept one step further. Telephones and even digital watches may soon be turned into small versions of lie detectors. Such miniature Psychological Stress Evaluators (PSEs) would, unlike current polygraphs, detect lying by picking up "microtremors" in a person's voice. Microtremors, which are movements of the voice too slight to be noticed by the human ear, vary according to the degree of stress. Imagine having a PSE on your home phone or on your wristwatch! You would usually know if someone was avoiding the truth!

1. *What is the one main topic of the paragraph?*
   a. *microtremors*
   b. *PSEs*
   c. *the police department, the FBI, and the CIA*
   d. *technological advances in lie detecting*

2. *What details about the topic does the paragraph provide?*
   a. *Polygraphs have been used for years to check the truth of what someone is saying.*
   b. *A recent technological advance, a PSE is a very small lie detector that might be used on a telephone or watch.*
   c. *PSEs never make a mistake; they are always accurate.*
   d. *PSEs detect lying by picking up microtremors in a person's voice.*

3. *The main idea of the paragraph is that* _____
   _____

C   However, many people have serious questions about the ethics of PSEs, and if moral values are a problem, there are likely to be legal problems too. The almost limitless variety of uses of PSEs is truly frightening. Employers might use them while interviewing job applicants. Teachers might use them on students who are suspected of cheating. Husbands and wives, friends and relatives might begin to use them on each other for "fun," which would likely lead to anger and a break in relations. One ethical problem of PSEs involves the fact that a person who is accused of lying may actually be telling the truth; the stressfulness of the situation might cause microtremors in the voice. There is also the problem of unprofessional use of PSEs; many users might not be able to interpret correctly the signals from the detectors. A serious legal question involving PSEs is that of our private lives. Doesn't the use of such equipment violate our right to privacy? Fortunately, lawmakers are aware of these questions and are moving to create new laws to limit the use of this new technology.

1. *What is the one main topic of the paragraph?*
   a. *problems*
   b. *ethical and legal questions about PSEs*
   c. *the use of PSEs*
   d. *the unprofessional use of PSEs*

2. *What details about the topic does the paragraph provide?*
   a. *People have been using PSEs for many reasons.*
   b. *There is an almost limitless variety of uses of PSEs.*
   c. *There are ethical and legal problems with PSEs.*
   d. *Lawmakers are moving to create new laws to limit the use of PSEs.*

3. *The main idea of the paragraph is that* _____
   _____

D   In the medical profession, technology is advancing so fast that questions of law and ethics cannot be discussed and answered fast enough. Most of these questions involve ending or beginning a human life. For example, we have the medical ability to keep a person technically "alive" for years, on machines, after he or she is "brain dead", i.e., after the "new brain" has stopped functioning. But is it ethical to do this? And what about the alternative? In other words, is it ethical *not* to keep a person alive if we have the technology to do so? And there are many ethical questions involving the conception of a human baby. *In vitro* fertilization, for example, is becoming more and more common. By this method of conceiving a baby outside a woman's body, couples who have difficulty conceiving a child may still become parents. This possibility brings joy to many families, but it also raises important questions. At a cost of between $70,000 and $75,000 for the delivery of one such baby, should society have to pay for this—especially when there are many orphaned children who need parents? A fertilized human egg might be frozen for a long time—perhaps decades—before it is implanted in the mother's body; is this fertilized egg a human being? If the parents get a divorce, to whom do these frozen eggs belong? And there is the question of surrogate mothers. There have been several cases of a woman who is paid to carry (for the nine months of development) the baby of another woman who is medically unable to do so. After delivering the baby, the surrogate mother sometimes changes her mind and wants to keep the baby. Whose baby is it? Is it the surrogate's because she gave birth? Or is it the biological parents'?

1. *What is the one main topic of the paragraph?*
   a. *in vitro fertilization and surrogate motherhood*
   b. *new methods of giving birth*
   c. *ethical and legal questions brought about by new technology in medicine*
   d. *ethical questions about keeping a person alive who is "brain dead"*

2. *What details about the topic does the paragraph provide?*
   a. *Technological advances in the medical profession are bringing about ethical and legal questions.*
   b. *There are ethical questions involving keeping a person alive who is "brain dead."*
   c. *It is easy these days to fertilize a human egg outside a woman's body.*
   d. *There are ethical and legal questions involving in vitro fertilization and surrogate mothers.*

3. *The main idea of the paragraph is that* _____

_____

After You Read

Making Inferences

exercise
On the short lines, put a check mark next to each statement that you can infer from the reading selection. Do not check the other statements, even if you think they are true. On the line after each statement that you check, write the phrases from the selection from which you inferred the information.

1. _____ Recent discoveries in technology are both good and bad. _____

_____

2. _____ Technology seems to be moving faster than ethics. _____

_____

3. _____ Experts in philosophy, ethics, and law believe that the new technology is dangerous. _____

4. _____ Polygraphs can detect if a person is telling the truth. _____

_____

5. _____ Polygraphs are always accurate, but PSEs sometimes make mistakes.

_____

6. _____ The variety of uses of PSEs may be dangerous. _____

_____

7. _____ Several recent advances in medical technology are unethical. _____

_____

Going Beyond the Text

 *activity* ___ Bring to class recent newspaper and magazine articles about problems that have arisen from technological discoveries in the areas of communication and medicine. Share the articles with the class. Discuss the important information and learn new vocabulary.

WHAT DO YOU THINK?

Considering Medical Ethics

There are many controversial issues (questions to argue about) in the field of medicine. Here are some of them. What do you think about each issue—and *why*?

1. Is euthanasia ethical? In other words, is it moral to painlessly kill a person who is incurably sick or brain dead? Why or why not?
2. If a married couple has fertilized eggs frozen in a medical laboratory, and then they decide to get a divorce, what should happen to the eggs?
3. It is now possible for a woman in her fifties or even sixties to give birth to a baby. What do you think about this?

PART three

Building Vocabulary and Study Skills

Words with Similar Meanings

exercise ▶▶▶

The words in each of the following groups have similar meanings, but they are not exactly the same. Match the words with their definitions by writing the letters on the lines. If necessary, check your answers in a dictionary.

1. _____ brain

2. _____ mind

3. _____ memory

a. a way of thinking or feeling
b. the ability to remember
c. an organ of the body that controls thought and feeling

4. _____ equipment

5. _____ machine

6. _____ device

a. an instrument
b. the things that are needed for an activity
c. a man-made instrument that needs power (e.g., electricity) in order to work

7. _____ insight

8. _____ knowledge

9. _____ logic

a. a way of thinking with formal methods (using the left brain)
b. understanding that comes from experience and learning
c. the power of using one's mind (especially the right brain) to understand something suddenly

Categories (Content Areas)

It often helps to learn words in groups (words with the same stem, words with similar meanings, words with opposite meanings, etc.). One method of grouping words is to put them together in categories, such as people, animals, buildings, and so on. One kind of category is a "content area"— the subject with which all the words are associated.

example: The following are words associated with the content area of science: *laboratory, neuroscientist, subjects, experiment.*

Cross out the word in each line that does not belong, as in the example. Write the category or content area of the words that belong together.

1. polygraphs   ~~microtremors~~   lie detectors   PSEs

      machines that detect lies
_____

2. discoveries   changes   problems   advances
_____

3. ethics   morals   values   questions
_____

4. doctor   neuroscientist   biologist   surrogate
_____

5. creativity   cerebrum   hypothalamus   subcortex
_____

6. drinking   breaking   writing   eating
_____

7. meditation   ulcer   insomnia   headache
_____

8. loneliness   depression   allergy   helplessness
_____

9. reading   writing   mathematics   dreams
_____

Word Roots and Affixes

It is often possible to guess the meanings of new words from word roots (also called "stems") and affixes (prefixes and suffixes). There is a list of many affixes on page 152. Here are some more word roots and affixes and their meanings.

prefixes	meanings
a-, an-	no, without
ante-	before
micro-	small
poly-	many

suffixes	meanings
-ism	belief in; act or practice
-ist	a person who believes in or performs a certain action

word roots	meanings
anthro, anthropo	man, human
ced	go, move
chrom	color
chron	time
graph	write, writing
hetero	different
homo	same
metr, meter	measure; an instrument for measuring
morph	form
phil	love
psych	mind
somn	sleep
sphere	round; ball-shaped
tele	far
theo, the	god

exercise Without using a dictionary, guess the meaning of each underlined word. Use the list of word roots and affixes.

1. It is believed that an earthquake <u>anteceded</u> the fire.
    a. caused
    b. happened after
    c. happened before
    d. put out; worked against

2. There were some <u>amorphous</u> clouds in the sky.
    a. without form or shape
    b. thick and dark
    c. beautiful
    d. related to rain

3. Many ancient peoples were <u>polytheists</u>.
    a. very well educated
    b. people with many culture centers
    c. people who studied many languages
    d. people who believed in many gods

4. Movies often <u>anthropomorphize</u> creatures from other planets.
   a. study
   b. give human form or characteristics to
   c. present in a terrible way
   d. depict

5. They wore <u>polychromatic</u> body paint.
   a. beautiful
   b. of many colors
   c. complex
   d. made of natural dyes

6. My teacher didn't appreciate my <u>heterography</u>.
   a. talking a lot in class
   b. different ideas in the speech that I gave in class
   c. logic
   d. spelling that was different from the rule

7. He sometimes has a problem with <u>somnambulism</u>.
   a. sleepwalking
   b. drinking
   c. lying
   d. breathing

8. He used a <u>telemeter</u>.
   a. instrument for seeing something very small
   b. instrument for finding directions
   c. instrument for measuring time
   d. instrument for measuring how far away an object is

PART four
Reading in the Real World

Marking a Book; Summarizing
Academic Reading

Students—especially college students—often need to read so much material that they don't have time to reread it before an important exam. For this reason, it's necessary to learn how to mark a book. If you mark the topics, main ideas, and important details as you read, you can go back later and look over your markings to study for a test—without reading the whole passage again. After marking a passage, it's also easier to summarize it (tell the main ideas and a few important details in as few words as possible). However, it's important to note that there is no one "right" way of marking a book. You need to find a style that is comfortable to you. Here is how one student might mark the following paragraph and summarize it:

example: We can follow a baby's intellectual development by observing how she perceives objects. An infant of about 6 months will look at a toy, reach for it, and maybe put it in her mouth. But if someone hides that toy behind a cloth, the baby does not remember it at all and shows no sign that she realizes it even exists. She doesn't think of looking for the toy behind the cloth because she cannot yet imagine a thing that she can't see or touch. However, by the age of 2, a baby will go in search of a hidden toy because she can now understand that objects exist even if she cannot see or touch them.

Summary: The development of a baby's thought process can be traced by a comparison of the way in which 6-month-old infants perceive things with the way 2-year-old children perceive them. At 6 months, babies understand the existence only of objects that they can see or touch, but by the age of 2, they are able to understand that things they can't see or touch do exist.

The reading selection in Part Four is from a textbook called *Understanding Psychology,* by Richard A. Kasschau. It presents information about discoveries in the acquisition of language.

exercise Mark each of the following sections as shown above—with circles and underlining. Then write a summary of each section. When you finish, compare your markings and summaries with those of your classmates.

The Development of Language

A   Psychologists believe that chimpanzees must develop at least as far as 2-year-old humans because, like 2-year-olds, they will look for a toy or a bit of food that has disappeared. They can represent the existence of that toy or bit of food in their minds. Can they be taught to "talk" about it? One husband and wife team, the Gardners, raised a baby chimp named Washoe in their home and—since chimps are very good with their hands—taught her to use the American Sign Language for the deaf. At 3½ years of age, Washoe knew at least 87 signs for words like "food," "dog," "toothbrush," "gimmee," "sweet," "more," and "hurry." By age 5, Washoe knew and used more than 160 signs.

Chimp and human in "conversation"

Summary:

B Making these signs at the appropriate times would not be enough to be called language, though. A dog or a parrot might make signs that its owner could interpret as demands for a walk or food. Washoe's remarkable achievement was that some of her signs had abstract meanings and that she could put signs together in new ways to produce new meanings. Productivity is a key feature of language use. For example, Washoe learned the sign for "more" (putting her fingertips together over her head) because she loved to be tickled and wanted more. But she was not simply doing something like a dog does when it rolls over to be tickled; she was able to use the same sign later in entirely new circumstances—asking for more food or more hair brushing.

Summary:

c   Since the original experiments with Washoe, several chimpanzees have been taught to "talk" in other ways. Lana the chimpanzee was trained on a special typewriter connected to a computer. The machine has 50 keys, each marked with a different symbol which stands for a word in Yerkish, a special monkey language devised just for this study. When Lana presses a key, the symbol appears on the screen in front of her. Lana has learned to type out sentences and thus converse with the experimenters. Sometimes, she types a word out of order, reads the sentence on the screen, and erases it (by pressing the erase key) before she has been corrected. In other cases, Lana has made up phrases to describe objects she's never seen before. For example, the first time Lana saw a ring, she identified it as a "finger bracelet."

Summary:

D   The example of Washoe shows that there are several steps in learning language. First, one must learn to make the signs—whether by hand or by mouth. Then, one must give them meaning; and finally, one must learn grammar. Each child takes these steps at his or her own rate. During the first year of life, the average child makes many sounds. Crying lessens, and the child starts making mostly cooing sounds, which develop into a babble that includes every sound humans can make—Chinese vowels, African clicks, German rolled *r*s, and English *o*s.

Late in the first year, the strings of babbles begin to sound more like the language that the child hears. Children imitate the speech of their parents and their older brothers and sisters, and are greeted with approval whenever they say something that sounds like a word. In this way children learn to speak what becomes their native language even though they could just as easily learn any other.

Summary:

E | The leap to using sounds as symbols occurs some time in the second year. The first attempts at saying words are primitive, and the sounds are incomplete: "Ball" usually sounds like "ba," and "cookie" may even sound like "doo-da." The first real words usually refer to things the infant can see or touch. Often they are labels or commands ("dog!" "cookie!").

By the time children are 2 years old, they have a vocabulary of at least 50 words. Toward the end of the second year, children begin to express themselves more clearly by joining words into two-word phrases. From about 18 months to 5 years of age, children are adding approximately 5 to 10 words a day to their vocabulary.

Summary:

CHAPTER ten

Medicine, Myths, and Magic

in this chapter

The first reading selection discusses traditional healers: What do they do to make people well, and how can we explain their success? The second selection covers new discoveries in the mind-body relationship. The final selection reveals some surprising remedies that you can find in your own kitchen—without going to a drugstore or a doctor.

217

PART one

The Work of the Traditional Healer

Before You Read

Getting Started

Look at the pictures here and on the next page and discuss them.

1. What kinds of people and things are in the pictures?
2. Compare the pictures below with those at the right. What do all the pictures have in common? How are they different?

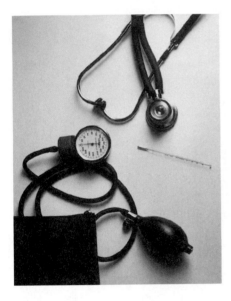

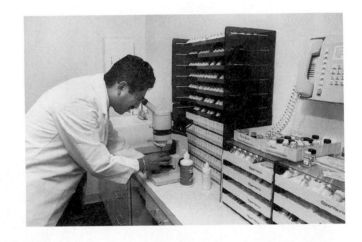

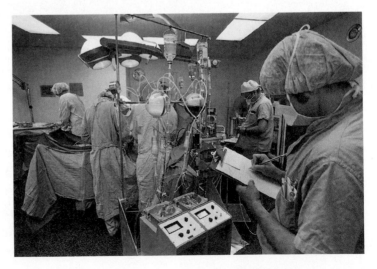

Preparing to Read

**exercise 1** Look again at the pictures on pages 218 and 219. Then survey the first reading selection by looking at the subheads. Put a check (√) by the topics below that you believe will be discussed in the reading.

1. _____ Asian Methods of Medicine As Compared to Western Ones

2. _____ Comparison of Traditional Medicine with Modern Medicine

3. _____ Why We Get Sick

4. _____ How to Prevent Sickness

5. _____ Supernatural Methods of Treating Disease

6. _____ Ceremonies of Traditional Healers

7. _____ New Research on Astrology

**exercise 2** Check the questions that you believe the reading selection will answer.

1. _____ How are the methods of traditional healers and modern doctors similar? How are they different?

2. _____ How do traditional healers view disease? How do modern scientists view it?

3. _____ What is the difference between methods of disease prevention in traditional societies and in modern urban ones?

4. _____ What are the steps in treatment of disease?

5. _____ How are tribal doctors learning the scientific methods of the West?

6. _____ What do traditional healers do in tribal ceremonies?

exercise 3 As you read the following selection, think about the answer to this question: How are traditional healers different from modern doctors?

Read the following selection quickly. Do not use a dictionary. Then do the exercises that follow the reading.

The Work of the Traditional Healer

Traditional Healers and Modern Doctors

In most urban and suburban areas throughout the world, sick people are taken to a doctor's office or to a hospital for treatment. But among tribal and village people in many countries, patients are taken, instead, to a local healer. This person is a combination of a doctor, a priest, and a psychologist. Some of his or her folk methods are similar to those of a doctor, but most are very different. The difference in methods is a result of the fact that disease—to the modern, scientific mind—is viewed as something natural; it is caused by viruses, bacteria, and other small things that we can't see without a microscope. By contrast, in much of the world, disease is considered to be something *super*natural; in other words, sickness is not caused by something physical but instead is the result of deep anger, broken religious laws, the hatred of enemies, and so on. A physician knows how to treat a specific disease. A traditional healer, however, treats the whole person—and often the patient's family and friends as well.

Prevention of Disease

Of course, there may be no need for treatment if people know how to take care of themselves to prevent sickness. A modern physician might tell patients what to eat, how much to exercise, when and how to relax, and the like. A traditional healer, on the other hand, might tell patients to wear amulets—special necklaces for protection against bad spirits. Nevertheless, in both villages and urban societies, people do become ill and sometimes need medical help.

The Diagnosis

The first step in any treatment, of course, is the diagnosis: The doctor or the healer has to find out why the patient is ill and decide what to do about it. For the diagnosis, both ask about symptoms. (Is the patient complaining about headaches? Stomachaches? Insomnia? Skin rash?) But the similarity in methods ends there. The doctor's next step is to give blood tests, take X-rays, etc., while the healer might use supernatural methods. Healers might ask patients about their dreams, use astrology to find the cause of the problem in the stars, or go into a trance (a condition of deep concentration in which they don't function normally) in an effort to contact spirits or other beings outside the world.

The Cure

After the diagnosis comes the cure. In modern medicine, this solution usually means one or more of the following: the same methods that are used for prevention (healthful food, rest, exercise), perhaps warm baths or massage, drugs, or surgery. Likewise, folk medicine includes some of the same cures. As in the diagnosis, however, a healer also uses a wide variety of supernatural methods in his or her cures. Two of the most common are *exorcism* and *soul hunts*. Exorcism is based on the belief that disease is caused by bad spirits. Thus, in an exorcism ceremony, the healer performs a number of traditional activities to take the evil beings out of the victim's body. Songs, dances, and prayers are part of any exorcism, and soul hunts include them as well. In these ceremonies, the healer tries to persuade the victims' souls, which are believed to have left their bodies, to return.

A Typical Tribal Ceremony

The Ndembu people of Central Africa believe that illness is often the result of the anger of a relative, friend, or enemy. This emotion, they say, causes a tooth to enter the body of the person who is the target of the anger and to create disease. When the healer decides which body part contains the evil tooth, he calls together the victim's relatives and friends to watch a ceremony, at the end of which he "removes" it from the patient's throat, arm, leg, stomach, etc. Although the patient and the villagers know what has happened—that the tooth has been hidden inside the healer's mouth the whole time, the patient is often cured. The Ndembu ceremony is typical of treatments around the world, in which stones, insects, or small sharp objects are "taken out" of sick people. Despite scientific evidence that disproves the effectiveness of such methods, the fact remains that the treatments are often successful, and many villagers prefer to be cured in this way than by a modern physician.

The Success of Traditional Healers

Scientists ask how traditional healers can actually be successful in their treatments and why they are so popular. The answers probably lie in a combination of the following reasons. First, supernatural ceremonies are symbolic, and the people who participate in them believe deeply in the symbols. Even Western physicians agree that patients with deep faith—belief in God, their doctors, the drugs they take, images, or symbols—will regain their health faster than patients with little hope. Second, ceremonies may be effective because people come together for a common goal; patients see how many people in their communities care about the cure. In addition, these communal meetings provide socially acceptable opportunities for the people of the village to express what they feel. Social and psychological problems can be solved along with the physical ones of the sick person. Fourth, scientists theorize that the trance parts of the ceremonies produce certain chemicals in the body, which then work to help cure the disease. Finally, many of the healer's natural drugs, which come from his or her surroundings (a nearby forest, jungle, or desert), have been found to be medically effective. Scientists are fascinated by what they learn from the methods of traditional healers.

After You Read

Getting the Main Ideas

exercise 1  Write F on the lines before the statements about folk medicine and M before statements about modern medicine. In some cases, both answers are correct.

1. _____ Disease is thought to be produced by supernatural causes.

2. _____ People try to avoid getting sick by eating properly, exercising, and relaxing.

3. _____ The first step in treatment is the diagnosis of the illness.

4. _____ Spirits from other worlds are contacted through a trance.

5. _____ Rest, massage, chemical drugs, or surgery are possible cures.

6. _____ Through a ceremony, something bad is removed from the sick person's body.

7. _____ People get well more quickly if they believe they will regain their health.

8. _____ Social interaction and the help of relatives and friends are an important part of the cure.

Guessing Vocabulary from Context

exercise 2 On the lines, write words from the reading selection with similar meanings to the words listed. The numbers in parentheses refer to the number of *correct answers*.

1. doctor (1):_____

2. take care of (1):_____

3. sick (1):_____

4. disease (2):_____

5. sick person (2):_____

6. supernatural beings (1):_____

7. bad (1):_____

8. belief (1):_____

To understand the meaning of sentences or paragraphs, it is not always necessary to know the exact definitions of vocabulary items; in other words, often knowing the *general* meaning of a word is enough.

example: Modern doctors use scientific equipment such as <u>microscopes</u> to figure out the causes of disease. (What are <u>microscopes</u>? They are a kind of scientific equipment. For this context, it is unnecessary to know exactly how they look or what they do.)

exercise 3 What is *essential* about the following vocabulary items—i.e., what do you need to know to understand their meaning in these contexts? Complete the general definitions as in the example.

1. In most urban and suburban areas throughout the world, sick people are taken to a doctor's office or to a hospital for treatment.

   A hospital is a place *where sick people are taken.*

2. Disease is caused by viruses, bacteria, and other small things that we can't see without a microscope.

   Viruses and bacteria are _____

   _____

3. For the diagnosis, both the modern doctor and the traditional healer ask about symptoms. (Is the patient complaining about headaches? Stomachaches? Insomnia? Skin rash?)

   Insomnia and skin rash are _____

   _____

4. In modern medicine, the same methods that are used for prevention—healthful food, rest, and exercise—are often part of the cure (as well as warm baths, massage, drugs, or surgery).

   Massage and surgery are _____

   _____

5. In a soul hunt, the healer tries to persuade the victims' souls, which are believed to have left their bodies, to return.

   Souls are something _____

   _____

6. Many of the healer's natural drugs, which come from his or her surroundings (a nearby forest, jungle, or desert), have been found to be medically effective.

Surroundings may be a forest, jungle, or desert that is _____

_____

exercise 4 Reread the selection "The Work of the Traditional Healer" carefully. Try to guess the meanings of new words from the context. Use your dictionary only when absolutely necessary. Check your answers to the Getting the Main Ideas exercise. Correct your errors if necessary.

Understanding Reading Structure

The following outline shows the organization of the comparison of the two kinds of medicine in the reading selection.

I.   Traditional Folk Medicine
  A. Theory of Disease
  B. Prevention of Disease
  C. Diagnosis
  D. Cure
II. Modern Scientific Medicine
  A. Cause of Disease
  B. Prevention of Disease
  C. Diagnosis
  D. Cure

exercise 5 The following points are details of comparison from "The Work of the Traditional Healer." Show where they fit into the outline above by writing the appropriate roman numerals (I or II) and letters (A, B, C, or D) on the lines as in the examples. Then look back at the reading to check your answers.

1. _II A_ Disease As a Result of Bacteria or Viruses

2. _I B_ Prevention of Illness with Amulets

3. _____ Giving Blood Tests and Taking X-Rays

4. _____ Songs, Dances, and Prayers

5. _____ Prevention of Sickness Through Healthful Food, Exercise, Relaxation

6. _____ Trances to Contact Supernatural Spirits

7. _____ Disease Caused by Evil Spirits

8. _____ A Tooth-Removing Ceremony

9. _____ Sickness As a Result of Broken Religious Laws

10. _____ Using Dreams and Astrology to Find Causes of Sickness

11. _____ Exorcism and Soul Hunts

12. _____ Use of Massage, Drugs, or Surgery

Various paragraphs in most reading selections provide different kinds of supporting details. Besides points of comparison, these might include steps in a process and reasons.

exercise 6 Complete the following paragraph outlines of the reading selection by adding the kinds of details asked for in parentheses.

A TYPICAL TRIBAL CEREMONY

(Write four steps in a process.)

I. The healer decides which body part a tooth is in. _____

_____

II. He or she calls together friends and relatives for a ceremony. _____

_____

III. _____

_____

IV. _____

_____

THE SUCCESS OF TRADITIONAL HEALERS

(Write five reasons.)

I. _____

_____

II. _____

_____

III. _____

_____

IV. _____

_____

V. _____

_____

Making Inferences

exercise 7

Write T before the statements that are true, according to the information that is stated or implied in the reading. Write F before those that are false. Write I (impossible to know) before the statements that are not proven, disproven, or implied by the reading.

1. _____ Until recently, modern doctors have not respected the work of traditional healers.

2. _____ Traditional healers work to cure more than just a person's body.

3. _____ Both modern physicians and traditional healers try to prevent disease.

4. _____ Amulets are believed to help protect people against disease.

5. _____ Both modern physicians and traditional healers use only natural methods to make a diagnosis.

6. _____ People in tribal societies would prefer a modern physician to a traditional healer.

7. _____ Healing ceremonies that are led by traditional healers are often successful.

8. _____ It is the trance of the ceremonies that cures the patients, not the songs, dances, or prayers.

9. _____ Traditional healers work on solving social problems.

10. _____ Traditional healers' methods have no basis in psychology or science.

exercise 8

Turn back to the Preparing to Read section on page 220 and answer the questions you checked in Exercise 2. Then answer the question in Exercise 3.

Discussing the Reading

activity

In small groups, talk about your answers to these questions.

1. Which facts in the reading make sense to you? Which theories do you believe? Why?
2. In what situations might a traditional healer help more than an urban physician can? In what situations might modern medicine be necessary? Why?
3. What are your personal theories about health, illness, and cures?

PART two

The Mind-Body Relationship

Before You Read

Main Idea and Summary

exercise

For each paragraph below, practice what you have learned about finding the main idea and summarizing paragraphs. First, read each paragraph quickly, without using a dictionary. Mark the information in any way that helps you to understand it. (For example, you could circle the main topic, underline the important words of the main points, and number the supporting details.) Then write the *main idea* in one sentence. To *summarize* the paragraph, write the main idea and add the important details in as few words as possible. (You might need to write more than one sentence.) The *Main idea* and *Summary* parts for paragraph A are given as examples.

The Mind-Body Relationship

A **W**estern doctors are beginning to understand what traditional healers have always known—that the body and mind are inseparable. The World Health Organization, in fact, recommends that in some countries, urban doctors might have greater success if they take a traditional healer with them as they visit patients. Until recently, modern urban physicians healed the body, psychiatrists the mind, and priests or ministers the soul. However, the medical world is now paying more attention to holistic medicine—an approach based on the belief that people's state of mind can make them sick or speed their recovery from sickness.

Main idea: Western doctors are beginning to understand that the body and mind are inseparable.

Summary: Traditional healers have always known that the body and mind are inseparable. Now Western doctors are paying more attention to holistic medicine.

B Several studies show that the effectiveness of a certain drug often depends on the patient's expectations of it. For example, in one recent study, psychiatric patients at a major hospital were divided into two groups. One group was given a tranquilizer to make them calm. The other group received a placebo; the members of the second group did not know, of course, that their "tranquilizer" actually had no medication in it at all. Surprisingly, *more* patients were tranquilized by the placebo than by the actual tranquilizer. It seems likely that a person's hope of a cure and belief in the physician influence the effect of medication.

Main idea: _____

_____

Summary: _____

_____

_____

C   In study after study, there is a positive reaction in almost exactly one-third of the patients taking placebos. How is this possible? How can a *placebo* have an effect on the body? Evidence from a 1977 study at the University of California shows that several patients who received placebos were able to produce their own, natural "drug." That is, as they took the placebos (which they *thought* were actual medication), their brains released enkephalins and endorphins—natural chemicals that act like a drug. Scientists theorize that the amount of these chemicals released by a person's brain quite possibly indicates how much faith the person has in his or her doctor.

Main idea: _____

_____

Summary: _____

_____

_____

D   Another study demonstrates the importance of environment on patients' recovery from sickness. A group of doctors and health experts recently changed a Veterans' Administration hospital from a crowded, colorless building into a bright, cheerful one. Although the doctors expected some improvement, they were amazed at the high rate of recovery. After just three months in this pleasant environment, many patients who had been in the hospital for three to ten *years* were healthy enough to be released and to lead normal lives.

Main idea: _____

_____

Summary: _____

_____

_____

E   It is even possible that there is a connection between a person's mind and the risk of developing cancer. Doctors are learning that people who express their emotions by occasionally shouting when they're angry or crying when they're sad might be healthier than people who suppress their feelings. Scientists at the National Cancer Institute studied a large group of patients who had had successful operations for cancerous growths. The scientists discovered that those in the group whose cancer later returned were people who suppressed their emotions, felt angry but denied their anger, and refused to admit that their illness was serious.

Main idea: _____

_____

Summary: _____

_____

_____

After You Read
Distinguishing Facts from Theories

exercise 1   Which of the following statements have been proven, and which are only beliefs that some people hold? On the line, write *fact* or *theory* for each statement, according to the presentation of the information in the reading selection "The Mind-Body Relationship."

1. _____ Urban doctors have greater success if they take a traditional healer with them as they visit patients.

2. _____ A person's state of mind can make him sick or speed his recovery.

3. _____ The effectiveness of a certain drug often depends on the patient's expectations of it.

4. _____ A person's hope of a cure and belief in the physician influence the effect of medication.

5. _____ In a 1977 study, several patients who took placebos were able to produce their own, natural "drug."

6. _____ The amount of natural chemicals released by a person's brain indicates how much faith the person has in his or her doctor.

7. _____ There is a connection between a person's mind and the risk of developing cancer.

Applying Information

Use paragraphs B, C, D, and E of the reading selection to answer this question: If you are very sick, what three things can *you* do to increase your chances of getting well?

1. _____

2. _____

3. _____

Discussing the Reading

In small groups, talk about your answers to these questions.

1. In your culture, do physicians practice holistic medicine, or do most of them heal just the body?
2. Do you know of any people whose emotions have affected their physical health?

WHAT DO YOU THINK?

Discussing Folk Cures

Each culture has some traditional cures for certain common illnesses or conditions. These are cures which can't be found in a drugstore; instead, people learn them from their parents and grandparents.

1. If there are students from different cultures in your class, move around the room and ask them about traditional cures in their cultures. If all the students in your class are from the same culture, compare your ideas on traditional cures; do these differ from region to region or family to family? Write your answers in the chart on the next page. Then ask your teacher if she or he knows some folk cures from North America. Add any illnesses or conditions to the chart that you want to.

2. After you have filled in the chart, consider the various cures. How are they similar? How are they different? Compare them to the medicine that we find in an urban drugstore. Are there advantages to each, or is one kind better? What do you think?

Folk Cures

Illness/Condition	student: country:	student: country:	student: country:	student: country:
a cold				
a cough				
nausea				
itchy skin				
hiccups				
a headache				
a hangover				

PART three
Building Vocabulary and Study Skills

Categories

exercise

Circle the words in each item that belong in the underlined category.

1. body parts:

target   (tooth)   exorcism   (throat)

2. emotions:

anger   sadness   effect   cure   hatred

3. symptoms of illness:

insomnia   blood   trance   rash

4. things that cause disease:

amulets   virus   bacteria   deep anger

5. methods of diagnosis:

blood test   relaxation   X-ray   stomachache

6. groups of people:

organization   tribe   community   society

7. places to live:

suburbs   village   mosque   solstice

8. types of structures:

pyramid   amulet   cave   monument

9. types of meetings:

evil   spirit   ceremony   celebration

10. words in medicine:

patient   priest   physician   treatment

11. words in religion:

prayer   soul   faith   worship

Word Forms

**exercise** Complete the sentences with the appropriate forms of these base words.

diagnose
treat
√combine
nature
be
effective
tradition
accept

1. In most urban and suburban areas of the world, sick people go to a doctor for treatment .

2. The healer is a _____ of doctor, priest, and psychologist.

3. In _____ village societies, disease is viewed as something outside the world—something _____ .

4. During the _____ , a doctor asks about symptoms.

5. While he or she is in a trance, the healer tries to contact spiritual _____s.

6. Folk medicines are often successful, and scientists are trying to find out the reasons for their _____ .

7. At communal ceremonies, villagers can express their feelings in a socially _____ way.

Word Roots and Affixes

Here are some more word roots and prefixes and their meanings.

prefix	meaning
hyper-	above, beyond
hypo-	beneath, under

word root	meaning
corp	body
derm	skin
gam	marriage
mort	death
ortho	straight, correct
spir	breathe

Without using a dictionary, guess the meaning of each underlined word. Use the list of word roots and affixes. (Look back at the list in Chapter Nine, Part Three on pages 208 and 209 for additional help.)

1. He went to a <u>dermatologist</u> for help with his problem.
   a. person who studies bones
   b. eye doctor
   c. skin doctor
   d. person who helps people with mental problems

2. The <u>mortality</u> rate is very high in that village.
   a. birth
   b. death
   c. marriage
   d. divorce

3. The child began to cry when the doctor took out a <u>hypodermic</u> needle.
   a. large
   b. for use in the stomach
   c. for use on the skin
   d. for use under the skin

4. The little girl is <u>hyperactive</u>.
   a. very quiet, shy
   b. more active than is normal
   c. less active than is usual
   d. having difficulty with breathing

5. He's in the hospital on a <u>respirator</u>.
   a. strict diet
   b. special bed to help his back problems
   c. machine to help him breathe
   d. machine that pumps blood (as the heart does)

6. The physician looked at the <u>corpse</u>.
   a. dead body
   b. amulet
   c. ceremony
   d. rash

7. People in that village believe in <u>polygamy</u>.
   a. many gods
   b. marriage
   c. marriage to more than one person
   d. the necessity of marrying someone from a different village

8. They took their child to an <u>orthodontist</u>.
   a. doctor
   b. dentist
   c. dentist who straightens teeth
   d. doctor who helps people with breathing problems

Improving Reading Skills: Predictions

Because good reading requires an active mind, fluent readers make use of "predictions" about the material they are reading. They try to guess quickly—without thinking about it—what is going to come next.

exercise 1 In each of the following sentences, complete the last word. Work as fast as you can and write your time (the number of seconds it takes you to finish) on the line after each group. Try to improve your time with the second group. The first one is done as an example.

1. You should take care of yourself to prevent ill<u>ness</u> _____ .

2. A healer might give an amulet to his or her pat_____ .

3. A trance is a condition of deep concen_____ .

4. Many patients prefer to be cured by traditional methods rather than by a
   modern physi_____ .

5. Some scientists think that the trance produces healing body
   chemi_____ .

   Time: _____

6. Some natural cures for pain are warm baths and

mass_____ .

7. Some people believe that illness is the result of the hatred of a friend or

rela_____ .

8. The patient felt weak; he didn't have any ener_____ .

9. Some illnesses are emotional, and some are phy_____ .

10. This is a difficult problem; is there any sol_____ ?

Time: _____

exercise **2**   In these sentences, fill in the last word. (There may be more than one correct answer.) Work as fast as you can and write your time (number of seconds) on the line after each group. Try to improve your time with the second group.

1. Disease is usually caused by _____ .

2. In a tribal society, if a man is sick, he may believe that he has broken a

_____ .

3. Both healers and physicians treat _____ .

4. The patient has been feeling terrible; she has bad _____ .

5. Some people believe deeply in _____ .

Time: _____

6. Psychiatrists heal _____ .

7. The doctor gave him a tranquilizer to make him _____ .

8. Environment seems to influence a person's recovery from

_____ .

9. It might be beneficial if we shout when we're _____ .

10. Doctors are learning that it's not good if their patients suppress their

_____ .

Time: _____

Understanding Analogies

As you saw in Chapter Five, some standardized tests have a section on analogy. Many of these have multiple-choice answers. You need to (1) understand the two words that are given, (2) understand the relationship between the two words, and (3) choose the pair of words that has the same relationship.

example: illness: sickness::
- **a.** well:health
- **b.** doctor:physician
- **c.** sleeplessness:symptom
- **d.** disease:condition

The best answer is b because *illness* and *sickness* are both nouns and are synonyms. a is incorrect; these two words have different parts of speech. c is incorrect. The two words are both nouns but not synonyms; sleeplessness is one possible symptom. d is incorrect; both words are nouns, but disease is only one kind of a condition.

exercise Take this practice test. Work as quickly as possible (as you would on an actual test) and don't use a dictonary. Your teacher might decide to time you on this test.

1. art:painting::
- **a.** cosmetics:makeup
- **b.** mosque:building
- **c.** music:jazz
- **d.** statue:artist

2. nomad:migration::
- **a.** doctor:treat
- **b.** patient:sick
- **c.** hunter:follow
- **d.** physician:diagnosis

3. depict:painting::
- **a.** write:book
- **b.** see:photograph
- **c.** watch:movie
- **d.** predict:future

4. exorcism:ceremony::
- **a.** dance:sing
- **b.** amulet:protection
- **c.** symptom:insomnia
- **d.** trance:music

5. rank:military::
- **a.** society:status
- **b.** power:politics
- **c.** status:society
- **d.** politics:power

6. beautiful:pretty::
- **a.** ugly:unattractive
- **b.** thin:slim
- **c.** plump:fat
- **d.** nice:handsome

Reading in the Real World

Scanning for Information
Magazine Articles

Read the following article from *McCall's* magazine and do the exercises that follow. (*Hint:* It's always a good idea to look through the questions *first* and have them in mind as you read.) This article may seem difficult to you, but *don't worry* about the words you don't understand. Instead, concentrate on understanding the main ideas and answering the questions.

Home Remedies Even Doctors Use

The next time you're sick, you might be able to avoid a trip to the doctor's office by simply pulling something out of the refrigerator. Or the kitchen cabinet. Or even the spice rack. More and more studies are finding that certain foods, spices, and other household staples provide effective

5   relief from common health problems. In fact, many physicians, concerned about the overuse of antibiotics and the trend toward treatment overkill for even minor medical problems, are recommending these simple cures. And patients are more than willing to give them a try, considering today's soaring medical costs and shrinking insurance coverage.

10   The treatments here are more than just folklore—all of them come from doctors with decades of experience, and many even boast the kind of scientific credentials usually reserved for prescription medicines. And all are likely to be in your house already. So try one out the next time you or your kids are hit with an everyday illness or injury. But keep in mind

15   that, just like prescription medicines, treatments involving natural substances *can* cause side effects. If you experience any unusual reactions to the therapy, discontinue it immediately.

Baking soda nixes itches.

Adding about 1/4 to 1/2 cup per quart of cool water, or half a box in the

20   bathtub, will often calm down rashes, chicken pox, or poison ivy. You can soak in it or apply it with compresses, says Lorraine Stern, M.D., an associate clinical professor of pediatrics at the University of California, Los Angeles and a pediatrician in practice for 21 years, but be aware that

it may be drying to the skin. These treatments or a paste made from baking soda and water are also effective for insect bites and bee stings.

Ginger quiets queasy stomachs.

If your mother gave you ginger ale for an upset stomach, she was onto something. Ginger has a calming effect on the stomach—a fact verified by a study finding that ginger capsules helped counteract the effects of motion sickness. Most of the grocery store varieties of ginger ale and ginger snaps (cookies) are very light on real ginger, but they may have enough to settle slight queasiness. For a more powerful punch, though, you can boil a few slices of ginger root in about 2 cups of water to make yourself a batch of ginger tea. (Ginger tea is also available at some health food stores.)

Garlic fights colds and flu.

The trade-off here is obvious—the unwelcome scented aftereffects— but studies have confirmed that some of garlic's chemical constituents can kill disease-causing germs. Add two to three cloves per serving to whatever you're making or, for maximum healing power, make this special soup: Toss garlic (again, two to three cloves per serving) and a bit of ginger into a potful of vegetable soup that is heavy on ingredients loaded with vitamins A and C (e.g., carrots, broccoli, spinach, tomatoes, red and green peppers). The latest studies have named vitamins A and C as two of the most effective nutritional infection fighters, and the soup's steam helps clear congestion, covering all approaches on the cold front. To avoid the odor of garlic, try the pill form found in many pharmacies and health food stores.

Acupressure alleviates nausea and pain.

Above your wrist is a point you can press into medical service to relieve nausea, according to Bruce Pomeranz, M.D., a professor of neuro- biology at the University of Toronto. Six studies confirm the effect, although *why* it works is still unclear. Find the groove (long, narrow channel) between the two large tendons on the inside of your wrist that run from the base of the palm up to the elbow. About 2 inches above the wrist, press down hard with a thumb or finger for a minute or two until the spot feels slightly achy. Mild queasiness may be relieved immediately; relief of more intense nausea may require about 20 minutes of repeated pressing.

Another acupressure point—the web of flesh between the thumb and forefinger—seems to moderate pain sensations. Find a spot about an inch into that triangle where you've got muscle, not just skin, and squeeze it

65 | until it aches a bit. Repeat two or three times, or hold the pressure for a few minutes. It's especially effective for relieving pain in the head or neck area but can relieve any pain because it triggers the release of endorphins, the body's natural painkiller.

 **exercise 1**

According to the article, what home remedy (cure) might you try for each of these conditions?

CONDITION   CURE

1. You have a sore throat, watery eyes,   _____
and are having difficulty breathing.

2. You have a queasy (upset) stomach;   _____
i.e., you feel seasick.

3. You have a headache.   _____

4. You have a problem with your skin;   _____
for example, your skin itches because
of an insect bite.

exercise 2

Find words or phrases that mean the same as the following.

1. something (caused by a medicine) that is in addition to the purpose (second paragraph):

_____

2. put something (or yourself) in water or liquid (third paragraph): _____

3. effects (usually unpleasant) that follow another action (fifth paragraph):

_____

4. bacteria (fifth paragraph): _____

5. motion sickness; a stomach problem (two words) (sixth paragraph):

_____ and _____

6. the body's natural painkiller (seventh paragraph): _____

exercise 3

In paragraph A, the writer says that patients are happy to try these home remedies ". . . considering today's *soaring* medical costs and *shrinking* insurance coverage." What do you suppose she's saying about medical costs? In other

words, what can you guess that *soaring* means? _____

_____

What does *shrinking* mean? _____

_____

Going Beyond the Text

Bring to class newspaper and/or magazine articles about medical or health-related issues that interest you. Discuss new vocabulary. Tell the class about the most interesting information.

CHAPTER eleven

The Media

in this chapter

The first selection discusses the history of motion picture technology. You will also learn to read movie reviews in newspapers so that you can choose good movies to go to and stay away from bad ones.

PART one

Movie Magic: Then and Now

Before You Read

Getting Started

Look at the pictures on pages 244 to 246 and discuss them.

1. What is happening in each scene?
2. Which scene happened the furthest in the past? Which happened most recently?
3. Have you seen any of the movies in these pictures?

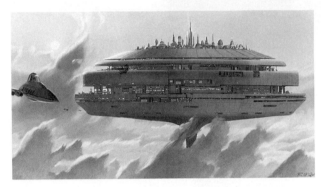

Preparing to Read

exercise 1 Look at the pictures again and then survey the first reading selection. In addition to the subheads, look quickly at the first and last sentences of each paragraph. Then check (√) the following questions that you believe will be discussed in the reading.

1. _____ When did the earliest movies appear?

2. _____ Were there illusions in the first films?

3. _____ How was the movie business different from television?

4. _____ How did people become movie stars?

5. _____ What is the history of film lighting?

6. _____ Why is there so much crime in movies?

7. _____ What was used for blood in black and white movies, and what is used now?

8. _____ How is the computer used in making movies?

9. _____ Why are stars' salaries so high?

10. _____ What are some substitutions that have been used in movie illusions?

11. _____ Who are some of the most famous directors of modern films?

12. _____ What might we expect from movie technology in the future?

exercise 2 As you read the following selection, think about the answer to this question. What are some ways in which motion picture technology has changed?

Read the following selection quickly. Do not use a dictionary. Then do the exercises that follow the reading.

Movie Magic: Then and Now

The Birth of the Motion Picture Industry

The enormous film industry of today had a relatively simple beginning. The first public showing of a motion picture—on May 22, 1891, at Thomas Edison's workshop in New Jersey—consisted of a polite man who bowed to the audience, smiled, waved, and took off his hat. Then in 1895, the Lumière brothers presented their first film; it depicted workers as they left the Lumière factory in France. Soon afterward, in 1896, three films were shown at Koster and Bial's Music Hall in New York City: one of a man walking his dog, another of a train arriving at a station, and a third of a balloon flying in the air. Each film was only about 30 to 90 seconds long; the quality was poor, and the images were jumpy, but these early moving pictures were a great success. They soon led to the creation of longer films (of about ten minutes each), such as George Méliès' *A Trip to the Moon* and Edwin S. Porter's *The Life of an American Fireman* and *The Great Train Robbery,* made between 1902 and 1905. These films, for the first time, told a story, and the motion picture industry was born.

The First Movie Illusions

Since its birth, the movie industry has been filled with illusion—i.e., things that seem to be real but actually aren't. The early movie makers and their audiences were as fascinated by the creation of illusions as film viewers are today. George Méliès, for example, was excited about the camera's ability to create "supernatural" images. He surprised his audience by showing people disappearing or objects flying through the air. His art seemed to be magic! Although the methods used then were very simple, the viewers accepted the images on the screen and believed them. In *The Great Train Robbery,* for instance, there was a lot of shooting; smoke came out of the guns, and men "dropped dead." The audience couldn't *hear* the gunshots because there was no sound at the time. (The first "talking" motion picture—*The Jazz Singer*—didn't appear until 1927.) But even so, women in the audience of *The Great Train Robbery* put their fingers in their ears to shut out the "noise" of the guns. The imagination of the viewers, added to the pictures on the screen, made the illusion seem real.

Film Lighting

The reason that the American film industry moved to southern California early in the twentieth century was simple: the good weather. In the East, it rained, snowed, or was cloudy for several months every year, but in the West, it was sunny year-round. "Inside" scenes were filmed outdoors in "rooms" with only two or three walls, so that the sun could light the scene. Unfortunately, this illusion was a poor one; the light looked exactly like what it was—sunlight—and not like the light inside a building. Nevertheless, when powerful lights came into existence and indoor scenes were actually shot inside, not all the problems were solved. On the one hand, good weather was no longer essential, and movie makers could decide how to use the lighting in a scene. On the other hand, the heat of the huge lights made actors very uncomfortable. Among other problems, it caused ice cream to melt very quickly. Thus, film producers began looking for new solutions to create illusion. In this case, mashed potatoes, which didn't turn to liquid, were used instead of ice cream.

The Appearance of Blood

One of the most common illusions throughout the history of film has been the use of "blood." Because of the popularity of murder mysteries, war stories, horror movies, and westerns, there has always been an enormous amount of blood on the screen. Movie producers were challenged by two problems: *what* to use and *how* to use it. When movies were filmed in black and white, it was possible to use chocolate syrup as a substitute for real blood. These days, in color films, "blood" is a combination of Karo syrup, food dye Red. No. 33, and food dye Yellow No. 5. "How?" is a more difficult problem. In old westerns, when the "bad guy" was shot by the "good guy," he used to hit the place where he had been shot, say, "You got me," and drop to the ground. Though not very realistic, it was essential for the actor to hit himself in this way because "blood" was hidden in a small packet under his shirt. When he did this, the packet would break, and blood would come out through his fingers. These days, however, "bleeding" is a matter of technology. Sometimes, as in *The Godfather,* a performer may be shot over a hundred times! In such cases, the many packets hidden on the victim's body are attached to thin wires which, in turn, are connected to a computer. The computer causes each packet to explode at exactly the right moment.

Substitutions

Movie illusions include a wide variety of substitutions. Instead of letting actors or actresses fall off a building, producers use dummies (large dolls). Stunt people usually take the place of movie stars for the action of dangerous scenes. Instead of paying thousands of people to appear in a scene, movie makers—until recently—have often made use of miniature figures to create the illusion of a crowd. Once, during the filming of *The African Queen,* many mosquitoes were needed in a scene. However, the little insects couldn't be persuaded to perform, so the filmmakers stirred tea leaves around in a glass of clear water and brought the camera up close to the glass. The illusion worked just fine. Some of the most creative substitutions can be found in sets from war movies. In one very early film, *The Battle of Santiago Bay,* miniature ships were put into inch-deep water. Smoke was essential in the battle scene, so the artist's wife offered to smoke a cigarette and an office boy added a cigar. The film was a great success.

Special Effects

Today, of course, such simple methods of creating special effects would not be accepted by audiences who are used to seeing very believable action. Nowadays, especially in science-fiction films, very realistic-looking scenes are made possible by modern technology. Viewers who are fascinated by this "movie magic" often ask how it is produced. For many years in recent times, most of the illusions in these scenes combined the *real* (live performers) with the *imagined* (e.g., miniatures and painted scenes). The actors and actresses were filmed separately from a picture of a spaceship; then a view of stars and planets was shot. After that, miniature figures of creatures from outer space might be filmed, and so on. Afterward, these separate elements were all combined on the same piece of film. In one "simple" 5- to 10-second piece of action, as many as eighteen different elements might have been required.

The Influence of Computers

Today, much of the "magic" on the screen is a result of computer technology. In *Who Killed Roger Rabbit?,* live actors and cartoon characters were combined as they had never been before. *Forrest Gump* allowed long-dead celebrities—such as John Lennon and presidents of the United States—to interact in scenes with modern-day actors. In *Jurassic Park,* people ran for their lives from very realistic-looking dinosaurs. In a TV commercial from the early 1990s, even *cars* at a gas station appeared to dance with amazingly human-like movement. This effect was created by starting with actual dancers who had special sensors attached to different parts of their bodies: wrists, elbows, shoulders, knees, hips, and so on. These sensors recorded each movement and translated the information to a computer program. The cars were then drawn on the computer screen following the exact movements of the dancers.

What's Next?

Computers are also making *virtual reality* experiences possible. With special gloves and headsets, people are able not only to *see* a movie but to *feel* as if they are in the middle of a scene, themselves. Perhaps Aldous Huxley was predicting something like virtual reality in his 1932 novel, *Brave New World.* In this futuristic science-fiction book, the characters go to "feelies" instead of "movies" for entertainment. They sit in theater seats that allow them to see, hear, smell, taste, and feel everything on the screen. When we consider what may soon be possible, we realize how far we have come since that first film of a man smiling, waving, and taking off his hat.

After You Read

Getting the Main Ideas

 Write T on the lines before the statements that are true, according to the reading. Write F before the statements that are false. Write I before the statements that are impossible to know from the reading selection.

1. _____ Thomas Edison made the first motion picture.

2. _____ The first movies had many interesting sound and special effects.

3. _____ Even early movies included illusion.

4. _____ The lighting in early films came from the sun.

5. _____ In early movies, tomato ketchup was used for "blood."

6. _____ To create illusions, movie makers have used dolls, miniatures, and substitutions.

7. _____ Combinations of special effects have been an important part of modern science-fiction movies.

8. _____ Virtual reality is exactly what Aldous Huxley predicted in *Brave New World*.

Guessing Vocabulary from Context

 On the lines, write words or expressions from the reading selection "Movie Magic: Then and Now" that fit these definitions.

1. a small package: *packet* _____

2. people or things taking the place of other people or things: _____

3. large dolls used in movies: _____

4. people who do dangerous things in movies: _____

5. very small: _____

> To understand sentences or paragraphs, it is often enough to know only the general meaning of vocabulary items, rather than the exact definitions.

 On the lines, write the items from the reading that correspond to these general meanings. The number in parentheses indicates the number of possible answers.

1. moving pictures (3): _____

2. words that describe things that seem real but aren't (3): _____

3. kinds of weather (4): _____

4. kinds of food (3): _____

5. people in movies (4): _____

6. a kind of insect (1): _____

7. things to smoke (2): _____

 Reread the selection carefully. Try to guess the meanings of new words from the context. Use your dictionary only when absolutely necessary. Check your answers to the Getting the Main Ideas exercise. Correct your errors if necessary.

Understanding Reading Structure

> Time words often show the relationships between events and their order in time. Here are just a few examples:
>
> | | | |
> |---|---|---|
> | first | next | after that |
> | beginning | later | finally |
> | at present | until now | |

 List the time words from the reading selection "Movie Magic: Then and Now."

_____

_____

_____

exercise 6 Number in order these events in the reading selection.

1. _____ The motion picture industry moved to California.

2. __1__ With the first films that told stories, the movie industry began.

3. _____ A variety of substitutions were added to scenes for the purpose of illusion.

4. _____ Audiences were surprised by simple illusions of flying or disappearing objects.

5. _____ *Virtual reality* became possible.

6. _____ Through technology, separate elements were combined to create special effects.

Match each of the following lists with a paragraph from the reading selection by writing the paragraph's subhead on the line. Then number the events of the list in order.

1. Film Lighting

   a. __3__ Objects were substituted for other objects to solve the problems of hot lights.

   b. __1__ Inside scenes were filmed in sunlight.

   c. __2__ Powerful lights were invented.

2. _____

   a. _____ Movies added sound.

   b. _____ Smoke came out of guns.

   c. _____ "Supernatural images" of objects seemed magical to the audiences.

3. _____

   a. _____ George Méliès made a film about a trip to the moon.

   b. _____ On film, a man walked his dog, a train arrived, and a balloon flew into the air.

   c. _____ A film showed workers as they were leaving a factory.

   d. _____ A man in a film bowed to the audience and took off his hat.

4. (two subtopics) _____

   a. _____ Live actors interacted with cartoon characters.

   b. _____ Virtual reality experiences became possible.

   c. _____ Aldous Huxley wrote *Brave New World*.

Turn back to the Preparing to Read section on page 247 and answer the questions you checked in Exercise 1. Then answer the question in Exercise 2.

Discussing the Reading

In small groups, talk about your answers to these questions.

1. What is the oldest movie that you can remember seeing? How was it different from movies today?
2. What are some movie illusions other than those talked about in the reading? Can you guess how they were created?
3. Which do you prefer—old movies or modern ones? Why?
4. Are there theaters in your city that show mainly old movies?

PART two

Movie Reviews: The Critics' Choice

Before You Read
Skimming for Main Ideas

Readers often glance at material quickly before they read it, to get a general idea of what it is about.

As quickly as you can (try to do this in about 30 seconds), look over the following four newspaper articles. Then write the appropriate article letter next to the corresponding description.

1. _____ a positive review of a science-fiction movie

2. _____ a negative review of a mystery film

3. _____ a negative review of a science-fiction movie

4. _____ a positive review of a mystery film

exercise 2   Quickly read each paragraph again, without using a dictionary. Mark the information in any way that helps you understand it. Then use the information that you marked to write a summarizing statement.

Movie Reviews: The Critics' Choice

A

A CLASSIC

Murder, She Says is a classic mystery that will be received most enthusiastically by people who enjoy folk culture. The film is like a traditional folk story, one that has been told and retold through the centuries by expert storytellers. Like a folk story, *Murder, She Says* contains little that is new or surprising. Instead, it has all the elements of the best whodunits—predictable elements, to be sure, but the beauty of this movie lies in the *way* the story is presented. The photography is good, the music is exciting, and the special effects are realistic but do not overpower the film itself. Best of all, the acting is wonderful. The stars succeed in being believable and in making their art look easy

B

MUSEUM PIECE

It's easy to predict the ending of *Murder, She Says* within the first fifteen minutes of the movie. In fact, nothing in this film is surprising. It is, of course, a whodunit. An archeologist is murdered deep inside a Mesoamerican pyramid, and absolutely everyone in the film—his assistant, his wife, his brother, another archeologist, as well as the traditional healer of a nearby village—has a good reason to want him dead. A well-known detective is asked to come and solve the mystery, and, in the end, the murderer is found to be the only person who did not act like a killer. Every character in *Murder, She Says* is a stereotype from the old-fashioned movies of the '40s. We've seen it all before, again and again. This film belongs in a museum, not a theater. There is nothing unique or creative about it—no reason for even making

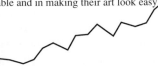

C

PIX EFX WOW 'EM

Astrostation XZ901 is the latest science-fiction film to come out of Zonar Studios. It presents a fascinating view of the universe in the year 2103, when spaceships are as common as jet planes, solar power is the only kind of energy, and science is the only religion. Scientists are the priests of this future world, and satellites are their churches. Human beings have enormous physical strength and mental power, but they have lost the ability to feel any emotion. All feelings—sadness, happiness, nostalgia, excitement, fear, etc.—are considered to be taboo and are carefully exorcised in ceremonies which include the use of chemicals and X-rays. More important than the story, however, is that *Astrostation XZ901* offers the most exciting, believable effects that have ever been seen on a movie screen. Spaceships zoom realistically toward the audience, human beings

D

XZ901 DISAPPEARS IN EFX

The biggest disappointment of the year is Zonar Studios' *Astrostation XZ901*. A huge amount of money has been spent on technology, but the movie is still not a success. It offers almost no acting, no story, and no ideas. The performers cannot move the audience emotionally because they have nothing to say and no ability to say it. The main character (played—badly—by Kurt Cute) is laughable and his co-star, Suzanne Slick, has the personality of a mosquito. With its total absence of value, the whole film consists of special effects that have no purpose; these shots cannot affect the audience in any way because there is no *reason* for them. This enormous failure is another typical case of the issue of expensive film illusion to try to hide the fact that the film makers have nothing to say.

After You Read
Distinguishing Facts from Opinions

Even in readings that are *fiction* (not real), there is information that can be considered *fact* (true according to what is stated or implied) and statements that are the *opinions* of the writer.

example: *Astrostation XZ901,* made by Zonar Studios, is a purposeless film consisting of nothing more than badly presented special effects.

(*Facts:* The movie *Astrostation XZ901* was made by Zonar Studios. It contains special effects. *Opinions:* The film has no purpose. It contains nothing of value, and the special effects are badly presented.)

exercise 1 On the short lines, write F before the statements that are *facts,* according to what is stated or implied in the reading. Write O before the statements that are (or may be) the *opinions* of the writers of the articles. The first two are done as examples.

MURDER, SHE SAYS

1. __F__ *Murder, She Says* is about an archeologist who is murdered.

2. __O__ This film belongs in a museum.

3. _____ In the movie, the archeologist's assistant was one person who had a good reason to want the archeologist to die.

4. _____ The elements of this mystery have appeared in many other films.

5. _____ The movie has music and special effects.

6. _____ Because there is nothing new or surprising in it, audiences will be bored.

ASTROSTATION XZ901

7. _____ *Astrostation XZ901* is a science-fiction film.

8. _____ There are spaceships, scientists, and X-rays in the movie.

9. _____ The characters in the film have lost the ability to feel emotion.

10. _____ The actors and actresses who starred in the film have lost the ability to think or express their ideas.

11. _____ The film has no meaning because feelings cannot be exorcised in ceremonies.

12. _____ The special effects are fascinating.

13. _____ The stars of the film are not very effective.

14. _____ Special effects are expensive.

15. _____ Movie studios should not spend much money on special effects.

Discussing the Reading

activity In small groups, talk about your answers to these questions.

1. Do you watch movie reviews on TV or listen to them on the radio? Do you read them in the newspaper? Why or why not?

2. What effect do you think reviews have on the success of the movies they describe?

3. If you see the movie, do you usually agree or disagree with the opinions of the reviewer?

4. Do you think that movie reviews are good or bad for the motion picture industry? Why?

PART three

Building Vocabulary and Study Skills

Hyphenated Words

Hyphens (-) have several meanings. For instance, a hyphen can replace the word *to*.

example: Each film was only 30–90 seconds long. (30–90 = 30 to 90; i.e., between 30 and 90 seconds)

Hyphens often connect word parts, especially of adjectives.

example: In the West, there is <u>year-round</u> sunshine. (<u>Year-round</u> means "throughout the year.")

exercise 1 Complete the sentences with the missing hyphenated words as in the example. Choose from these:

part-time	inch-deep	up-to-date
self-discipline	one-third	well-known
X-rays	old-fashioned	realistic-looking

1. This mystery takes place in a hospital. A doctor kills patients by taking

   <u>X-rays</u> .

2. When performers become famous, they do not forget their difficult pasts.

   One _____ actor friend of mine, for example, remembers

   that he used to spend about _____ of each day looking for

   work. He had to take many _____ jobs in fields other than

   entertainment. Acting is difficult work that requires a lot of

   _____ .

3. In the past, illusions were created simply; in one war movie, for instance,

   miniature ships were put in bowls of _____ water.

   Nowadays, however, audiences expect that _____ special

   effects will be created by _____ technology. They are no

   longer satisfied with simple, _____ stories and good

   acting.

Improving Reading Skills

To be a good reader, it is not necessary to understand exactly every word or even every sentence of a selection. In fact, good readers usually accept some amount of uncertainty when they read; i.e., they decide which words and sentences are essential for understanding the main ideas and important details. Instead of worrying about the other elements of the selection, they then go on to other, more important material.

The Summer House (selected theaters). Wry, delightful British comedy starring a radiant Jeanne Moreau as a half-Egyptian, half-English Tallulah Bankhead type who descends upon the household of an old friend (Julie Walters) whose daughter (newcomer Lena Headey) is about to make a disastrous marriage. With Joan Plowright as Walters' wise and formidable neighbor. (K.T.) (1:20)

example: What is important about a movie review? Perhaps the name of the film, the main actors, the type of film (comedy, documentary, action, drama, romance, science fiction, or musical), something about the story, and the opinion of the critic (the person who wrote the review). In the review above, we find the following information:

Title:	*The Summer House*
Actors:	Jeanne Moreau, Julie Walters, Joan Plowright
Type of film:	comedy
Story:	a woman visits an old friend whose daughter is about to make a disastrous marriage
Opinion of the critic:	good ("delightful")

exercise

Because they were written for a big-city newspaper, the following movie reviews contain vocabulary that may seem difficult to nonnative speakers of English. Nevertheless, it is not necessary to understand every word or sentence to get the meaning of the reviews. Underline the words and phrases that seem important. Then answer the questions about each movie.

1. What is the title of this film?_____

Who are some of the actors?_____

_____

What type of film is it?_____

What is it about?_____

What is the critic's opinion?_____

Tombstone (R, general release). Overlong Western about the Earps, Clantons and the Gunfight at the O.K. Corral. Some stirring action but mostly aggressively unbelievable. Kurt Russell heads the cast as Wyatt Earp. Sam Elliott, Val Kilmer, Dana Delany, Powers Boothe

Interactions II • Reading

> **Twogether** (Times-rated: Mature, Monica 4-Plex). Andrew Chiaramonte's engaging love story, uncommonly reflective as well as romantic and sensual, could prove to be a sleeper. Nick Cassavetes and Brenda Bakke are its exciting stars. (K. T.) (2:02)

2. What is the title of this film? _____

   Who is the director? _____

   Who are the actors? _____

   What type of film is it? _____

   What is the critic's opinion? _____

> ★ **Visions of Light** (Monica 4-Plex, Saturday-Sunday at 11 a.m.) This documentary on the art and craft of cinematography does more than overflow with some of the most gorgeous images in the history of American film: it successfully attempts to give directors of photography their rightful place as prime creators. (Turan) (1:30)

3. What is the title of this film? _____

   What type of film is it? _____

   What is the critic's opinion? _____

> ★ **What's Love Got to Do With It** (R, selected theaters). A high-energy compendium of spectacular music, vigorous acting and clichéd situations, rock star Tina Turner's life story has been adroitly tailored to fit the glossy, audience-pleasing contours of the show-biz biopic. Powered by the energy of Tina's (and ex-husband Ike's) music, the films' biggest assets are show-stopping performances by Angela Basset (Oscar nominee for actress) and Laurence Fishburne (Oscar nominee for actor) as the unhappy couple. You may not respect this film, but enjoying it is inevitable. (Turan).

4. What is the title of this film? _____

   What type of film is it? _____

   What is it about? _____

   What is the critic's opinion? _____

Going Beyond the Text

activity

Bring to class the movie section of a local newspaper. Discuss the new vocabulary. Then choose one film that interests you and summarize the review for the class. Go to see the movie and tell the class about it.

Figurative Language

In Chapter Six, you saw that some words have figurative meanings in addition to their basic, literal meanings. In the phrase "the *birth* of the motion picture industry," for example, *birth* is a noun that means "beginning."

On vocabulary and reading tests, *all* the answers for an item might be synonyms or near-synonyms of the underlined word in the sentence. Read the sentence carefully and choose the answer that has the same meaning of the word as it is used in that particular context.

exercise For each underlined word or expression below, circle the letter of the appropriate meaning for its context.

1. The actress <u>melted</u> into the arms of her lover when he arrived alive from the war.
   a. disappeared
   b. became liquid
   c. hugged and kissed
   d. fell; fainted

2. I don't like <u>syrupy,</u> old-fashioned love stories.
   a. with sugar and water
   b. sentimental
   c. containing a thick liquid
   d. medicinal

3. They <u>shot</u> that movie in just two months.
   a. fired a weapon
   b. filmed
   c. saw
   d. went first

4. "Get out of here and never come back!" the actor <u>exploded</u>.
   a. shouted in anger
   b. blew up like a bomb
   c. said
   d. was angry

5. That documentary <u>brought to light</u> the problems of refugees.
   a. was filmed outside, under the sun
   b. took to other countries
   c. made known
   d. was made with powerful lights

Reading in the Real World

Scanning for Information
Movie Listings

Before viewers go to the movies, they often check the entertainment section of a newspaper to find out what is available. Besides names of movies, theaters, producers or directors, and performers, this guide from an urban newspaper contains "mini-reviews" of the films.

exercise 1

Movies in the United States are given *ratings:* G, PG, PG-13, R, and NC-17. These ratings are a guide for parents who might not want their children to see a movie with too much sex or violence. Look at the explanation before the first mini-review on the top of page 262 to find out what these mean; then write the meanings on the lines.

G = _____

PG = _____

PG-13 = _____

R = _____

NC-17 = _____

exercise 2

Scan the movies on pages 262 to 265. Then, on the chart below, write the rating for each film and check (√) its type.

movie	rating	western	comedy	drama	romance	action
Cabin Boy	PG-13		√			
Cool Runnings						
The Fugitive						
Geronimo						
Gunmen						
In the Name of the Father						
The Piano						

■ *Capsule reviews are by Kenneth Turan (Turan), Peter Rainer (P.R.), Kevin Thomas (K.T.) and Michael Wilmington (M.W.). Films considered especially noteworthy by a majority of the reviewers are designated with a ★.*

■ *Ratings are by the Motion Picture Assn. Categories: (G) for general audiences; (PG) parental guidance urged because of material possibly unsuitable for children; (PG-13) parents are strongly cautioned to give guidance for attendance of children younger than 13; (R) restricted, younger than 17 admitted only with parent or adult guardian; (NC-17) no one younger than 17 admitted.*

★ **The Accompanist** (PG, Music Hall, through Tue.). An assured and psychologically acute French film about the complex relationship between a diva and her pianist that is as carefully done and beautifully mounted as the operatic pieces by Berlioz, Massenet, Strauss and the like that make up the score. Claude Miller deftly directs, and Romane Bohringer, the hottest new French actress, gives a crack performance. (Turan) (Running Time: 1 hour, 50 minutes)

Ace Ventura: Pet Detective (PG-13, general release). Every body movement and facial tic of Jim Carrey (of "In Living Color" fame) is so broadly exaggerated here, he makes goofy Jim Varney look like stoic Charles Bronson by comparison. A movie centered around as manic a presence as Carrey's sounds like it could be hell, but his starring debut proves surprisingly capable of provoking unexpected giggle fits. The movie is uneven, but his cartoonish inhumanness is nearly heroic. (Chris Willman) (1:28)

★ **The Age of Innocence** (PG, general release). The fashionable world of 1870s New York City as depicted in Edith Wharton's Pulitzer Prize-winning novel and seen by director Martin Scorsese; starring Michelle Pfeiffer, Daniel Day-Lewis and Winona Ryder. Scorsese's adaptation (co-written with Jay Cocks) is beautifully done, polished, elegant and completely cinematic. It is also a bit distant, a film that doesn't wear its feelings on its sleeve; but given the effects it's after, that would be counterproductive. Nominated for five Academy Awards including supporting actress (Ryder). (Turan) (2:13)

The Air Up There (PG, general release). Perhaps the first film to be high concept both literally and metaphorically, this story of an American college coach (Kevin Bacon) determined to recruit a 6-foot-10 African basketball player is a feeble and simplistic attempt at an adventure comedy. Narrative clichés and bathroom humor keep it very far from the final four. (Turan). (1:46)

Baraka (Times-rated: Mature, Sunset 5, Sunday at 11 a.m.). Ron Fricke's awesomely beautiful visionary collage, filmed in 24 countries in Todd AO 70mm, urges a return to timeless spiritual values in salvaging our endangered planet. Affecting but too similar to "Koyannisqatsi," which Fricke photographed, co-wrote and co-edited. (K.T.) (1:37)

Beethoven's 2nd (PG, general release). It's just as funny and appealing as "Beethoven" the first. This time the messy Saint Bernard falls in love, which could mean more dogs to rile Charles Grodin's nice but fussy family man. Debi Mazar is hilarious as the nasty owner of Missy, the object of Beethoven's desires. A family film that can actually be enjoyed by the entire family. (K.T.) (1:26)

Blank Check (PG, general release). Lame Disney kids' film about a tyke who finds a blank check and uses it to shower himself with presents before the inevitable moralizing sets in. (P.R.) (1:34)

Blink (R, selected theaters). The best—the only—reason to check out this muddled thriller is for Madeleine Stowe's extraordinary performance as a formerly blind woman who regains her sight and witnesses (sort of) a murder. It's a first-rate piece of acting in a second-rate shocker. Aidan Quinn, as a police detective, looks like he's prepping to be Columbo's nephew. (P.R.) (1:46)

Blue (R, selected theaters). Polish director Krzysztof Kieslowski, working with the shattering Juliette Binoche and haunting composer Zbigniew Preisner, has turned a conventional story of a woman's search for meaning after tragedy unhinges her life into an intensely emotional display of virtuoso filmmaking. Dense with feeling, this is a project in which no shot is ordinary and no moment taken for granted. (Turan) (1:40)

Body Snatchers (R, selected theaters). Director Abel Ferrara has reimagined and reinvigorated the classic science fiction story about sinister pods from outer space who get you when you sleep, using the best of special effects talent and cool directorial skill to turn out a creepy and unsettling piece of genre filmmaking that knows how to scare you and isn't afraid to try. The most adult horror film in quite some time. (Turan) (1:30)

Cabin Boy (PG-13, general release). Chris Elliott has developed such a wonderfully perverse comic persona that he's earned a good movie vehicle. This isn't it, not by a nautical mile. There's a constant aura of bemusement in this loose parody of old coming-of-age-at-sea pictures, but surprisingly few actual gags written in to make good on the promise. Ex-Elliott boss David Letterman contributes a hilarious cameo early on, helping the movie peak in its first 15 minutes. (Chris Willman) (1:20)

Car 54, Where Are You? (PG-13, general release). Dumb movie about dumb cops, based on the '60s TV series and on the shelf for two years, where it should have remained. David Johansen, John C. McGinley, Fran Drescher and Rosie O'Donnell star. (K.T.) (1:29)

Cool Runnings (PG, general release). Blithe, infectious comedy with serious underpinnings about a Jamaican bobsledding team competing in the Olympics and coached by John Candy. A beautifully crafted film for all ages. With Leon, Doug E. Doug, Rawle D. Lewis and Malik Yoba. (K.T.) (1:37)

Death Wish V: The Face of Death (R, general release). Charles "Vengeance Is Mine, Sayeth the Bored" Bronson—now in his 70s—returns, more absurdly stoic than ever, for this snoozer 20th-anniversary sequel. Once again, bad things happen to good Bronson mates, though this time his fiancee (Lesley-Anne Down) is the victim of a crime lord (Michael Parks), causing the hero to track down and eliminate the New York Mafia, all six of 'em. (Chris Willman) (1:31)

262

Faraway, So Close! (PG-13, Music Hall, through Tue.). An allegory on the reunification of Germany and the sacrifice involved in achieving it. Wim Wenders' sequel to his 1987 "Wings of Desire" operates on many levels as an angel (Otto Sander) becomes human—only to discover how terrible that condition can be. The film is slow to take off but soars when it does. With a cast that includes Horst Buccholz, Peter Falk, Lou Reed and Mikhail Gorbachev. (K.T.) (2:20)

★ **Farewell My Concubine** (R, selected theaters). A gorgeous, intoxicating epic, set in the exotic world of Chinese opera and covering more than half a century of Chinese history. This Chen Kaige-directed film, the deserving co-winner of the Palme d'Or at Cannes, marks the coming of age of Chinese cinema artistically and politically. Starring Leslie Cheung and Gong Li as rivals for the affection of the same man, it features exceptional performances and superb visuals to complement its stately pace. Oscar nominee for foreign film. (Turan) (2:36)

★ **The Fugitive** (PG-13, general release). Dr. Richard Kimble (Harrison Ford) never stops to catch his breath, and neither would you if fearsome U.S. Marshal Sam Gerard (Tommy Lee Jones) was on your trail. A crisp and jolting melodrama that screws the tension pitilessly tight, director Andrew Davis' superadrenalized version of the old TV show about the innocent man simultaneously fleeing the law and trying to find his wife's murderer is one movie that more than delivers on expectations. Nominated for seven Academy Awards including picture and supporting actor (Jones). (Turan) (2:07)

Geronimo: An American Legend (PG-13, general release). The latest film from director Walter Hill, a handsome and respectful Western that wants to echo and modernize the myths of the past, is most impressive as a physical piece of filmmaking but difficult to warm up to on an emotional level. Wes Studi is especially fierce as the legendary Apache war chief who hated to be fenced in and forced the Army to chase him all over the Southwest. (Turan) (1:55)

The Getaway (R, general release). Roger Donaldson does a perfectly respectable job directing the holdups and shoot outs, but the best reason to see this remake of the violent Sam Peckinpah film are Alec Baldwin and Kim Basinger standing in for Steve McQueen and Ali MacGraw as partners in love and crime. Featuring romantic scenes that will make interesting viewing for future grandchildren, these two have a chemistry that brings a pleasant buzz to the proceedings. (Turan). (1:55)

Golden Gate (R, selected theaters). "M. Butterfly's" David Henry Hwang throws light on the persecution of Chinese Americans by the FBI during the McCarthy Era only to drown his important subject in an increasingly ludicrous, soap opera-style love story. With Matt Dillon, Joan Chen. (K.T.) (1:32)

Grumpy Old Men (PG-13, general release). Walter Matthau and Jack Lemmon play a pair of long-time feuding friends who square off over the same woman (Ann-Margret). It's a cantankerous romp without much wit or point. (P.R.) (1:47)

Gunmen (R, selected theaters). Numbskull exploitation of violence, a murky, stale action picture teaming Mario Van Peebles and Christopher Lambert in a quest to locate a fortune in drug funds in a fictional South American country. (K.T.) (1:31)

★ **Hard-Boiled** (Times-rated: Mature, Sunset 5, Fridays-Saturdays, midnight). This film from veteran Hong Kong action director John Woo, a filmmaker who never leaves you begging for more, shows you why he has been embraced both by fickle critics and the financiers of Hollywood. One of the premier orchestrators of large-scale mayhem ever to fill a screen, Woo's carnivals of carnage are as close to pure cinema as anything on the market today. The director's cut. (Turan) (2:12)

Heaven and Earth (R, selected theaters). In his third film on Vietnam, Oliver Stone's point of view (that of nearly four decades of cataclysmic life experience for a Vietnamese woman) is different, but his overwrought and insistent storytelling style remains unchanged. Although the passion and verve Stone brings to filmmaking are enviable, one wishes his hectoring style left more room for trusting the audience. (Turan) (2:20)

★ **Highway Patrolman** (Times-rated Mature, Nuart). Finest film yet from "Repo Man" and "Sid and Nancy's" Alex Cox, a classic odyssey involving a young Mexican highway patrolman's coming of age under severe testing of the spirit. A beautiful, gritty, superbly structured film—in Spanish with English subtitles—in the manner of John Ford and John Huston. With the slight but formidable Roberto Sosa in the title role. (K.T.) (1:44)

House Party 3 (R, general release). Hair of the dog that bit hip-hop fans? No, this holdover is more like a hip-hop hangover, rendering the first film's great fun four years ago as blurrily remembered as a drunken blackout. A few up-and-coming black comics liven up the party in supporting roles, but this time Kid 'N Play are underwhelming, the stereotypes are overwhelming and the big gags uniformly fall flat. (Chris Willman) (1:33)

I'll Do Anything (PG-13, citywide). Part romantic comedy, part skewering of Hollywood, part tribute to actors and part prickly father-daughter relationship, the first film by writer-director James L. Brooks in seven years is too many parts in search of a whole. Funny, well-acted (especially by Nick Nolte, Albert Brooks and newcomer Whittni Wright) and filled with laugh-out-loud moments though it is, it is a triumph of individual parts that falls short of overall satisfaction. (Turan) (1:55)

★ **IMAX Films** (Times-rated Family, IMAX Theater, Museum of Science and Industry, (213) 744-2014). **Blue Planet.** The technology behind this IMAX documentary, shot aboard the space shuttle and around the globe, is so extraordinary it may knock most audiences breathless. Director Ben Burtt and writer-editor Toni Myers' film have some strong pro-conservation ideas that lend meaning and impact to the potent images. (M.W.) **The Discoverers.** The latest IMAX presentation takes off from Daniel Boorstin's book about pathfinders throughout history with big-screen images of Isaac Newton, Magellan and others interspersed with footage of modern-day scientists and adventurers. Despite some World's Fair movie blandness, the vistas are great. (P.R.) **Fires of Kuwait.** This Oscar-nominated IMAX documentary, directed and shot by David Douglas, gives us amazing sights, staggering sounds. A record of the unprecedented joint international effort to battle hundreds of blazing oil-well fires left after Iraq's Kuwait invasion. (M.W.) **Grand Canyon: The Hidden Secrets.** The unprecedented scope and intimacy of Reed Smoot's cinematography makes this film a great travelogue. **Chronos.** Of all the IMAX movies, Ron Fricke's New Age travelogue, obviously inspired by "Koyaanisqatsi," which Fricke photographed, is the most ambitious, conceptually and artistically. In every way, it's a genuinely original feast for the eyes and senses. You're unlikely to see a more beautiful movie all year. (M.W.)

★ **In the Name of the Father** (R, selected theaters). The crack creative team responsible for "My Left Foot"—director Jim Sheridan and star Daniel Day-Lewis—combine again for this crackling politically charged melodrama based on the true story of an Irishman falsely accused of a murderous bombing. Besides steamrolling the audience with the power of polemical filmmaking, "Father" adds the emotional truth of a moving father-son relationship. Nominated for seven Academy Awards including picture, director, actor (Lewis) and supporting actor Peter Postlethwaite. (Turan) (2:07)

Intersection (general release, R). A dithering romantic drama about a self-absorbed dolt of a husband going through yet another mid-life crisis, this Mark Rydell-directed film has a glamorous cast (Richard Gere, Sharon Stone, Lolita Davidovich) but no real idea of how to involve an audience. (Turan) (1:40)

Iron Will (PG, general release). A charming live-action fairy tale set in 1917 about a boy, his dogs, and a darn tough sled race, this is sweet and sentimental family filmmaking of a kind that Walt himself would have loved. Mackenzie Astin is perfectly cast as the charmingly innocent, physically fit hero, director Charles Haid has directed with appropriate simplicity, and you've never seen a happier group of mushing huskies. (Turan) (1:49)

Jurassic Park (PG-13, general release). The poor little rich kid of the summer of '93 movies. Enormous amounts of money and attention were expended on making the film's half-dozen dinosaur species awfully impressive (though much too intense for small children), but very little was done to make any of the puny human beings equally involving. In fact, when the big guys leave the screen, you'll be tempted to leave with them. (Turan) (2:07)

★ **Like Water for Chocolate** (R, selected theaters). One of the most sensuous and visually alluring Mexican films in years. Writer Laura Esquivel's adaptation of her century-spanning period novel, directed by husband Alfonso Arau, is a 10-course feast of magic realism: a rapt tale of a cursed upper-class family whose sexual repressions are exorcised in sumptuous banquets, while lovers wait a lifetime for a moment of bliss. There's just one word for it: scrumptious. (M.W.) (1:53)

Mrs. Doubtfire (PG-13, general release). Robin Williams can't help but be funny in this situation born in high-concept heaven: divorced dad disguises himself as a nanny to spend more time with his kids. But the rest of the film, although unobjectionable enough, underlines Williams' recent desire to appear in warm, cuddly and terminally bland motion pictures. (Turan) (2:08)

★ **Much Ado About Nothing** (PG-13, selected theaters). The crowning glory of this high-spirited version of Shakespeare's romantic comedy of lovers at cross-purposes is that it gives us Kenneth Branagh (who also directed) and Emma Thompson, the English-speaking world's reigning acting pair, performing at the top of their game. Also starring Denzel Washington, Michael Keaton, Keanu Reeves and Robert Sean Leonard, "Much Ado" is a model of popular Shakespeare, enormously entertaining

without a note of condescension. (Turan) (1:51)

My Father, the Hero (PG, general release). Gerard Depardieu is enjoyable trying to get his mouth around the English language in this otherwise tepid farce about a 14-year-old on vacation with her dad (Depardieu) who pretends he's her lover to get a boy jealous. Smarmy premise. (P.R.) (1:46)

My Girl 2 (PG, general release). Only for those who really enjoyed "My Girl." Anna Chlumsky is once again the adorable malcontent who, in this sequel, goes in search of The Mother She Never Knew. (P.R.) (1:42)

My Life (PG-13, general release). Written and directed by "Ghost" screenwriter Bruce Joel Rubin. It attempts to deal with big picture issues like life and death in a tale of an L.A. adman (Micheal Keaton) who is dying of cancer as his wife (Nicole Kidman) prepares for the birth of their first child. If this sounds glib, manipulative and sappy, you have no idea. (Turan) (1:52)

★ **Naked** (Times-rated Adult, Sunset 5, Goldwyn Pavilion). An astonishing character study and a double winner at Cannes (best director for Mike Leigh, best actor for David Thewlis). This story of a sullen drifter who descends into as hellish a London as Dickens ever imagined is an attempt to stretch the emotional boundaries of truth on film as far as they will go. Painful to sit through at times, but unlike anything else you're likely to see. (Turan) (2:12)

Nothing but a Man (Times-rated Mature, Monica 4-Plex Saturdays-Sundays at 11 a.m.). Revival of Michael Roemer and Robert Young's extraordinary depiction, warm but unflinching and critical, of what it's like to be black in America. Superb performances by Ivan Dixon and Abbey Lincoln as newlyweds beleaguered in a small Southern town. With Julius Harris, Gloria Foster. (K.T.) (1:32)

Once a Cop (Times-rated: Mature, Monica 4-Plex). Lively Hong Kong martial arts movie, while entertaining, might have been more involving had the romance between a top Beijing cop (Michelle Khan) and her colleague-turned-crook (Yu Rong-Guang) had as much screen time as the spectacular action sequences. (K.T.) (1:41)

Orlando (PG-13, Monica 4-Plex, Friday-Saturday midnight, Saturday-Sunday 11 a.m.). Elegant and beautifully assured visually, this if-looks-could-kill version of Virginia Woolf's time-travel fantasy starts out strongly, with Quentin Crisp delightful as Queen Elizabeth I, but writer-director Sally Potter's themes of the arbitrariness of sexual roles and the price of sexual discrimination are presented in a way that is more hollow and artificial than emotionally involving. (Turan) (1:33)

The Pelican Brief (PG-13, general release). Although it's taken from a thriller by John Grisham and stars Julia Roberts and Denzel Washington, this story of the aftermath of two Supreme Court assassinations is never more than sporadically exciting. Especially when compared to the better-acted film version of Grisham's "The Firm," this is more fizzle than sizzle. (Turan) (2:21)

A Perfect World (PG-13, general release). With Kevin Costner as a con on the run with a 7-year-old hostage and director Clint Eastwood co-starring as the man on his tail, this chase movie ought to be less lethargic than it is. Costner gives his most affecting performance to date, but a dose of the Geritol Eastwood's character prefers would be a good idea all around. (Turan) (2:17)

Philadelphia (PG-13, general release). Nothing is so fatal to effective drama as the air of do-goodism that hangs over Hollywood's first attempt to deal with the AIDS crisis. Tom Hanks plays a high-powered lawyer who feels he's been fired because of the disease, and Denzel Washington co-stars as the initially homophobic lawyer who takes his case. Not intended to be subtle, with the good and bad guys clearly labeled, this is mainstream socially conscious filmmaking that is not worried about sacrificing nuance to make its points. Nominated for five Academy Awards including actor (Hanks). (Turan) (1:59)

★ **The Piano** (R, selected theaters). Using Holly Hunter and Harvey Keitel in ways never seen before, writer-director Jane Campion has given a sweepingly romantic 19th-Century tale an almost avant-garde edge. In telling the story of Ada, a mute arranged bride who comes to primitive 1852 New Zealand with her piano and powerfully affects the lives of Keitel and Sam Neill, Campion shows herself to have a command of the visual and the emotional that is fearless and profound. Winner of two prizes at Cannes, and deservedly so. Nominated for eight Academy Awards, including picture, director, actress (Hunter) and supporting actress (Anna Paquin) (Turan) (2:01)

★ **The Remains of the Day** (PG, general release). Anthony Hopkins and Emma Thompson turn an unspoken relationship between two people who refuse to acknowledge even the existence of emotional attachments into the year's most moving tandem performance. Created by the team (director James Ivory, co-producer Ismail Merchant, screenwriter Ruth Prawer Jhabvala) responsible for "Howards End," this version of Kazuo Ishiguro's Booker Prize-winning novel about a butler and housekeeper in 1930s England is a beautifully melancholy piece of work, a fine romance, as the song goes, with no kisses. Nominated for eight Academy Awards including picture, director actor (Hopkins) and actress (Thompson). (Turan) (2:14)

Romeo Is Bleeding (R, general release). (rating, location). Choked by style, this would-be avant-garde *film noir* is graced by a tip-top villainess played by Lea Olin. She's the only reason to wade through the gore and the hyperstylistics. Co-stars Gary Oldman as a cop playing both sides of the fence. (P.R.) (1:53)

Saviors of the Forest (unrated, weekend mornings at the Monica 4-Plex). This self-consciously irreverent documentary follows two director-cameramen who head down to Ecuador to take a look at the decimation of the rain forests. Their overly loose narrative does a decent enough job of making educational agitprop user-friendly, but the "saviors" don't have quite the wits to make good on their aspirations toward making the "Roger & Me" of environmentalism. (Chris Willman) (1:38).

★ **The Scent of Green Papaya** (selected theaters). This delicate, evocative film, Vietnam's first official selection for the best foreign language film Oscar, is a beautiful memory film, an idealized tribute to the spirit of that country's pre-war days and a culture whose concern for textures, colors, tastes and smells turned everyday life into a complete aesthetic experience. Oscar nominee for foreign film. (Turan) (1:44)

★ **Schindler's List** (R, general release). A most unlikely director, Steven Spielberg, tells the quietly devastating story of the most unlikely of Holocaust heroes, Oskar Schindler, a convivial sensualist, gambler and war profiteer who rescued 1,100 Jews and ended up the only Nazi Party member to be buried in Jerusalem's Mt. Zion cemetery. Put together with care, emotion and, most important, restraint, this is as good a film on the Holocaust as we are likely to get. Nominated for 12 Academy Awards, including picture, director, actor (Neeson) and supporting actor (Ralph Fiennes) (Turan) (3:15)

 **exercise 3** What country is each of these films probably from?

1. *The Scent of Green Papaya:* _____

2. *Once a Cop:* _____

3. *The Age of Innocence:* _____

4. *Like Water for Chocolate:* _____

5. *Blue:* _____

 **exercise 4** Match the following movies with their stories. Write the letters on the lines.

1. _____ *Philadelphia*

2. _____ *Faraway, So Close!*

3. _____ *Geronimo: An American Legend*

4. _____ *The Air Up There*

5. _____ *Blink*

6. _____ *The Piano*

7. _____ *Blank Check*

8. _____ *Beethoven's 2nd*

a. An American college basketball coach tries to get an African player on his team.

b. A man with AIDS sues his employer who fired him because of the disease.

c. A child finds a check and uses it to buy himself a lot of presents.

d. A dog falls in love and causes problems for his owner.

e. The army chases an Apache war chief.

f. A blind woman regains her sight and sees a murder.

g. An angel becomes human.

h. A bride (who never speaks) goes to New Zealand in 1852.

 Answer these questions.

1. Have you seen any of these films? If so, which ones?_____
   _____

2. What did you think of them?_____

3. Did you agree or disagree with the critics?_____

WHAT DO YOU THINK?

Censoring Sex and Violence

In some countries, government censors remove from movies scenes that have sex or violence. Is censorship good or bad? Why do some cultures believe it is necessary? What do you think?

CHAPTER twelve

Prejudice, Tolerance, and Justice

in this chapter

The first reading selection discusses systems of justice in different societies. The second selection gives a humorous glimpse into the U.S. trend of lawsuits. Finally, you will read two newspaper articles about an unusual punishment intended to change the ways of two young criminals.

PART**one**

The Concept of Law

Before You Read

Getting Started

Look at the picture and discuss it.

1. Where does this scene take place? Who are the people and what are they doing?
2. What might have happened before this scene began? What might happen next?
3. Would a comparable scene in your culture be similar? Why or why not?

Preparing to Read

If you ask questions before and during the reading process and then think about the answers, your reading will be more active; you will probably better understand and remember the material you have read.

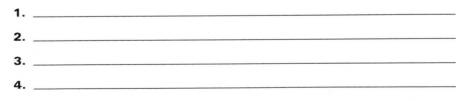

exercise 1   Look at the picture again and then scan the first reading selection. List questions that you think the reading might answer.

1. _____

2. _____

3. _____

4. _____

5. _____

6. _____

7. _____

 As you read the following selection, think about possible answers to the questions that you wrote above.

Read the following selection quickly. Do not use a dictionary. Then do the exercises that follow the reading.

The Concept of Law

The Idea of Law

*T*he idea of "law" exists in every culture. All societies have some kind of law to keep order and to control the interactions of people with those around them. The laws of any culture tell people three things: what they *can* do (their rights), what they *must* do (their duties), and what they may *not* do (illegal actions). In addition, there are usually specific types of punishment for those who break the law.

What Prevents Crime?

Although all societies have laws, not all have the same idea of justice— what is "right" and "wrong" and how "wrong" should be punished. In most Western cultures, it is thought that punishing criminals will prevent them from committing other crimes. Also, it is hoped that the fear of punishment will act as a deterrent that prevents other people from committing similar crimes; in other words, people who are considering a life of crime will decide against it because of fear of punishment. In most non-Western cultures, by contrast, punishment is not seen as a deterrent. Instead, great importance is placed on restoring balance in the situation. A thief, for example, may be ordered to return the things he has stolen instead of, as in Western societies, spending time in prison.

Kinds of Law

Another difference in the concept of justice lies in various societies' ideas of what laws are. In the West, people consider "laws" quite different from "customs." There is also a great contrast between "sins" (breaking religious laws) and "crimes" (breaking laws of the government). In many non-Western cultures, however, there is little separation of customs, laws, and religious beliefs; in other cultures, these three may be quite separate from one another, but still very much different from those in the West. For these reasons, an action may be considered a crime in one country but be socially acceptable in others. For instance, although a thief is viewed as a criminal in much of the world, in a small village where there is considerable communal living and sharing of objects, the word *thief* may have little meaning. Someone who has taken something without asking is simply considered an impolite person.

Civil Law and Society

Most countries have two kinds of law: criminal and civil. People who have been accused of acts such as murder or theft are heard in the criminal justice system, while civil justice deals with people who are believed to have violated others' rights. The use of the civil system reflects the values of the society in which it exists. In the United States, where personal, individual justice is considered very important, civil law has become "big business." There are over 700,000 lawyers in the United States, and many of them keep busy with civil lawsuits; that is, they work for people who want to sue (bring legal action against) others. If a man falls over a torn rug in a hotel and breaks his arm, for instance, he might decide to sue the hotel owners so that they will pay his medical costs. In a country like Japan, by contrast, there is very little use of the civil justice system. Lawsuits are not very popular in Japan, where social harmony (peaceful agreement) is even more important than individual rights, and where people would rather reach agreements outside court.

The Judgment of Disputes

In most cultures, when people cannot reach agreement on their own, a judge might be called on to make a decision. In North America, a case might be heard in a court of law before a judge chosen by the government and, perhaps, a group of citizens in a jury. In some tribal societies, however, a man or a woman who is thought to have special supernatural power might be chosen by the people to judge disputes. In the 1950s, among the Gisu people of Uganda, the inhabitants of a village had great faith in a man who was believed to have the ability to cause smallpox, a serious disease. On Sundays, they went to his "court," where he charged a fee for his judgments of cases. Although the Ugandan government considered this practice illegal, he was very popular with the people.

Social Justice

In societies where courts and judges simply don't exist, self-help is necessary and socially acceptable in disputes. If a cow has been stolen, the owner's friends and relatives may get together and help him get the animal back. In small villages, everyone, in a sense, becomes a judge; in such societies, where people's neighbors are also friends, members of their families, or co-workers, the opinions of the villagers are very important. Social disapproval of people's activities can serve both as powerful punishment for and as strong deterrent to crime.

Modern and Traditional Justice

In some countries, traditional and modern justice exist side by side. A good example of this combination can be found in Tanzania, where people usually take their legal disputes first to family leaders or the representatives of their village "age-set," a group of people of about the same age. If the disagreement cannot be settled by these leaders, then the case is taken to a modern court. The people who are part of the dispute will argue until both sides agree, for the goal is to restore a situation of balance and social harmony. Another example occurred in the United States in the summer of 1994. Two Indian teenagers pleaded guilty to attacking a man in Washington State.* Instead of sentencing the boys to prison, the judge sent them back to their people in Alaska for traditional tribal punishment. It was believed that prison would turn them into hardened criminals but that tribal justice might help them become functioning members of society.

---

*For more about this, see Part Four of this chapter.

After You Read
Getting the Main Ideas

 exercise 1

Write T on the lines before the statements that are true, according to the reading. Write F before the statements that are false. Write I before the statements that are impossible to know from the reading.

1. _____ The concept of law and justice is the same in all cultures.

2. _____ Punishment brings back balance to situations and prevents other crimes.

3. _____ Every country's laws are based on historical customs and religious beliefs.

4. _____ In urban societies, crimes are usually judged in the criminal law system, while personal disagreements are resolved by other methods.

5. _____ In every society, it is illegal and socially unacceptable to commit murder.

6. _____ Traditional justice is more effective than modern justice.

The reading selection gives examples of concepts of justice in the United States and other Western countries, Japan, and traditional village societies. Choose the important ideas about these systems and write them on the lines, without mentioning the specific society. Then exchange books with a classmate. Write <u>US</u> in the parentheses before the statements about the United States, <u>J</u> before those about Japan, and <u>tr</u> before those about traditional societies. Exchange books again to check the answers. The first one is done as an example.

1. (US) <u>Punishment is considered a deterrent to crime.</u>

_____

2. (   ) _____

_____

3. (   ) _____

_____

4. (   ) _____

_____

5. (   ) _____

_____

6. (   ) _____

_____

7. (   ) _____

_____

8. (   ) _____

_____

Guessing Vocabulary from Context

Here are some vocabulary items that might be new from the reading selection "The Concept of Law." Try to determine the definition of each item from the context and write it on the line. Then check your answers in a dictionary.

1. concept = _____

2. punishment = _____

3. justice = _____

4. deterrent = _____

5. commit = _____

6. restore = _____

7. balance = _____

8. order = _____

9. prison = _____

10. sin = _____

11. lawsuit = _____

12. sue = _____

13. harmony = _____

14. dispute = _____

15. sentence = _____

 Are there other vocabulary items in the reading that are new to you? If so, write them in a list on the left-hand side below. Then try to determine their meanings from the context, write definitions, and check your answers in a dictionary.

_____

_____

_____

_____

_____

_____

 Now reread the selection carefully.

Understanding Reading Structure

exercise **6** Write your own outline for each paragraph of the reading selection. (There may be several correct possibilities.) Then compare your outlines with those of your classmates and explain the reasons for your organization of the information.

    I.   The Idea of Law

         A. What People Can Do _____

         B. What People Must Do _____

         C. What People May Not Do _____

         _____

         _____

         _____

II. What Prevents Crime?

_____

_____

_____

_____

_____

_____

III. Kinds of Law

_____

_____

_____

_____

_____

_____

IV. Civil Law and Society

_____

_____

_____

_____

_____

_____

V. The Judgment of Disputes

_____

_____

_____

_____

_____

_____

VI.   Social Justice

_____

_____

_____

_____

_____

_____

VII. Modern and Traditional Justice

_____

_____

_____

_____

_____

_____

 Turn back to the Preparing to Read section and answer the questions you wrote in Exercise 1.

Discussing the Reading

 In small groups, talk about your answers to these questions.

1. In Exercise 2 of the Getting the Main Ideas section, which follows the reading, you listed statements about various systems of justice. In your opinion, what other cultures or countries do these statements refer to?
2. What else do you know about the system of law and justice in the United States or Canada? Compare it with the system in your culture.
3. What kind of justice system seems most advantageous to you? Why?
4. Are there any famous trials going on now? If so, what are they about?

Going Beyond the Text

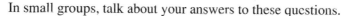 Bring to class newspaper and magazine articles about famous legal trials—past and/or present. Share the articles with the class. Discuss the important information and learn new vocabulary.

PART two

My Lawsuit That Wasn't

Before You Read

Skimming for Main Ideas

exercise

Read the following selection quickly, without using a dictionary. Then list the main ideas (the important events) of the story as in the example.

1. <u>A friend talked to the writer about lawsuits.</u> _____

2. _____
   _____

3. _____
   _____

4. _____
   _____

5. _____
   _____

My Lawsuit That Wasn't

A few weeks ago, I went to a party at my friend Carl's house. I hadn't really wanted to go. I had a backache and would have preferred to stay home, but I knew that if I didn't show up, Carl would be disappointed.

I decided not to stay very long, so I explained to Carl about my back and told him that I wanted to go home early. That was my first mistake. Carl immediately looked interested.

"How did you get that backache?" he asked.

"Well," I said, "I'm not sure. Maybe I just need to buy a new bed; the mattress on mine might be too soft. Or—oh, I don't know—it doesn't hurt very badly. Maybe it happened when I fell down."

"Aha!" he said with enthusiasm. "When did that happen?"

"As I was coming out of Anita's Health and Beauty Place."

"That's it!" Carl shouted. "I'm sure you hurt your back when you fell. I have just one word of advice for you: *sue.*"

"What?" I said. "Why? Perhaps all I need is a good massage and a little rest. Then I'll be fine."

"Don't miss this opportunity," he said excitedly. "My cousin Michael was in a traffic accident a few years ago, and he sued the driver who caused the accident. He won the lawsuit, and the driver not only had to take care of all of Michael's medical treatment, but he also had to pay Michael $10,000 in cash."

"You're kidding," I said.

Carl shook his head. "No. It's true."

My second mistake was letting Carl persuade me to see his lawyer, whom I'll call "Harvey."

"This will be a great case," Harvey told me after I had explained the situation. "Your backache began when you fell over something just outside the door to Anita's. It seems clear that this was Anita's fault. Probably the entrance to the shop was slippery or was in bad condition."

"I'm not sure about that," I answered. "I don't think that's exactly what happened."

Harvey smiled. "But that's the best way to present the case to the judge."

To me, Harvey seemed a little too enthusiastic. This made me uncomfortable because I wanted to settle this problem without "stretching the truth."

Going to the next lawyer, "Scott," was my third mistake. As soon as he had heard my story, he grinned from ear to ear.

"This will be a challenging case," Scott said. "But I think we can win. First, you have to learn one basic fact about lawsuits: If you want to win a lot of money, you have to choose the right person to sue."

"What?"

"Sure. In this situation, for example, we won't even try to sue Anita. Her beauty shop is small, so she can't be very wealthy. Instead, we'll have to find some evidence that you fell on the city sidewalk—not on private property. The city government," he smiled, "has lots of money. The possibilities are limitless."

I did not want to get into a long conflict with the city government; I just wanted to solve the problem of my aching back. So I visited a third lawyer, who had successfully helped another friend of mine settle his case out of court.

At first, this lawyer seemed helpful. "Hmmm," said "Louise" after she had heard the facts, asked a lot of questions, and thought about the problem for a long time. "You probably won't want to go through a long lawsuit—that can take years. But after we begin filing our papers, we can probably settle this case out of court, and get some money for you."

"That sounds reasonable," I said. "What do we do first?"

"About my fees," Louise continued, "of course you will have to pay direct costs—there's the cost of filling out forms, secretarial time, the price of copying, mail, parking at the courthouse, and so on. I charge an hourly rate—some now, some later. Now if you will just write out a check, and sign here. . ."

"Uh . . . ," I answered, as I reached for my coat. "Let me think about it a little more, and I'll call you. . . ."

"Don't forget," said Louise as I was on my way out. "You mustn't talk about the case to anyone—anything you say could be held against you later on. And of course, don't go to Anita's until this is settled. You can do your own hair, and . . . ."

Finally, I did something right. I went to "Richard," a lawyer who didn't say much, but who seemed very certain about his opinions. After he had listened to my story, he looked at me across his desk and shook his head.

"You may not appreciate my advice," he said, "but here it is. If I were you, I'd get some rest and then a good massage. Then, if I had a few hundred dollars, I'd buy a new bed with a very good mattress. Of course, I'm not a doctor, but I think this could be a very effective cure for your backache. In short, I see no basis for a lawsuit."

I grinned. "Thanks for your opinion," I answered, "but you're wrong about one thing. I do appreciate your advice very much!"

After You Read
Making Inferences

 What can you infer about the American legal system from the reading? List the possibilities.

_____

_____

_____

_____

_____

Discussing the Reading

activity

In small groups, talk about your answers to these questions.

1. In your opinion, what are the author's feelings about the American legal system? Do you agree or disagree? Why?
2. Have you or someone you know ever been involved in a lawsuit? If so, what happened?
3. In what situations would you go to a lawyer? In what situations would you sue? Why?
4. How do you usually solve disagreements? Are you usually satisfied with the solutions? Why or why not?

PART three

Building Vocabulary and Study Skills

Categories (Content Areas)

exercise

What categories (content areas) are the following words usually connected with? Write _ed_____ on the lines before the words about education; _rel_____ before the words about religion; _med_____ before words about medicine; _l_____ before words about law; and _bus_____ before words about business and money. In a few cases, more than one answer may be correct.

1. _ed_ classroom	**9.** ____ priest	**17.** ____ bargain
2. _l_ jury	**10.** ____ account	**18.** ____ crime
3. ____ virus	**11.** ____ symptoms	**19.** ____ disease
4. ____ budget	**12.** ____ prayer	**20.** ____ advertise
5. ____ justice	**13.** ____ ceremony	**21.** ____ worship
6. ____ blackboard	**14.** ____ treatment	**22.** ____ instructor
7. ____ courtroom	**15.** ____ patient	**23.** ____ judge
8. ____ sue	**16.** ____ merchandise	**24.** ____ lesson

25. _____ dispute	33. _____ credit	41. _____ exam
26. _____ assignment	34. _____ sin	42. _____ cash
27. _____ punishment	35. _____ worship	43. _____ deterrent
28. _____ lecture	36. _____ physician	44. _____ consumer
29. _____ memorize	37. _____ prison	45. _____ hospital
30. _____ marketing	38. _____ salesclerk	46. _____ graduate
31. _____ cure	39. _____ faith	47. _____ surgery
32. _____ illegal	40. _____ charge	48. _____ discount

activity

Divide into groups. The class chooses a content area, such as the law, travel, city life, work, art, geography, movies, etc. Within a given time limit, each group writes a list of as many words as possible connected with the content area. Then the class discusses the words. The winner is the group with the most correct words. Then repeat the activity with another content area.

Improving Reading Skills: Prediction

Fluent readers often make use of prediction when they read; they try to guess, without thinking about it for very long, what is going to come next. The following exercises may improve your ability to predict.

exercise 1

Fill in the words missing from the following paragraphs as in the example. There may be several correct answers. When you are finished, discuss the reasons for your choices.

In disputes in which a reasonable _agreement_____ seems impossible, it

may be _____ to get the help of a lawyer.

_____ a good one is not easy. You might want to ask friends for

_____ , but their suggestions may help only if their cases were

_____ to yours. There may also be _____ in

your area that provide lists of _____ with their specialties. It is

important to choose a lawyer who _____ a lot about the

particular _____ that you are worried about.

Your first _____ is to call the lawyer and

_____ an appointment to see him or her. During this first

Interactions II • Reading

_____ , you may not get answers to specific legal

_____ , but you can find out about the lawyer's

_____ and fees, and you can see if you get a positive

_____ from the conversation. If you ask, you may not have to

pay _____ for this first meeting. Its purpose is to help you

_____ whether or not this lawyer is the best one to take care of

your _____ .

     Lawyers make most of their money by _____ for their time.

They usually charge by the hour, and add up _____ for phone

calls, writing _____ , filling out legal _____ ,

and so on. To save yourself _____ , always be prepared before

you call or _____ your lawyer: Write a _____

of your questions and _____ before you begin your discussion.

Then, during the session, listen _____ , take notes, and

_____ organized. Always be honest with your

_____ and tell him or her all the _____ . In

addition, provide the lawyer with all the written _____ you have

on the case.

exercise 2

Find sections from reading selections at the level of the class; that is, they should be neither too easy nor too difficult. Rewrite the material, but leave out every eighth word. Have copies made for everyone in the class. You and the other students try to figure out the missing words from clues in the reading. Then discuss the reasons for your choices.

focus on testing

Finishing Timed Tests

On any test, some questions will seem easier to you than others. If you are taking a *timed* test, it will help you to answer the easy questions first and then to come back to the harder ones later. In this way, you will be able to finish more—or all—of the test without wasting time.

Reading in the Real World

Scanning for Information
Magazine Articles

exercise ▼▼▼▼ The following two articles are about an unusual punishment for a crime. Read the first article and answer the questions about it. Work as quickly as possible, as you would on a test. (Your teacher might decide to give you a time limit.) Remember to answer the easy questions first. If you finish before the time limit, don't begin the second article. Instead, check your answers. Your teacher will tell you when to begin reading the second article.

Tribal court may banish teens to Alaskan islands

■ **Admitted robbery:** Indians making restitution to Washington victim.

KLAWOCK, Alaska (AP)—A panel of Tlingit elders began a hearing Thursday to decide whether two Indian teen-agers should be banished to uninhabited islands
5 for severely beating and robbing a pizza deliveryman in Washington state last year.

Cousins Adrian Guthrie and Simon Roberts, both 17, pleaded guilty to robbery in May for attacking Tim Whittlesey of
10 Everett, Wash., with a baseball bat. Whittlesey's hearing and eyesight were permanently damaged.

Rather than sending the teens to prison, a Washington state judge agreed to send them
15 north to face the Kuye'di Kiuu Kwaan Tribal Court. The youths could still get prison time later.

Rudy James, a tribal elder who proposed the alternative at the behest of the youths'
20 parents, says the punishment probably will be banishment for up to two years to separate, isolated islands in Alaska's vast Alexander Archipelago. The hearing in this southeast Alaska fishing village may last
25 through today.

The tribal elders held court in the Alaska Native Brotherhood-Alaska Native Sisterhood hall, a single-story building used for weddings, funerals, town meetings and
30 bingo games. It was the first time the Klawock court was convened to determine a sentencing referred from a state court.

About 75 people attended Thursday's hearing, which lasted two and a half hours
35 and was scheduled to resume this morning. No one was allowed into the hall until it had been ritually cleansed with branches of devil's club, a thorny plant native to the region.
40 Everyone entering the room submitted to purification by being brushed with a cedar bough and wiping their feet at the door.

Guthrie and Roberts entered the room through an "entrance of shame," wearing their tribal regalia turned inside out.

Each boy was allowed to speak and had a tribal advocate at his side. The boys testified that they had gotten drunk on rum at a party the night of the attack. Guthrie said they got the idea from another boy who bragged that he had mugged pizza deliverymen "to make quick cash."

Both were vague when asked about certain details of the crime, including whether it was premeditated.

"It wasn't very planned-out," Guthrie said. "We just went."

Both expressed regret.

"I feel sorry what happened to him, the victim, and the shame I've put my family through and having to be here today," Roberts said.

1. A hearing (line 2) is probably
   a. a conversation
   b. similar to a trial
   c. the sense by which one perceives sound
   d. a kind of punishment
   e. listening

2. Banished (line 4) probably means
   a. sent away (as punishment)
   b. punished
   c. put in prison
   d. beaten (as punishment)
   e. not allowed to go to

3. Mugged (line 51) means
   a. borrowed money from
   b. killed
   c. hit
   d. beaten and robbed
   e. bought (something) from

4. The tribal elders held court to decide
   a. if the boys were guilty
   b. how to help the victim
   c. on a sentence for the teenagers
   d. if the boys should go to a state court
   e. which island to send the boys to

5. The teenagers committed the crime when they
   a. were drunk
   b. had heard another boy brag about a similar crime
   c. had carefully planned it
   d. a and b only
   e. a and c only

Muggers face year in island isolation

■ **Teens banished:** No contact with outside world.

KLAWOCK, Alaska (AP)—They'll have sleeping bags, and tools for cutting firewood and gathering food. But they'll have no way to contact the outside world
5 during a year or more of exile to offshore islands whose only inhabitants are wild animals.

Two 17-year-old Tlingit Indian boys, Adrian Guthrie and Simon Roberts, were
10 banished to separate islands by tribal elders for beating and robbing a pizza delivery man.

It is the first case of a state court referring a criminal case to an American
15 tribal panel for a traditional Indian punishment.

Guthrie and Roberts were held aboard a fishing boat Saturday pending their move to the sprawling Alexander Archipelago of
20 hundreds of mountainous islands off the coast of southeastern Alaska. Tribal officials will not disclose their final destinations.

On Saturday, the teen-agers were lounging in the sun. One listened to music
25 on a Walkman as two tribal guards stood watch. The boys would not talk to reporters.

They probably would be taken to their islands during the night for security, said
30 elder Byron Skinna Sr.

The teen-agers pleaded guilty in May to robbing Tim Whittlesey and beating him with a baseball bat while he was working as a pizza delivery man in Everett, Wash. They
35 stole $47 and a pizza. Whittlesey, 25, suffered permanent damage to his hearing and eyesight.

Twelve tribal elders deliberated for $3\frac{1}{2}$ hours Friday night before banishing the two
40 for a year to 18 months.

Elder Skinna said each boy would be given forks for digging up clams, axes and saws for cutting firewood, and some food to carry them through the first few days. He
45 said they would have sleeping bags and each will build a small shelter, which will be equipped with a wood stove for cooking and heat.

Guthrie and Roberts look much like
50 teen-agers anywhere else in the United States, wearing reversed baseball caps and MTV-inspired clothes. But their elders say the boys have been taught how to live off the land since they began to walk.

6. <u>Exile</u> (line 5) is probably
   a. punishment
   b. banishment
   c. being forced to leave home
   d. all the above
   e. none of the above

7. We can infer that for the next year or more, the teenagers
   a. won't have conversations with other people
   b. will have no electricity for cooking or heating
   c. may have to work hard to survive
   d. all the above
   e. a and b only

8. For the next year or more, the teenagers
   a. will have only each other for company
   b. won't have a radio
   c. will need to gather their own food
   d. all the above
   e. b and c only

9. The victim of the crime
   a. will have problems hearing for the rest of his life
   b. will have problems seeing for the rest of his life
   c. was a baseball player
   d. a and b only
   e. b and c only

10. It is stated or implied that the teenagers who committed the crime
   a. are similar in many ways to other teenagers in the United States
   b. play baseball
   c. know how to survive in the wilderness
   d. all the above
   e. a and c only

131 ©Worldsat International/Science Photo Library/Photo Researchers, Inc.; *132* © Culver Pictures, Inc., photo from Winter Pond Collection, courtesy Alaska State Library; *133* (top) © David Simeon/Stock, Boston; *133* (bottom) Robert Isaacs/Photo Researchers, Inc.; *135* © Porterfield/Chickering/Photo Researchers, Inc.; *142* © Gale Zucker/Stock, Boston; *163* © Walter Gilardetti; *164* Jose Clemente Orozco, Mexican, 1883–1949, *The Epic of American Civilization: Hispano-America,* (Panel #16), 1932–1934, Fresco, size 120 × 119 in., P.934.13.16, commissioned by the trustees of Dartmouth College, © trustees of Dartmouth College, Hanover, New Hampshire; *165* (top) © Scala/Art Resource, NY; *165* (bottom left) © Pablo Picasso, *Guernica,* 1937, oil on canvas, 350 × 782 cm., Centro de Arte Reina Sofia, Madrid, Spain, © Giraudon/Art Resource, NY; *165* (bottom right) © Elliot Elisofon Photographic Archives, National Museum of African Art; *166* (top) © The Bettmann Archive; *166* (bottom) The Metropolitan Museum of Art, Rogers Fund 1956 (56.44); *177* © Peter Menzel/Stock, Boston; *178* (top) The Bettmann Archive; *178* (bottom) © Owen Franken/Stock, Boston; *181* (top) © Walter Meayers Edwards/National Geographic Society Image Collection; *181* (bottom) © Michael Gilecco/Stock, Boston; *193* © Alfred Pasieka/Science Photo Library/Photo Researchers, Inc.; *195* (top left) © Walter Gilardetti; *195* (top right) © John Fung; *195* (bottom left) © Michael Dwyer/Stock, Boston; *195* © Walter Gilardetti; *212, 213* © T. J. Kaminski/Studios Kaminski Ltd., Reno; *217* (left) The Bettmann Archive; *217* (right) © Beringer/Howard Pratch/The Image Works; *218* (left) © Will and Dehi McIntyre/Photo Researchers, Inc.; *218* (top right) Liama Druskis/Stock, Boston; *218* (bottom right) © Spencer Grant/Stock, Boston; *219* (top) © Jack Jacka; *219* (bottom left) © Martin Rogers/Stock, Boston; *219* (bottom right) © Rick Smolan/Stock, Boston; *243* © Douglas Kirkland/Sygma; *244* (top) © The Kobal Collection; *244* (bottom) © 1972 by Paramount Pictures Corporation, all rights reserved; *245* © Everett Collection; *246* (top, Middle) © Everett Collection; *246* (bottom) © Walter Gilardetti; *267* © Bob Daemmrich/Stock, Boston; *268* © Spencer Grant/Stock, Boston.

Text credits: *Page 37* from LONGMAN DICTIONARY OF AMERICAN ENGLISH, copyright © 1983 by Longman Publishers, reprinted with permission; *100, 101, 102* from LONGMAN DICTIONARY OF AMERICAN ENGLISH, copyright © 1983 by Longman Publishers, reprinted with permission; *105(#1)* reprinted by permission of The Venice Beach House; *105 (#3)* "Careers for People" reprinted by permission of Dr. Joseph Simms, PhD., licensed Psychologist; *128* from "The Global Crime Wave" by Gene Stephens, THE FUTURIST, July-August, 1994, reproduced with permission from The Futurist, 7910 Woodmont Ave., Suite 450, Bethesda, MD 20814; *157* from LAME DEER: SEEKERS OF VISIONS, copyright © 1972 by John Fire/Lame Deer and Richard Erdoes, reprinted by permission of Simon & Schuster, Inc.; *189* "Scientists Say Aromas Have Major Effect on Emotions" by Carla Kallan, LOS ANGELES TIMES, May 13, 1991, © Carla Kallan, reprinted by permission; *211* from UNDERSTANDING PSYCHOLOGY by Richard A. Kasschau, reprinted by permission of publisher; *239* from "Home Remedies Even Doctors Use" by Catherine Clifford, MCCALL'S, August 1992, © 1992 by Catherine Clifford as appeared in MCCALL'S, reprinted by permission; *262* from "Now Playing," LOS ANGELES TIMES, February 13, 1994, copyright 1994, Los Angeles Times, reprinted by permission; *282* "Tribal Court May Banish Teens to Alaskan Islands," STAR FREE PRESS, September 2, 1994, reprinted by permission of Associated Press; *284* "Muggers Face Year in Island Isolation," STAR FREE PRESS, September 4, 1994, reprinted by permission of Associated Press.